Boundless Worlds

Boundless Worlds

An Anthropological Approach to Movement

Edited by
Peter Wynn Kirby

Berghahn Books
New York • Oxford

First published in 2009 by
Berghahn Books
www.berghahnbooks.com

Library of Congress Cataloging-in-Publication Data
Boundless worlds : an anthropological approach to movement / edited by Peter Wynn Kirby. -- 1st ed.
p. cm.
Includes bibliographical references and index.
ISBN 978-1-84545-538-5 (alk. paper)
1. Space--Social aspects. I. Kirby, Peter Wynn, 1968-

HM654.B68 2008
304.2'3--dc22

2008046805

British Library Cataloguing in Publication Data
A catalogue record for this book is available from the British Library

Printed in the United States on acid-free paper

ISBN 978-1–84545-538-5 hardback

This book is dedicated to Jean Kirby and Bob Kirby.
Thanks, Mom and Dad, for everything.

And to the memory of my oldest friend, Mark Holmer Burnett (1968–2008),
whose cheery, but unyielding, integrity touched all who knew him.

Contents

Acknowledgements

This volume's journey began long, long ago and far, far away. I embarked on this book project while in England and then took it overseas to two successive postings in Japan while returning to Cambridge annually to lecture. Now I work in France. All this upheaval, with added research in libraries on three continents, certainly served as a frequent reminder of contemporary mobility and displacement. But I was sustained by much generous collaboration and encouragement along the way, and the book would not have succeeded without the help and patience of numerous friends and colleagues whom I would like to thank briefly here.

The origins of *Boundless Worlds* lie in wide-ranging early discussions with Phil Withington at Jesus College, Cambridge, while planning a conference that would interrogate contemporary space-focused scholarship. The conference, at first envisioned as an intimate affair, grew into a lively gathering that followed Phil to the University of Aberdeen, in Scotland. Entitled 'Space, Culture, Power' (10–11 April 2001), the conference had nearly 100 presenters on 24 panels. This event would not have been a success without the hard work of coorganizer Phil there on the ground, aided that week by the intrepid duo of Cathy Shrank and Hau Ming Tse. Tim Ingold deserves warm thanks for his early support and participation, as does Liz Hallam.

The theoretical positioning of the volume drew inspiration from the work of the contributors selected from the conference. It was also grounded in early research I conducted on 'space' and European ocularcentrism under the supervision of Keith Hart at Cambridge. Keith, also now Paris-based, has been a ready source of shrewd advice and friendly support over the years, and he and I have long discussed the possibilities and significance of movement, particularly in interpreting contemporary social transformations. Keith, in addition, kindly read and commented on two drafts of the introductory chapter. Jerry Eades, for his part, cheerfully lent me access to his voluminous personal library – and to mnemonic resources, conveyed through evocative stories – while in Japan and gave helpful publication advice and support. The introductory chapter also improved after careful reading by Rob Kirby and Mitch Sedgwick, respectively. While my work benefited greatly from this and other assistance, any shortcomings remain my own.

I would also like to thank Marion Berghahn, editor and publisher at Berghahn Books; Anna Wright, editorial assistant; and Mark Stanton, editorial manager, for their professional help in publishing the book.

Artists Christian Grou and Tapio Snellman, founders and principals of the design firm **neutral**, generously contributed several of their movement studies to the volume's Visual Appendix. Their participation and friendship are much appreciated.

And, finally, I thank my wife, architect Hau Ming Tse, for her encouragement and patience throughout all of this. Her expert assistance with the Visual Appendix and with the cover design was instrumental; but far more important was her loving participation in this semi-nomadic intellectual journey – and her help in keeping the momentum going – which brought the book to where it is today.

Peter Wynn Kirby
Ecole des Hautes Etudes en Sciences Sociales (EHESS)
Paris, 2008

Chapter 1

Lost in 'Space': An Anthropological Approach to Movement

Peter Wynn Kirby

> *More than thirty years after our first encounter, both Belleville and I have changed. But Belleville is still a place, while I am afraid I look more like a flow.*
>
> Manuel Castells (2000: 454)

The tension between place, memory, and change lies at the heart of human existence and, as Manuel Castells's quotation cited above indicates, sometimes place allows us to understand just how mutable and protean our lives become. But that is not to say that places are fixed or even durable, save in relative terms. We live in a world shaped by flux. Islands of apparent stability are engulfed by a sea of human and animal peregrinations, linguistic and cultural change, emergent social institutions, traffic in goods as well as flows of 'bads' (such as disease and pollutants), circuits of material culture, exchange of images and ideologies, slow motion tectonic shifts, and climate change. Not least, our bodies are in constant motion with organs pumping fluids, lungs expanding and contracting with air, hair regenerating (or receding), bodies building and losing tissue, and cells undergoing continual birth and decay. Subject to buffeting motion and change in a broad sweep of socio-cultural contexts, it is not surprising that anthropologists find enduring attempts to create armatures of stability out of the vagaries of existence. Even the edifices we construct, which in comparison to flesh seem the essence of permanence and solidity, are effectively architectural illusions obscuring ongoing negotiation between dwellers, materials, design, and use. Movement and change – aggressively regulated, channelled, and even denied in the creation and maintenance of social institutions and the structuration of social relations – are the reviving undercurrent circulating throughout social life.

Yet while anthropology and other social sciences have long acknowledged the importance of addressing flux in socio-cultural inquiry, albeit with a diversity of approaches,[1] attention to the ramifications of movement remains

1. Some important earlier work that laid the foundations for current research on this topic includes Redfield 1941; Malinowski 1944; Lewis 1951, 1965; Gluckman 1955, 1958; Turner 1957; Harris 1968; Mitchell 1969, 1987; Fletcher 1971; Wolf 1971, 1982; Castells 1977, 1983; Bourdieu 1977; Hannerz 1980; Hopkins and Wallerstein 1982; and Worsley 1984.

relatively lopsided. Extensive work on migration and diaspora cultures and on social 'movements' provides important insights into the fluidity of people, culture, and ideas, as I detail below; and, indeed, the current emphasis in scholarship on transnational flows of everything from labour and images to pollution and contagion in our mediated, globalizing world reveals keen interest in certain specific forms of movement as objects of analysis (e.g., A. Ong 1999; cf. Tsing 2000, 2005). Nevertheless, a focus on certain emblematically transnational or 'global' movements exposes lacunae in, or neglect of, other elements of mobility and flux worthy of anthropological purview (e.g., Piot 1999). As 'users' are drawn into the compressed space of mediated communication and accelerated travel corridors, or folded into the altered temporalities to which hypertext and split-second electronic transactions give rise – creating discontinuities between the immediacy and rootedness of lived surroundings and distant or virtual planes – so social scientists often seem seduced by the immense speed and 'flow' (and novelty) of new circuits into paying less attention to more quotidian themes or settings (e.g., Castells 2000; cf. Harvey 1990). And as some accounts begin to discern metonymic traces of global processes in many forms of social movement (cf. Strathern 1995 and Tsing 2000, 2005 for salient critiques), human-scale experience of movement is neglected.

Globalization and globalism (the latter indexing discourse on the global) signal important and historic transformations in our world, transformations that beg careful anthropological analysis. Yet, as I explore below, ways of thinking about and addressing globalization expose problems in how anthropologists confront questions of movement that pose great difficulties for the discipline. Some of these interpretive obstacles have been created by the historical legacy of 'space' in Euro-American discourse.

Social scientists' keen interest in 'space' in recent years stems, to a considerable extent, from the belief that spatial knowledge, architectures, symbolism, and action comprise an analytical cross-section of social phenomena that can help lead to a deeper, more insightful understanding of varied social contexts. Unfortunately, this chimera of 'space' often leads to vastly divergent results. Recent work in anthropology and other social science (detailed in the sections below, as well as in subsequent chapters in this volume) has made it increasingly clear that what is generally termed 'space' is guilty by association with a wide array of concepts from the European intellectual tradition that in fact lead us away from a clearer understanding of the multiplicities of social life. Indeed, far from being an unlucky bystander, 'space' has lain, in many ways, at the very heart of brutal European (and other) encroachments on less powerful societies, not to mention domination of domestic populations. Cartesian-influenced conceptions of space and linked technologies of power, such as cartography and development schemes, have etched political notions of segregation, domination, and control onto the surface of the world, reshaping the globe itself to 'Western' specifications – so much so, in fact, that it has become difficult to countenance use of this term without severely undermining research objectives. Against the backcloth of contemporary social developments, with stewardship of planetary ecology and responses to infectious disease pandemics complicated by uneven geopolitical terrain; with transnational flows of migrants, capital, and 'culture' making state frontiers seem increasingly arbitrary, obstructive, and anachronistic; with creation of far-flung social networks via communications technologies, expanded travel corridors, and other means of social and intellectual exchange continuing apace; and with heavy-handed counter-jihadist measures, however understandable at times, provoking public outcry at lost freedoms and unfortunate excesses, a sustained interrogation of 'space' and a renewed appreciation of movement seem particularly timely.

The collection's attention to the politics of demarcation penetrates straight to the heart of these issues, particularly the tension between social boundaries and social movement reflected to some extent in the volume's title. The political ramifications of 'marking one's territory', common both to the competitive spraying of territory in the animal world and to the (often equally bestial) erection of boundaries between human groupings, are undeniable. But beyond these rites of possession and division, human engagement with the world consists of a ceaseless marking, and remarking, of our environs, a circulating interplay between the trammelled routes and existing toponyms that accrete to 'places' through history-laden social contact with terrain and the daily embodied iterations and symbolic interchange that transpire in the simplest journey or sensory immersion in a social milieu.[2] As several of the book's contributors vividly illustrate, autochthonous notions of place, interval, and (topo)genealogy are, to be sure, laden with power.[3] Yet Cartesian ideas of space seem particularly culpable in denying relations between 'objects' contained within its abstracted field. Therefore, while attuned to the important socio-political dimensions of

2. I discuss Augustin Berque's theorization of 'milieux' in a later section.
3. Indeed, this volume rejects the notion that all 'non-Western' reckonings of surroundings constitute a monolithic category, opposed to space, in which power vectors, demarcation, fortification, and segregation somehow do not exist. As historical examples such as the Great Wall of China, monumental Japanese castle architecture, and Incan military fortifications demonstrate with persuasive archaeological materiality, societies have long created sharp, fixed, well-policed demarcations between themselves and others. And brutal imperialistic impulses are hardly exclusively European or American in origin. Furthermore, as explored in the Conclusion to this volume, as well as in the contributed chapters, societies all over the world are marked by social boundaries of a (usually) less material nature that create divisions between women and men, between ethnic groups, and between citizens and 'aliens' that undermine any such simplistic characterization of ideas of place, relation, and exclusion in social milieux.

topologies of hierarchy and exclusion and control in a range of societies, this volume remains sensitive to how the axes of space have been extended and overlaid on top of existing notions of relation, proximity, and affect, replotting in x,y,z co-ordinates alternative social mappings, and facilitating proliferation of a certain culturally-anchored set of political relations that have long been assumed as givens in all too many scholarly analyses.

This volume of essays brings together nine scholars whose thoughtful, rigorous, and penetrating socio-historical investigations give the lie to conventional understandings of space and its interpretation. These scholars have, each in their own way, distinguished themselves as shrewd investigators of alternative understandings of spatial phenomena specifically and as bold critics of 'conventional wisdom' in socio-cultural inquiry more generally. Taken together, the collected essays comprise a subtle and concerted assault on the constellation of familiar notions that combine to make 'space/place' not only a considerable hurdle impeding understanding of varied social groupings but, to some, an epithet reviling simplistic, ethnocentric or hackneyed thinking.

Significantly, this collection does not propose abandoning the term 'space' entirely (though one contributor, Tim Ingold, has argued that this is an essential first step (Ingold 2001)). Rather than coin new jargon or produce convoluted intellectual formulations, we prefer to construct a coherent and many-pronged attack on flawed invocations of this concept while pointing the way towards a more sensible and socio-historically sound account of the rich complexities of practical and symbolic interventions into human environs. A strong thread weaving through the contributions is the importance of movement: movement as an essential component of the effervescence and improvisation of social life, movement in defiance of political strictures, indeed, the inevitability of movement across or along spatio-political structures or boundaries intended to restrict movement, control dissent or difference, and pacify populations. The collected essays, in relating their research findings, reveal important dimensions of 'topo-logics' of richly varied provenance and, in turn, identify the ways in which human lives belie the cold, empty, passionless rationality of space as imposed in social settings and as implicated in some structuring of human thought itself.

One criterion for selecting essays – aside from a demonstrated sensitivity to the spatial politics of occupation, demarcation and movement – was a willingness to look beyond disciplinary boundaries. (To be sure, many of the volume's critiques of policed geopolitical frontiers and enforced spatial/cultural protocols could be directed at overly zealous boundary maintenance between scholarly disciplines.) Another was the ability to combine broad theoretical sophistication with original and specialist research. The result is nine essays that consider appropriations and engagement in social milieux as diverse as contemporary Palestine, hinterland Mongolia, community Tokyo, and Island Melanesia; spatial dynamics of cross-cultural contact in colonial South Asia, on the one hand, and in multinational corporate France, on the other; and frictions between spatio-temporally localized traditions and global ambitions in both networked knowledge industries in rural Finland and in politically mobilized 'post-diaspora' Tibet. The essays taken as a whole comprise a concerted and coherent attempt to interrogate (largely 'Western') occupations and manipulations of space against the backdrop of how people actually move through, exist in, conceive of, and represent these spaces in their everyday lives in varied social contexts. Many anthropological collections analysing 'space' and/or 'place' (e.g., Low and Lawrence-Zúñiga 2003; Gupta and Ferguson 1997; as well as Feld and Basso 1996, to a lesser extent – Hirsch and O'Hanlon 1995 stands as a notable exception) dive into theoretical analysis of ethnographic subjectivities and experiences of place in our contemporary age without grappling much (if at all) with the social/political/historical roots of these important socio-cultural phenomena. In order to lay sturdy foundations for this discussion, I review and interpret below the rise of 'space-thinking' in European and diaspora societies (and its imposition on other parts of the world) before moving on to engage with alternative means of approaching the study of bodies and surroundings in a range of socio-cultural settings.

Making 'Space'

Space has been in the making for millennia, and yet it is clear that the origins of 'Cartesian' space, as presently leveraged and experienced, extend back at least to Greek civilization's intellectual achievement of creating rationality and abstraction out of the heterogeneity and unevenness of the world. While the intellectual roots of this process took sustenance from linguistic developments[4] and a logic imposed on philosophical questions of all stripes, the trope of space grew most clearly out of mathematical advances (cf. Jonas 1982),[5] perhaps most vividly illustrated by Euclidian geometry. Chief among

4. It is important to recognize that this intellectual leap probably did not occur out of the blue. Havelock (1982: 6), for example, argues that the rational, analytical 'alphabetic mind' took approximately three millennia to develop out of a confluence of sources.
5. Jonas argues that the ocularcentrism of Greek civilization created the reflective distance necessary to distinguish subject and object, leading to abstraction and intertwined with developments in geometry. Whether this is the sole origin of the Greek ability to objectify, though, is up for debate (e.g., Havelock 1982) and is, of course, difficult to ascertain retrospectively with any great certainty. Adding to this ambiguity is Ivins (1946), who, for his part, argues that Greek society and even its geometry were not vision-centred but moulded by tactility. Jay (1993: 23), an eloquent and persuasive supporter of Greek ocularcentrism, discerns spatio-visual cues in the Greek language: 'The word *theater*, as has often been remarked, shares the same root as the word *theory*, *theoria*, which meant to look at attentively, to behold. So too does theorem, which has allowed some commentators to emphasize the privileging of vision in Greek mathematics, with its geometric emphasis'.

these was the Greeks' success in severing relations between objects, denying characteristics of place and creating infinite division and transferability within two-dimensional surface-planes and three-dimensional cones, spheres, polyhedra, and so on, in conceptual 'space' (Euclid 1990 [*c*.300 BCE]). Implicated in Greek metaphysics' objectification and logic of conversion was a system of mnemonics, pioneered and refined into an 'art' (Yates 1966) by the Greeks, in which visualized spaces (often in fact places, rooms and corridors from actual buildings visited by devotees and etched in their mind's eye through long hours of practice) became festooned with interchangeable images of objects and personae used to symbolize, store, and conjure up complex information (Yates 1966; Fabian 1983). Though these cavernous precincts of the mnemonically trained mind generally remained fixed, the contents of the architectonic spaces could be altered at will.[6] This cold, rational conception of space – refined through subsequent centuries to the present day and resulting in a 'spatialization of consciousness' (Fabian 1983, emphasis removed) that shapes rhetoric, conceptions of the world, and their presentation (Fabian 1983; cf. Havelock 1982: 9, 311–12) – has had a pervasive influence on academic and other engagement with the world. Not only do memory and rhetoric and pedagogy bear the stamp of this spatialized approach to knowledge (W. Ong 1958), with spatio-cultural forms such as taxonomies, grids, kinship diagrams, and so forth shaping encounters with social data (Fabian 1983), but a complex of space-focused biases and stances and predispositions has created pervasive distortions in how social scientists, and others, interpret surroundings and the societies they study. Amid these conditions of persistent intellectual disengagement from lived experience, people continue to 'see' the world through the filter of space.

Developments of spatial representation in art and architecture both reflected and reinforced this process. To take painting, for example: from classical times through the Middle Ages there was extensive, though crude, use of two-dimensional media to represent three-dimensional scenes. But the refinement of linear-perspectival composition in Renaissance painting signalled an expansion of 'space-thinking' (and ocularcentrism)[7] that would have important ramifications for European and other engagements with and representations of

6. That this system of memory readily appropriated the cultural legacy of Greco-Roman architectural space in ordering and recalling minutiae with great precision begs the question of how construction of knowledge might be different in societies with vastly different social histories and a more ecological orientation, for example, something that this collection addresses only indirectly.
7. This introduction, though attentive to the ocularcentrism inextricably embedded in English (and many other languages), is as riddled with spatio-visual metaphors and ocularcentrist constructions and etymologies as any other piece of writing (e.g., Jay 1993: 1–2).

their surroundings. Leon Battista Alberti characterized perspective as a '*velo*' (veil) of threads stretched across a frame and allowing the pyramid-shaped perspective of the scene to be perceived as a grid extending from the vanishing-point to the surface of the painting (from Alberti's fifteenth-century *De Pictura*, cited in Edgerton 1975: 118) and then in a reverse pyramid from the surface of the painting to the viewer that implied (and imposed) a 'monocular, unblinking, fixed eye' (Jay 1993: 54; cf. Hirsch 1995). This Quattrocento perspectival reckoning framed the world in terms of a strict, sophisticated set of geometrical and optical principles – couched in the production of verisimilitude – and implicated the viewer in the structuring of the scene. In the hands of Florentine architect Brunelleschi and other artists and designers after him, the Albertian 'veil' of space-thinking began to transform the (re)production of space into an end in itself, prioritized over representing the objects contained within it.[8] This subtle shift from an embodied experience of the world (a multi-sensory complex of knowledge and orientation, of which vision is an important component) to the practice of interpreting the world as a 'field' (cf. Gibson 1950; Jay 1993)[9] is significant and wide-reaching. Naturally, lived sensory experience of body and surroundings is part and parcel of existence in any society, a point on which I elaborate in later sections. But the extensive diffusion of this form of space-thinking, a social logic otherwise known as the Cartesian perspective – from whose viewpoint the world is surveyed as an eerily disembodied zone, cross-cut with x,y,z axes designating human or material positions as co-ordinates on a conceptual grid – has had massive political ramifications that contributions to this volume address directly. Not only did spatialized thought shape Enlightenment philosophy and the development of modern science (Ong 1958; Yates 1966; Fabian 1983; Jay 1993; Casey 1997), but it has fuelled colonial, imperialist, and capitalist appropriation of territory framed in the peculiar social rhetoric of spatiality, a dimension I discuss below.

Marking the Territory

If historical study of past millennia on this planet can tell us anything, it is that human societies have long engaged in movement, exploration, intercultural

8. As Jay (1993: 51–52) writes, with reference to painting: '[N]ow it was possible to be concerned more with the rules and procedures for achieving the illusion of perspective than with the subject depicted'.
9. This use of terminology is indebted to Gibson's theorization of the 'visual world' (in which a dinner plate lying on a table, viewed obliquely, is perceived as round) versus the 'visual field' (in which the plate is perceived as an ellipsis) (cf. Wartofsky 1979). Jay avers that with ocularcentrist developments in perspectival representation, the 'visual field now replaced the visual world' (Jay 1993: 55).

contact, and often violent conflict and aggression (e.g., Gibbon 1983 [1781]; Frank 1998; Diamond 2005). Yet, partly by virtue of technological achievements (for example, in ship-building and navigation) that allowed states to project power far beyond their borders, recent centuries witnessed an explosion of political expansion, and predatory European states in particular appropriated distant territory with scant regard to populations suffering incursion. The political ramifications of space as a conceptual regime, described above, were tightly bound up in this process. Just as the spatial organization of knowledge from Ancient Greece onward led to discipline and control of facts to be manipulated by European and diaspora intellects, spatial ordering of societies was intended to wield and exert control over populations and resources for domestic stability and for geopolitical advantage. Most importantly, 'savage' regions came to be seen from colonial/imperial vantages as both 'empty', waiting to be filled (i.e., civilized), and as a woefully neglected and underdeveloped resource (Fabian 1983). In short, space existed to be *occupied* (Fabian 1983). Subjugation of far-flung lands, and occupation of territory, came to be justified under projects of colonial and imperial expansion in which this Cartesian spatial logic shaped how rapacious states viewed, approached, and justified encounters with other peoples and their domination. One key technology of this multilateral spatial regime was that of cartography. Several scholars (following Edgerton 1975) believe that the recovery of Ptolemy's *Geographia* and its grid-based approach to mapping land likely aided fifteenth-century Europeans in honing perspectival representation.[10] In turn, this dispassionate European conception of space as a homogeneous, ordered field also influenced the practice of map-making and map-thinking. On this latter point, Svetlana Alpers, for instance, notes the preponderance of the 'mapping impulse' in Dutch art and describes a dramatic increase in cartography in sixteenth-century Holland (Alpers 1983: 119, 134). But while early map-making betrayed a great deal of inaccuracy and artifice as inventive cartographers made up for gaps in knowledge and skill (Alpers 1983), in time mapping became a sophisticated instrument of power. As a conceptual field, 'the mapping impulse' was essentially a two-dimensional, vision-focused counterpart to the three-dimensional abstraction of space-thinking. And as societies and, in particular, elites began to conceive of the world as a flat, uniform surface in which the heterogeneity of societies and ecology were denied, so they also began to think in terms of bounded territories with clear borders – perhaps not so unlike a chessboard.

10. Alpers, however, notes that while Ptolemy's grid and Renaissance linear perspectival art share important characteristics, such as the homogeneous, geometrical projection of axes, mapping does not include the viewer in the structure of the composition, nor does it involve perspective's three-dimensionality or its window-like frame (Alpers 1983; cf. Hirsch 1995). Of course, some maps do include features rendered in at least rough perspective, but these are more common in vernacular maps, commercial or tourist maps, or map caricatures created for visual or humorous effect.

Once territorial space came to be viewed as a two-dimensional field whose contours could be calculated with precision, it could be filled and made productive.[11] Indeed, the marriage of space-thinking with the 'mapping impulse' led to a prevalent conception of the world as a uniform surface, marked by settlements and other features that became little more than dots on a map in the minds of elites. Not only was the diversity of topography reduced (or even eliminated) to the specifications of the type of map selected – layers of schematized data could be peeled away depending on whether the map was to be 'topographical', 'political', or otherwise, and could shift with respect to the legend and projection chosen – but maps began in turn to shape perception of landscape – for example, features (and peoples) not found on the map did not, in a sense, exist to the same degree for those for whom cartography had become ontology. (For an illustrative account of the cartographic biases of British officials in colonial South Asia, see Michael, this volume.)

The 'Western' colonialist/imperialist/capitalist legacy of occupation and appropriation of territory made adroit use of state technologies of knowledge, division and control. Naturally, this approach to power was not limited to foreign holdings, and the military and social motives for imposition of order that have shaped urban planning for centuries (e.g., Sennett 1994; Rabinow 2003) are just one example of how space and domination have had wider social application. (Eventual resistance against these disciplinary regimes, and related capitalist projects, came to a head in the postwar period, notably in neo-revolutionary, even 'situationist', post-1968 France (Debord 1983; Sadler 1998; De Certeau 1988), but such resistance has likely been pervasive in all manner of contexts, as banal as it may seem at times in less populated rural areas, for example (Scott 1985, 1976)). The numerous parallels we can discern in Foucault's work on power/knowledge through spatial and other discipline of bodies make it tempting to conclude that the impact of space-thinking on the wielding of state power was 'panoptical'. And, to be sure, the spatiality of knowledge that began as the memory palace and extended through the history of European art, architecture, and intellectual life reached a telling stage of development (and took a rather paranoid turn) when Jeremy Bentham in 1791 conceived of the 'Panopticon'.[12] Particularly in the ocularcentrist 'surveillance society' of the contemporary industrialized world, where state objectives of counter-terrorist security through control of space are invoked with new urgency to justify all manner of surveillance, examination, interrogation, and exclusion, it is unsurprising that the metaphor of the Panopticon remains so persuasive in conveying the cold, eerie precision of a

11. Though border areas sometimes remained ill-defined and hotly contested (Michael, this volume).

12. This (largely theoretical) prison design, in which all-seeing authorities wielded such knowledge of (and influence over) prisoners that inmates would self-regulate and 'normalize' their behaviour (Foucault 1979: 200 ff.), is no doubt well known to scholars of space and power, broadly defined.

theoretical space/power/knowledge complex. Yet we should also recognize that this Victorian project of omniscience and linked projects of power/knowledge, as convincing and seductive as they are, fit into a larger discourse of space, mapping, occupation, and control described throughout this introduction rather than the other way around. In order to do justice to the complexity of this theme, it is essential not only to scrutinize the ways in which this dominant yet acephalous spatial regime has influenced objectification, subjugation, and appropriation of diverse areas of the world (continuing today disguised in development and free trade initiatives pushed by industrialized powers onto less prosperous areas of the planet (cf. Escobar 1995)), but to look furthermore at how other societies conceive of their surroundings, articulate social engagement, and enact relations through movement, as a number of contributors to this volume succeed in doing with cogent ethnographic analyses. Before addressing these specific themes in greater detail, however, I discuss how related anthropological theory can help us foreground some disciplinary biases in anthropology that both aid and obstruct clearer understandings of social dynamics in myriad areas of the world.

The Place of Anthropology

Anthropologists have not always successfully peeled away the 'veil' of space-thinking from interpretations of social action in field encounters. Yet the discipline has been far more dedicated than its disciplinary cousins in seeking to understand topo-logics from 'native' points of view. This commitment stems, undoubtedly, at least in part from the common experience of long-term ethnographic fieldwork in small-scale settings or among relatively circumscribed groups of informants, often in social settings with divergent means of constructing social knowledge and markedly different socio-cultural 'reckoning' of relation, proximity, and surroundings. Importantly, growing attention in recent decades to communities in complex 'First World' settings, in the world's largest cities, and among dispersed, migrant, or itinerant groups has only served to underline the extremely resilient abilities of social groups to orient themselves even amid considerable dislocating forces (e.g., Hannerz 1969, 1980, 1992, 1996, 2004; Bestor 2001, 2004; A. Ong 1999; Yang 1997; Appadurai 1996; and Malkki 1995, to choose among many examples). Important work (e.g., Feld and Basso 1996; Gupta and Ferguson 1997; cf. Casey 1997) on 'senses of place' and the cultural underpinnings of place-orientation as key elements of ethnographic and ethnological analysis has brought field interpretations into the round, so to speak, allowing further understanding of the 'lived' and localized notions and actions through which peoples situate themselves in a range of societies. One glaring Cartesian hangover, however, is a lingering bias that imagines places as simply fitting into a container-like volume of space, including two-dimensional frames such as national or regional borders as inscribed on maps. (Meanwhile, a host of metaphorical invocations such as 'analytical space' or 'interpretive space', betraying at least the prevalence of the trope of space-thinking, if not always full awareness of its ramifications, appears all too commonly in anthropological work.) Amid the frequent interchangeable selection of 'space' and 'place', or 'space/place', and the array of different uses of these terms and approaches to these topics, it is hard to agree fully with the idea that there should be a sub-discipline called 'the anthropology of space and place' (see Low and Lawrence-Zúñiga 2003a, and especially Low and Lawrence-Zúñiga 2003b). Surely attunement to construction of, and engagement in, surroundings ought to be a component of any good ethnography. Indeed, as Ingold (2001) avers, the fact that these two terms, in English, rhyme and share 80 per cent of their letters must go a long way towards explaining why they crop up in stubborn proximity in sentences and titles far and wide. Perhaps worse (and no doubt due, in part, to the subtle, convincing arguments of 'place' scholarship described above), some eschew the term 'space' completely in favour of 'place' when describing social milieux. While on the surface this might seem like a refreshing step forward, 'place' when invoked on its own can become almost an un-reflexive, 'disciplinarily-correct', and flawed substitute for denigrated 'space' in less enlightened accounts, and links between the finite immediacy of locale and the broader experience of informants in wider social milieux can erroneously be assumed to be included within its narrower lexicographic scope. When this overemphasis on place is combined with a fascination for the global, a bizarrely schizophrenic theoretical 'bipolar disorder' materializes, with perhaps fewer social scientists even recognizing the need to stand astride the two extremes with theoretical consistency.

One way of projecting outward from place and taking account of broader horizons of experience is to reconcile place with landscape. (Of course, when immersed in the phenomenological flow of experience, moving through interpenetrating domains, there is no need for a theoretical 'bridge' between place and landscape – they transpose and modulate effortlessly and without reflection.) Landscape references a cultural 'perspective' on surroundings, particularly within the Euro-American intellectual and artistic tradition, which tends to *see* nature[13] as a view imbued with the social and cultural/linguistic spatiocentrism described above. Obviously, 'Western' views of landscape have been influenced by history and political economy, such as the growth of a landed gentry in England, freed from working the land and able to keep it at a remove, who could eulogize the 'natural' in poetry and speech and participate in its representation in gardens or paintings (Williams 1988).

13. Though a critique of this term can be expressed in great detail (as I attempt in Kirby 2002), 'nature' is laced with 'culture' and I do not choose this term as a simple designation of surroundings.

(Indeed, Martin Jay calls these 'aesthetic' landscapes: 'the real estate version of perspectival art' (Jay 1993: 59).) When this politico-historical background is taken into account, however, the term landscape offers a neat functionality in moving beyond the confines of place into the full ambit of human iterations and encounters. Crucially, place retains a perceiving subject, even if the subject in question exists outside of milieux firmly grounded in traceries of social relations, enduring paths of iteration, and mnemonic cues (e.g., Mondragón, this volume). While space is 'divorced as much as possible from a subject-position', place remains embedded in phenomenological experience, sensed 'from a specific (subjective) vantage point' (Hirsch 1995: 8). Landscape, alternatively, resonates with both subjective and cultural significance. The interplay between these crucial social and phenomenological dimensions of everyday enactments of, and navigations through, landscape gives the term, properly defined, a certain cogency when trying to convey the fluid character of localized practice and social movement, particularly in ethnographic terms – as demonstrated throughout this collection.

Hirsh's introduction to *The Anthropology of Landscape* (Hirsch and O'Hanlon 1995) provides an excellent distillation of the 'foreground' and 'background' qualities of social landscapes (Hirsch 1995: 3), demonstrating the subtle, emergent, processual nature of experiencing phenomena and interpreting the terminological constructs anthropologists and others use to convey the phenomenology of movement and action. In particular, the chapter succeeds in evoking the fluidity of human experience between the heterogeneous surfaces and horizons of day-to-day life – or 'landscape as … process' (Hirsch 1995: 5) in which a foreground of being and action points to 'actuality' while background augurs 'potentiality' – in other words, stages of action towards multiple futures (Hirsch 1995: 3). In discussing many of the terms common to spatial accounts in anthropology and elsewhere, Hirsch stresses the connections and semantic overlaps with which they resonate:

> They are … moments or transitions possible within a single relationship, analogous to the experience of a person momentarily losing his/her way on a familiar journey before relocating him/herself by reference to an external perspective; or to the 'empty place' which periodically fills the 'foreground' experience before receding to its customary 'background' location. … Landscape thus emerges as a cultural *process* (Hirsch 1995: 5–6, emphasis in original).

Hirsch, moreover, makes a convincing case for a positioning of landscape 'between place and space' (Hirsch 1995: 1) – importantly, in my opinion, he elects to preserve and refine the term space rather than abandon that conceptual register of analysis or fabricate a neologism. Space as 'background', 'horizon', 'potentiality' (Hirsch 1995: 4), remaining only relatively undefined in a processual landscape until becoming engaged with by subjective actors, seems truer to social experience and still allows for cognitive and mnemonic engagements with 'spaces' not presently inhabited, but conceived or remembered. The book's collective decision to take the 'conventional (Western) notion of 'landscape' … [as a] productive point of departure from which to explore analogous local ideas which can in turn be reflexively used to interrogate the Western concept' (Hirsch 1995: 2) is effective, even though the introduction's extensive play with the landscape metaphor creates a persistent vision-centred orientation in engaging with the material. And the book's emphasis on mobility and process and fluidity is an important beachhead for the social science of movement, a theme which is in many ways a logical extension of recent advances in anthropology but which is, nevertheless, a neglected research focus.

'Nomads of the Present': Anthropology and Movement

Anthropology has reverberated with frictions deep within the discipline (though rising more towards the surface of late) between those who wish to freeze the world they scrutinize and those more willing to move with that world. It perhaps goes without saying that, given the reifying instincts of the European intellectual tradition as well as prevalent disciplinary and institutional biases and pressures, the former approach has been far more prevalent than the latter.

Malinowski's pioneering work in particular launched a tradition of rigorous ethnography that still shapes contemporary anthropological practice. Though in his *Argonauts of the Western Pacific* (1922) Malinowski compellingly portrays the intricate, cyclical ritual movement of people and objects throughout a Melanesian archipelago and poses questions about the role of ethnographer that are still being pondered and answered in the present day, his account and those of other earlier ethnographers remain mired in theoretical ruts and narrative conventions that distort the lived and fluid character of social life. In addition to the many criticisms of classical anthropological work that raise valid questions about such important issues as 'Western' preconceptions regarding 'savage' behaviour (e.g., Stocking 1982), about gender bias (e.g., MacCormack and Strathern 1980), and about other flawed representation of the Other (e.g., Marcus and Fischer 1986; Clifford and Marcus 1986), we could also add a lingering ethnographic reflex for imposing spatio-analytical structure on the various lived ontologies of the field that endures in much contemporary ethnographic production. Tireless anthropological commitment to *writing through* problems of representation has produced numerous works that convey rather well the robust sense of being in another cultural realm, of speaking with, say, a cattle stockman on the range in Queensland or a spirit-medium in her Thailand home (Strang 1997; Morris 2000) with fluency in their languages and a strong 'sense of place'. Such varied ethnographies as Charles Piot's *Remotely Global* (1999), Michael Stewart's *The Time of the Gypsies* (1997), Stephan Gudeman and Alberto Rivera's *Conversations in Colombia* (1990), and Michael Taussig's *Shamanism, Colonialism, and the Wild Man* (1987) feature how the benefits of conveying ethnographic field data in evocative, experimental, or compelling narrative form can far outweigh the drawbacks of this disciplinary medium.

But while ethnographic writing strategies developed over the last two decades especially have managed to convey more faithfully the voices of informants and the rich flavour of field encounters, prevailing space-focused distortions nevertheless continue to miscast the immersive, motile, ever-becoming character of field-realms with more static, disembodied 'spaces' coloured by the analytical character and European intellectual provenance of scholarly interventions explored in detail earlier in this introduction. This continuing problem has been alleviated somewhat by the sorts of social groups innovative anthropologists have elected to study. More recently, for instance, there have been relatively more examples of ethnographers choosing to take on itinerant groups of informants – migrants, semi-nomadic professionals, or just 'ordinary' people who move a great deal – as a means towards understanding the unfixed, though hardly ungrounded, character of contemporary social lives (Ong 1999; Hannerz 2004; cf. Clifford 1997). These writers, building in part on the work of a small group of earlier scholars committed to portraying the shifting, processual, performative character of the field (e.g., Turner 1957, 1967, 1990; Schechner 1985; Schechner and Appel 1990; Fabian 1990; cf. also Melucci 1989; cf. Touraine 1981), have found ways to usher readers into the changing world in which their informants dwell and move. Ulf Hannerz's *Foreign News* (2004) is an excellent case in point, accompanying foreign correspondents along their actual and mnemonic journeys in search of 'stories'. In addition to drawing intriguing parallels between the work of these journalists and that of anthropologists themselves, Hannerz crafts a sophisticated and illuminating ethnographic study that probes into the fluid dynamics of life on the move. Aihwa Ong's *Flexible Citizenship* (1999), too, peers through contemporary murk surrounding shifting national identity and transnational linkages. Tracing the iterative and emigrant strategies of various Chinese and Chinese-diaspora groups, Ong succeeds in conveying the changing character of roots, identity, and affiliation in a world of porous borders and novel connections. Based on the best achievements of these and other examples, it seems abundantly clear that anthropologists are capable of well-rounded, innovative, even forward-looking or top(ont)ologically attuned portrayals of other worlds. Perhaps it is the experience of finding one's way through an often (though of course not always) 'foreign' world during fieldwork – or in some cases during graduate study abroad before returning 'home' – that makes anthropologists more sensitive to the spatial/cultural/political dimensions of social life. This may, indeed, be the source of some of anthropology's more unconventional insights, offering those who do research in more familiar settings with access to theoretical literature and a disciplinary focus shaped by this collective experience of feeling one's way through the dark, through the early stages of fieldwork, for the light switch.

It is to this end that the collection takes movement as its vehicle in analysing social experience of surroundings. Movement is, after all, life. Human lives unfold over socio-cultural terrain where history and language and experience congeal, and the liaison of bodies and environs brings endless adaptation and growth, with the land influencing denizens and travellers as much as the reverse. Movement is central to this engagement between being and surroundings. In contrast to the static, empty, soulless container conjured up by 'space', life transpires in organic dynamism, with social actors slowly influencing, through their corporeal and semantic iterations, the socio-cultural complex of elements that in turn shapes their development. Social knowledge of, and movement through, a social 'milieu'[14] is necessarily topo-mnemonic in character – memory is always influenced by spatial practice and spatial cues, and engagement in surroundings flows from embodied mnemonic interplay with characteristics of place in a community. Over time, a life spent in the same milieu can lead, as Bourdieu demonstrates, to a recursive cycle of practical adjustments that influence the dispositions of social actors there (Bourdieu 1977). The particular contours of a society's habitus can continue on in the conduct and articulations of social actors even when they move beyond the confines of the communities to which they have become habituated. But the very topography of these communities itself becomes a social matrix laden with embodied history and layers of mnemonic affect.

Both Bachelard's approach to the home and Casey's discussion of memory are informative here (Bachelard 1994; Casey 1987). Bachelard describes the physical and mnemonic rootedness that dwellers enjoy while living in and moving through the same abode: he writes that the place where we were born 'is physically inscribed in us' (Bachelard 1994: 14), and though he specifically describes the house, this characteristic of lived space is equally applicable to a neighbourhood or well-trammelled place. 'Space' is not an empty, Cartesian

14. For Berque (1997a: 8–10, 115–28; 1982), 'milieu' indexes a subjective, phenomenological, symbol-laden cultural topology in contrast with 'environment', which can denote a more objective, even scientific, view of surroundings.

medium, but a sequence of interpenetrating domains of affective significance to their inhabitants (Lefebvre 1994; Feld and Basso 1996). Space that has been lived and that has entered the imagination 'cannot remain indifferent space' (Bachelard 1994: xxxvi), unmarked by the subjective traces of the histories contained in it. Rather, 'space contains compressed time' (Bachelard 1994: 8), and its discovery and experience generate the recursive series of embodied adjustments that characterize a life lived in an intimately known nook – a lived embeddedness that develops quickly in a new home and in sterile hotel rooms. (Even the 'non-place' of metros, airport lounges, shopping malls, and so on (Augé 1995) – passages and nodes sometimes designed to eliminate characteristics of place entirely – has the potential to become emplacing and orienting once actors become habituated to routes travelled regularly. This is particularly the case for those who work in or otherwise inhabit 'non-places', who develop relationships with other functionaries in these flow corridors, and who develop something approaching intimate familiarity with these commodified spaces of transition, if not usually great affection.) Casey's account of 'place memory' and 'body memory' (Casey 1987: 181, 146) is important in conceptualizing the 'topoanalysis' (Bachelard 1994: 8) of, as it were, a living environment. Life in (that is, moving through) surroundings can be perceived as, though not reduced to, small, aggregating bodily acculturations to physical and social topography (Casey 1987: *passim*). But this clinical-sounding description seems almost to sterilize what is in fact a rich and dynamic process. As Bachelard points out, 'the word habit is too worn a word to express this passionate liaison of our bodies, which do not forget', with the places they experience (Bachelard 1994: 15). And the embodied history of a place is a powerful mnemonic register of associations that should not be neglected in assessing a social setting.[15]

Of course, contemporary lives often penetrate varied social milieux, wilfully or not, and the sites that these commuters and salesmen and smugglers, these travellers and migrants and 'nomads' encounter are rarely the stereotypical village community so often focused upon by early anthropologists. Against the backdrop of familiar tactics of state control – particularly after the jihadist strikes on New York City and Washington, D.C., on 11 September 2001 and attacks on 'failed' or 'rogue' states and stateless actors thereafter – one sense in which movement becomes constricted and impinged upon is when it passes through (or collides against) symbolic or concrete boundaries. Boundaries do not always disappear simply because of an increase of mobility, just as relations are not necessarily severed because of the presence of boundaries.[16] But at a time when industrialized nations in particular mobilize vast resources in the

15. Indeed, as Henri Lefebvre prophetically stated back in the 1970s, 'what is overlooked is the body' in analysing social space (Lefebvre 1994: 162).

name of counter-terrorism to prevent unsanctioned passage across geopolitical boundaries (Latour 2002), and when open public spaces and travel corridors have become monitored and controlled to a perhaps unprecedented degree, the conceit of free movement through myriad social spheres seems rather more distant and idealistic. In this era of relatively free Internet-facilitated exchange of ideas and transnational collaboration and trade (if not always camaraderie), the bleak-seeming prospect of nation-states as hermetically sealed 'gated communities' with members-only access – juxtaposed against other parts of the world (such as post-Intifada Palestine or HIV-beset Africa) as impoverished and/or plague-ridden Bantustans – occludes visions of a post-territorial world invigorated by movement. Indeed, against such a fragmented, even Balkanized, image of contemporary geopolitics, discussion of movement in general terms, and more particularly the idea of nomadism as a victory over repetitive, worn social traffic more typical of sedentary milieux (e.g., De Radkowski 2002; Deleuze and Guattari 1988), can smack of theoretical abstraction, idealism, and even naïveté (see Tsing 2005).[17] These accounts are, nevertheless, instructive. Theorists of social 'movements' have argued that as societies are composed of actors, and as social action is the basis of social life, then social life is constituted of and fuelled by social movements. Pioneering theorizations (e.g., Melucci 1989; Touraine 1981) of social movements as political action verge on reading like social movement as navigation – as if actors and societies were sharks that needed to keep plunging forward or risk drowning in stagnation. Yet movement (of social, political, and corporeal varieties) surely refreshes. Whether one views sedentarist navigations as Bachelard's 'passionate liaison' (above) or De Radkowski's shackled existence, movement stimulates through contact, creates familiarity and/or variety, and enables possibility. Keeping in mind the advantages of a 'processual approach, one alive to change' (Farmer 2006: xiii), as argued throughout this introduction, what anthropology is perhaps uniquely poised to offer among the social sciences is attention to the micro-scale, with ethnographic rigour and openness to fluidity, improvisation,

16. Based on his rigorous study of ethnic groups and their interactions, Barth's conclusion that social 'boundaries persist despite a flow of personnel across them' and that 'stable, persisting, and often vitally important social relations are maintained across such boundaries' (1969a: 9–10) is as true today as ever (see also Barth 1969b; Cohen 1986, 2000).

17. Anna Tsing (2005: 5-6) critiques this idea of liberation through movement that she finds prevalent in the 1990s in particular:

> By getting rid of national barriers and autocratic or protective state policies, everyone would have the freedom to travel everywhere. Indeed, motion itself would be experienced as self-actualization, and self-actualization without restraint would oil the machinery of the economy, science, and society. In fact, motion does not proceed this way at all…
>
> Insufficient funds, late buses, security searches, and informal lines of segregation hold up our travel; railroad tracks and regular airline schedules expedite it but guide its routes. Some of the time, we don't want to go at all, and we leave town only when they've bombed our homes.

and change. Good ethnographers remain attuned to how macro-scale shifts react against and interpenetrate the sites they scrutinize.

The contributors to this volume have interpreted these challenges in varying and important ways. It is the tension between restrictive, even claustrophobic, constructions of spatial order and the new potential for movement and exchange ushered in by recent social developments that contributors to this volume address collectively in their writing. The interplay of the existing and the emergent, the constricting and the liberating, furnishes an approach to human surroundings that can both help interpret where we are coming from and gauge where we are headed. From here on, I engage more directly with contributions to the present volume not only to introduce these chapters but to convey in greater detail the manner in which social worlds of vastly different kinds are experienced through movement.

The Chapters

Occupations and Divisions

Tim Ingold leads off with his polemical chapter 'Against Space', a scathing interrogation of familiar scholarly shibboleths entangled in ideas of space and knowledge. Ingold's contrarian analysis is guided not by static concepts like 'space/place' and 'occupation' – which he regards as misleading fictions resting on structures of power – but by a recognition of the essential movement and positionality of human interaction both with other bodies and with what he calls 'the land'. Ingold reminds us that 'places are defined by movement, not by the outer limits to movement', and he describes this 'meshwork' of experience as woven by 'lives that are never exclusively here or there, lived in this place or that, but always on the way from one place to another'. Ingold concludes that it is only through a persistent rational 'logic of inversion' that tapestries of knowing are unravelled or discarded in favour of an edifice of scientific knowledge constructed at a remove from the world it interprets. Ingold's frequently devastating critique of this knowledge-construction by scientists of varied disciplinary stripes (as well as the wider scope of political issues radiating outward from a space-focused orientation) not only exposes how wrong-headed much thinking about our world has become but, in turn, suggests an approach that conveys more faithfully the interpenetrating social domains, the dissolving horizons, and the perspectival fluidity of life and of knowing in human surroundings.

The book then plunges into several compelling socio-historical accounts of military, colonialist, and ritual action in which territorial infiltration and demarcation – and the spatial discourses from which they spring – betray imposition of sovereignty and the political ends of the state. First, **Bernardo**

A. Michael examines the territorial dynamics of political conflict in the context of colonial South Asia. In his ethnographically-inspired historical analysis, he examines how contrasting conceptions of territory and its demarcation led to extreme topo-social murk on the borders of the Empire. In a zone of ever-shifting allegiances, where obligations of military loyalty and tax liability could extend beyond the confines of a territory – and change not long after negotiation of treaties with ill-prepared colonial administrators – autochthonous political mappings of sovereignty along the Anglo–Gorkha frontier differed markedly from those imposed on the area by frustrated officials of the English East India Company. Michael's analysis of developments brought about by incessant political horse-trading, renegotiation of labyrinthine financial and kinship ties, and bursts of military action between 'sovereigns' raises important issues regarding the territorial fixations of imperialist European powers, their obsessive cartographic practice, and the incongruity of these vis-à-vis other social/political/territorial perspectives. This research not only exposes clear fissures between divergent socio-cultural understandings of human environs but, furthermore, allows considerable insight into the nature of boundaries and movement made more topical by contemporary social developments.

Next, **Richard Clarke**, in his 'Embodying Spaces of Violence', considers Israeli policies relating to 'the territories', and segregation of communities, in the context of the history of spatial production in Israel. His field research on both sides of the Green Line separating these two worlds examines how the region's fraught history has structured terrorism, terrorism discourse, and their corollaries of spatial separation, intrusion, and territorial control. Conducting ethnographic fieldwork during the (from our present vantage) stunningly amicable period of Oslo-Agreement cooperation between Palestinians and Israelis during the late 1990s, Clarke scrutinizes poignant narratives of former Israeli soldiers recalling their experience of the territories during military incursions. Very much an immersive and embodied experience, military training and later patrolling in hostile zones drilled specific forms of bodily practice that were reinforced during iterations through a variety of shifting domains: the winding alleyways of Kasbahs, the ambiguity of private homes selected for searches, and tranquil-seeming, yet parlous, desert expanses. Clarke interviews these former soldiers after they have returned from revisiting the occupied territories on organized tours (or otherwise); they interpret aloud their embodied rediscoveries of zones that stimulated tense responses during a surreal peace. Importantly for the volume, Clarke interprets these fecund social data against the backdrop of post-Oslo violence and the Israeli erection of a divisive security barrier and withdrawal from Gaza. Conceptions of space and identity here create very real implications for state (and resistance) projections of violence, as well as cognitive architectures of exclusion.

Martin Mills, in turn, confronts the globalization of the sacral state in 'post-diaspora' Tibetan Buddhism and the unmistakable nuances of conquest and domination that emanate from ostensibly peace-oriented rites. In this elegantly composed account, Mills argues that Tibetan-Buddhist rituals, practiced across the world since 1959, have been indispensable elements in the construction of Tibetan state legitimacy in the face of imperialistic encroachment by China and uncertain political limbo as a government-in-exile. Many rituals enacted in the name of 'World Peace' actually developed out of Tibetan-Buddhist practice marking the ritual subjugation of lived territory under the rule of the sacral state. To Mills, these are not mere innocuous anachronisms in the present day. In addition to considering the political and historical provenance of these ritual technologies of demarcation and power, Mills examines the contemporary exiled Tibetan use of concepts of 'World Peace' and juxtaposes post-Cold War Western interpretations of peaceful spiritual rhetoric with state-based Tibetan Buddhist understandings of geomantic authority and religious power. By doing so, he brings out important points of distinction between European understandings of inviolate national territorial sovereignty (and strong feelings of political identity drawn therefrom) and a perspective embracing a different (and still highly political) notion of projection of ritual authority across the boundaries of distant territories – 'a ritualized "galactic polity" … whose nexus is Tibet as a central sacred enclosure'.

Movement and 'Positionality'

The following chapters, in turn, explore more directly alternative ways of thinking about the politics of occupation and mobility, delving into the sometimes socially fettered, sometimes liberated, ways in which people move through, conceive of, and interact in spaces in an illustrative range of social settings. On a small island in Vanuatu, **Carlos Mondragón** finds a highly bounded set of domains interspersed with elements of fluidity. His rich ethnographic analysis depicts how Melanesian islanders' lived cosmologies reflect ideas about land, morality and social space that stand in marked contrast to (for example) Euro-American spatial discourse and practice. Bound up in a 'complex interweaving of land-(and sea-)scapes, personhood and genealogical "topographies"', islanders' cosmological prioritization of 'living growth' and 'processes of becoming' in language and spatial practice hints at a society open to lived improvisation and change. Yet at the same time, Mondragón's informants describe a social milieu in which movement throughout the island is severely curtailed by clan-controlled territory and taboo domains so extensive and intricate that only an outside ethnographer could have knowledge of a broad range of their features. Furthermore, islanders' local mappings of place, movement, and sociality suffered a collision with European missionaries' attempts over past decades to restructure islander settlements into more 'civilized' public aggregations. The island's contemporary predicament is a complex negotiation of all these above elements, with an attenuation of customary ways of conceiving of domains counterbalanced by the island's new-found place as a seaplane transportation hub for the archipelago, on the periphery of a variety of regional and transnational networks. Highlighting local conceptions of their environs and of interrelation, Mondragón points to islanders' alternative understandings of engagement and movement that offer insights into lived experiences of the world that lie underneath impositions of 'space' (missionary or otherwise) in social settings.

Morten Axel Pedersen's engrossing account of the nomadic practices and outlook of the Duxa, reindeer breeders of Northern Mongolia, privileges a dynamic fluidity in human action. Pedersen focuses on striking elements of Duxa 'landscape-ontology'. The Duxa herdspeople, fully nomadic and animist, view their world as a series of notable places radiating with spiritual energy surrounded by territory that is 'ontologically neutral' in social and spiritual terms. What Pedersen finds is that this 'nomadic landscape' is both physically and metaphysically heterogeneous, a feature inculcated by everyday navigations (and seasonal migrations) through the land and creation of, and engagement with, narratives that accrete over time to particular places associated with bizarre events, spirit-sightings, and topographical anomalies or irregularities. Armed with Latour's actor-network theory, Pedersen is able to interpret elements of this landscape-ontology and extrapolate from them to address wider issues of movement. As the world for a herdsman in Northern Mongolia may seem utterly boundless (to the extent that some Duxa may not even understand the very notion of boundaries or recognize their significance), Pedersen's ethnographic portrait of nomadic landscape-ontology goes some distance towards helping sedentarists apprehend a different understanding of the world, one made more topical in light of recent technological, social, and political shifts in 'developed' and 'developing' societies alike. In light of these latter concerns, the last three contributions to the volume engage more closely with such contemporary developments, assessing the impact of environmental pollution, globalization, and cross-cultural contact on movement and identity in more industrialized settings.

Peter Wynn Kirby's study scrutinizes the dislocation that victims of extreme toxic illness experience in contaminated communities. Kirby looks at the social and political fallout that emanated from the contested operations of a waste facility operating in the centre of a Tokyo community, from which approximately 10 per cent of the population contracted symptoms that were, in a number of cases, catastrophically debilitating. Grounding this case in Japanese society's complex logic of relationality – embedded in both traditional and contemporary ideas of place, hygiene, purity, and exclusion – Kirby delves into how the advent of toxic damage altered afflicted residents' spatial conceptions of their community, rerouting daily navigations (sometimes even eliminating mobility entirely) and prompting political agitation that further intensified victims' sense of alienation in a zone that became utterly transformed. This material not only furnishes examples of how deeply orienting, embodied 'senses of place' that accrue in a community can be subverted through a transformation in environment and bodily health, but demonstrates the disorientation that can occur when socio-cultural boundaries are collapsed or undermined.

Mitchell W. Sedgwick's study examines the politics of positionality in a large, protean office-space at a French subsidiary of a Japanese multinational corporation. Based on the responses and topo-strategies of French engineers working for Japanese management, ideas about position, prestige, and influence in the hierarchy of the organization played out clearly in personnel movements through the flexible membranes of the office. Sedgwick charts the rise and fall of executives' and engineers' fortunes in the subsidiary during a concatenation of organizational crises and cross-cultural displacements that made the political stakes in this emergent milieu all the more palpable. Against a backcloth of transnational flows of products and people and ideas writ large, in which this subsidiary was a deeply involved (though socio-culturally anchored) participant, the political jockeying and successive redeployments hint at the immense social adjustments that come hand-in-hand with processes of globalization and inter-cultural contact. In interrogating dimensions of spacing and movement in this well-chosen ethnographic site, the essay provides a penetrating insight into 'cross-cultural/social dynamics' as distilled within a specific organizational terrain.

The next chapter examines the experiences and challenges of a periphery remote from, and connecting up with, wider processes of globalization. **Eeva Berglund** focuses on the struggles of a rural outpost in contemporary Finland to reposition itself in the much-vaunted age of the network. In tough economic straits, an impoverished Finnish region, host to a small biotechnology lab and other ventures, attempts to balance aspirations for regeneration through entry into the global knowledge economy with nostalgia for the region's recent past as a mainstay of the nation's affectively resonant but economically declining forestry sector. Berglund immerses herself in the densely-forested environs of Kainuu as a Helsinki-born anthropologist exploring a provincial region after prolonged absence from her native Finland. The people she encounters there – very much concerned with preserving consciousness of forestry in, and passing on their childhood experience of 'moving in nature' (*kulkea luonnossa*) to, the next generation – transmit ideas of the 'Forest State' whose affective co-ordinates overlay national boundaries but which also exhibit differences in orientation that chafe at times against invocations of a networked world in which technological Finland now stands as a key node. In sketching this ethnographic tableau, Berglund exposes some elements of control and domination that are just as prominent in putatively liberating networks as in rigid social co-ordinates on the grid of state power.

What shapes movement and experience is, above all, *context*. The Conclusion to this book analyses the different topo-logics aired in the ethnographic studies presented by the volume's contributors and discerns in these an anthropological approach to movement that challenges the abstract conceit of 'space' so often invoked in scholarly accounts.

All of these chapters, indeed, put forward an anthropological sensitivity to movement and context that is, frequently, at odds with certain longstanding trends of ethnographic and knowledge production in anthropology and other social science. Importantly, it is the very practice of ethnography that furnishes a way through this impasse. That ethnography allows for the messiness of everyday life, and that ethnography furthermore tolerates (even rewards) adaptability and improvisation, gives anthropologists the methodological 'space' in which to move with, and understand, the murk of context, motile action, and social change around them. Writing in this spirit, the book's contributors, with varying methodological and theoretical choices – brought about largely by differences in the socio-historical topography of their selected arenas of study – remain open to the conceptual, positional, and social mutability that they encountered during their scholarly explorations.

In a sense, adaptability creates the conditions for successful socio-cultural analysis. In a shifting world, inhabited by social actors continually on the move, only an improvisational approach can hope to interpret the histories of human 'subjects' and the uneven 'meshwork' defined by their iterations. And while some may improvise better than others – as ethnomusicologist Paul F. Berliner's rich study of jazz musicians and their varied routes towards lyrical development, *Thinking in Jazz: The Infinite Art of Improvisation* (1994), vividly illustrates – we are all very capable of adapting as best we can along the journeys we choose. But improvisation takes serious work, a point that Berliner's book emphasizes repeatedly. Far from '"making something out of nothing"' (Berliner 1994: 492) or ad-libbing a few times a week in front of an audience, 'jazz as a way of life' (Berliner 1994: 486) involves a continual openness to material and surroundings honed by persistence, discipline, historical study, musicographic analysis, collaboration, social immersion, and lots of practice. While in the hands of gifted jazzmen improvisation can be elevated to an 'art', the craft of improvisation is accessible to all who choose it as a philosophy of living and as a means of knowing. For social scientists, then, whether through rigorous good ethnography itself or through a receptive approach to the histories and the presents of the peoples they study, seekers of social knowledge can peer behind the 'veil' of space-thinking to encounter fluid worlds as boundless as they must be.

References

Alpers, S. 1983. *The Art of Describing: Dutch Art in the Seventeenth Century*. Chicago: University of Chicago Press.

Appadurai, A. 1996. *Modernity at Large: Cultural Dimensions of Globalization*. Minneapolis, MN: University of Minnesota Press.

Augé, M. 1995. *Non-Places: Introduction to an Anthropology of Supermodernity*. London: Verso.

Bachelard, G. 1994 [1958]. *The Poetics of Space*. Boston: Beacon Press.

Barth, F. 1969a. 'Introduction', in Barth (ed.), *Ethnic Groups and Boundaries: The Social Organization of Cultural Difference*. London: George Allen and Unwin.

———. 1969b. 'Pathan Identity and its Maintenance', in Barth (ed.), *Ethnic Groups and Boundaries: The Social Organization of Cultural Difference*. London: George Allen and Unwin.

Berliner, P. F. 1994. *Thinking in Jazz: The Infinite Art of Improvisation*. Chicago and London: University of Chicago Press.

Berque, A. 1982. *Vivre l'Espace au Japon*. (*Living Space in Japan*. Published in French.) Paris: Presses Universitaires de France.

———. 1997a. *Japan: Nature, Artifice, and Japanese Culture*, trans. Ros Swartz. Yelvertoft Manor, Northamptonshire: Pilkington Press.

Bestor, T. C. 2001. 'Supply-Side Sushi: Commodity, Market, and the Global City', *American Anthropologist* 103(1): 76–95.

———. 2004. *Tsukiji: The Fish Market at the Center of the World*. Berkeley and Los Angeles: University of California Press.

Bourdieu, P. 1977. *Outline of a Theory of Practice*. Cambridge: Cambridge University Press.

Carsten, J. and S. Hugh-Jones. 1995. 'Introduction: About the House: Lévi-Strauss and Beyond', in Carsten and Hugh-Jones (eds), *About the House: Lévi-Strauss and Beyond*. Cambridge: Cambridge University Press.

Casey, E. 1987. *Remembering: A Phenomenological Study*. Bloomington and Indianapolis: Indiana University Press.

———. 1997. *The Fate of Place: A Philosophical History*. Berkeley and Los Angeles: University of California Press.

Castells, M. 1977. *The Urban Question*. London: Edward Arnold.

———. 1983. *The City and the Grassroots: A Cross-Cultural Theory of Urban Social Movements*. London: Edward Arnold.

———. 2000. *The Rise of the Network Society*, second edition. Oxford: Blackwell.

Clifford, J. 1997. *Routes: Travel and Translation in the Late Twentieth Century*. Cambridge, MA: Harvard University Press.

Clifford, J. and G. Marcus (eds). 1986. *Writing Culture: The Poetics and Politics of Ethnography*. Berkeley: University of California Press.

Cohen, A. P. (ed.). 1986. *Symbolic Boundaries: Identity and Diversity in British Cultures*. Manchester: Manchester University Press.

———. (ed.). 2000. *Signifying Identities: Anthropological Perspectives on Boundaries and Contested Values*. London: Routledge.

Debord, G. 1983. *The Society of the Spectacle*, trans. M. Prigent and L. Forsyth. London: Chronos.

De Certeau, M. 1988. *The Practice of Everyday Life*. Berkeley and Los Angeles: University of California Press.

Deleuze, G. and F. Guattari. 1988. *A Thousand Plateaus: Capitalism and Schizophrenia*. London: The Athlone Press.

De Radkowski, G.-H. 2002. *Anthropologie de l'Habiter: Vers le Nomadisme*. (*An Anthropology of Dwelling: Towards Nomadism*. Published in French.) Paris: Presses Universitaires de France.

Diamond, J. 2005 [1997]. *Guns, Germs, and Steel: The Fates of Human Societies.* New York: W. W. Norton.

Edgerton, S. Y. 1975. *The Renaissance Rediscovery of Linear Perspective.* New York: Harper and Row.

Escobar, A. 1995. *Encountering Development: The Making and Unmaking of the Third World.* Princeton: Princeton University Press.

Euclid. 1990 [*c.*300 BCE]. *The Thirteen Books of Euclid's* Elements (*Great Books of the World Volume X*). Chicago: Encyclopaedia Britannica.

Fabian, J. 1983. *Time and the Other: How Anthropology Creates its Object.* New York: Columbia University Press.

————. 1990. *Power and Performance: Ethnographic Explorations Through Proverbial Wisdom and Theater in Shaba, Zaire.* Madison: University of Wisconsin Press.

Farmer, P. 2006. 'From Haiti to Rwanda: Aids and Accusations' (preface to the 2006 edition). In P. Farmer, *Aids and Accusation: Haiti and the Geography of Blame*, second edition. Berkeley and Los Angeles: University of California Press.

Feld, S. and K. H. Basso (eds). 1996. *Senses of Place.* Santa Fe, NM: School of American Research Press.

Fletcher, R. 1971. *The Making of Sociology: A Study of Sociological Theory.* London: Michael Joseph.

Foucault, M. 1979. *Discipline and Punish: The Birth of the Prison.* Harmondsworth: Penguin.

Frank, A. G. 1998. *ReORIENT: Global Economy in the Asian Age.* Berkeley, Los Angeles, and London: University of California Press.

Gibbon, E. 1983 [1781]. *The History of the Decline and Fall of the Roman Empire.* London: Folio Society.

Gibson, J. J. 1950. *The Perception of the Visual World.* Cambridge, MA: Riverside Press.

Gluckman, H. M. 1955. *Custom and Conflict in Africa.* Oxford: Basil Blackwell.

————. 1958. *Analysis of a Social Situation in Modern Zululand.* Manchester: University of Manchester Press.

Goldmann, K., U. Hannerz, and C. Westin. 2000. 'Introduction: Nationalism and Internationalism in the Post-Cold War Era', in Goldmann, Hannerz, and Westin (eds), *Nationalism and Internationalism in the Post-Cold War Era.* London: Routledge.

Gudeman, S. and A. Rivera. 1990. *Conversations in Colombia: The Domestic Economy in Life and Text.* Cambridge: Cambridge University Press.

Gupta, A. and J. Ferguson (eds). 1997. *Culture, Power, Place: Explorations in Critical Anthropology.* Durham, NC: Duke University Press.

Hannerz, U. 1969. *Soulside.* New York: Columbia University Press.

————. 1980. *Exploring the City: Inquiries Toward an Urban Anthropology.* New York: Columbia University Press.

————. 1989. 'Notes on the Global Ecumene', *Public Culture* 1(2): 66–75.

————. 1992. *Cultural Complexity: Studies in the Social Organization of Meaning.* New York: Columbia University Press.

————. 1996. *Transnational Connections: Culture, People, Places.* New York and London: Routledge.

————. 2004. *Foreign News: Exploring the World of Foreign Correspondents.* Chicago and London: University of Chicago Press.

Harris, M. 1968. *The Rise of Anthropological Theory: A History of Theories of Culture.* London: Routledge and Kegan Paul.

Harvey, D. 1990. *The Condition of Postmodernity: An Enquiry into the Origins of Cultural Change.* Oxford: Blackwell.

Havelock, E. A. 1982. *The Literate Revolution in Greece and its Cultural Consequences.* Princeton, NJ: Princeton University Press.

Hirsch, E. 1995. 'Landscape: Between Space and Place', in E. Hirsch and M. O'Hanlon (eds), *The Anthropology of Landscape: Perspectives on Space and Place*. Oxford: Clarendon.

Hirsch, E. and M. O'Hanlon (eds). 1995. *The Anthropology of Landscape: Perspectives on Space and Place*. Oxford: Clarendon.

Hopkins, T. K. and I. Wallerstein. 1982. *World Systems Analysis: Theory and Methodology*. Beverly Hills and London: Sage.

Ingold, T. 2001. 'Against Space'. *Space, Culture, Power conference, Aberdeen,* 10 April 2001 [plenary lecture]. Aberdeen: University of Aberdeen.

Ivins, W. M., Jr. 1946. *Art and Geometry: A Study in Space Intuitions*. Cambridge, MA: Harvard University Press.

Jay, M. 1993. *Downcast Eyes: The Denigration of Vision in Twentieth-Century French Thought*. Berkeley and London: University of California Press.

Jonas, H. 1982. 'The Nobility of Sight: A Study in the Phenomenology of the Senses', in *The Phenomenon of Life: Toward a Philosophical Biology*. Chicago: University of Chicago Press.

Kirby, P. W. 2002. 'Environmental Consciousness and the Politics of Waste in Tokyo: "Nature", Health, Pollution, and the Predicament of Toxic Japan', Ph.D. dissertation. Cambridge: University of Cambridge.

Latour, B. 2002. *War of the Worlds: What about Peace?* Chicago: Prickly Paradigm Press.

Lefebvre, H. 1994 [1974]. *The Production of Space*. Oxford and Cambridge, MA: Blackwell.

Lewis, O. 1951. *Life in a Mexican Village*. Urbana, IL: University of Illinois Press.

———. 1965. *La Vida*. New York: Random House.

Low, S. and D. Lawrence-Zúñiga (eds). 2003a. *The Anthropology of Space and Place: Locating Culture*. Oxford: Blackwell.

Low, S. and D. Lawrence-Zúñiga. 2003b. 'Locating Culture', in Low and Lawrence-Zúñiga (eds), *The Anthropology of Space and Place: Locating Culture*. Oxford: Blackwell.

MacCormack, C. and M. Strathern (eds). 1980. *Nature, Culture and Gender*. Cambridge: Cambridge University Press.

Malinowski, B. 1922 [1961]. *Argonauts of the Western Pacific: An Account of Native Enterprise and Adventure in the Archipelagoes of Melanesian New Guinea*. New York: Dutton.

———. 1944. *A Scientific Theory of Culture and Other Essays*. Chapel Hill, NC: University of North Carolina Press.

Malkki, L. 1995. *Purity and Exile: Violence, Memory, and National Cosmology among Hutu Refugees in Tanzania*. Chicago: University of Chicago Press.

Marcus, G. and M. Fischer. 1986. *Anthropology as Cultural Critique: An Experimental Moment in the Human Sciences*. Chicago: University of Chicago Press.

Melucci, A. 1989. *Nomads of the Present: Social Movements and Individual Needs in Contemporary Society*. London: Hutchinson Radius.

Mitchell, J. C. 1987. *Cities, Society, and Social Perception: A Central African Perspective*. Oxford: Clarendon.

Mitchell, J. C. (ed.). 1969. *Social Networks in Urban Situations: Analyses of Personal Relationships in Central African Towns*. Manchester: University of Manchester Press.

Morris, R. 2000. *In the Place of Origins: Modernity and its Mediums in Northern Thailand*. Durham, NC: Duke University Press.

Ong, A. 1999. *Flexible Citizenship: The Cultural Logics of Transnationality*. Durham, NC: Duke University Press.

Ong, W. J. 1958. *Ramus, Method, and the Decay of Dialogue: From the Art of Discourse to the Art of Reason*. Cambridge, MA: Harvard University Press.

Piot, C. 1999. *Remotely Global: Village Modernity in West Africa*. Chicago: University of Chicago Press.

Rabinow, P. 2003. '*Ordonnance*, Discipline, Regulation: Some Reflections on Urbanism', in S. Low and Denise Lawrence-Zúñiga (eds), *The Anthropology of Space and Place: Locating Culture*. Oxford: Blackwell.
Redfield, R. 1941. *The Folk Culture of Yucatan*. Chicago: University of Chicago Press.
Sadler, S. 1998. *The Situationist City*. Cambridge, MA, and London: MIT Press.
Schechner, R. 1985. *Between Theater and Anthropology*. Philadelphia: University of Pennsylvania Press.
Schechner, R. and W. Appel (eds). 1990. *By Means of Performance: Intercultural Studies of Theatre and Ritual*. Cambridge: Cambridge University Press.
Scott, J. C. 1976. *The Moral Economy of the Peasant: Rebellion and Subsistence in Southeast Asia*. New Haven: Yale University Press.
———. 1985. *Weapons of the Weak: Everyday Forms of Peasant Resistance*. New Haven: Yale University Press.
Sennett, R. 1994. *Flesh and Stone: The Body and the City in Western Civilization*. London: Faber and Faber.
Stewart, M. 1997. *The Time of the Gypsies*. Boulder, CO, and Oxford: Westview.
Stocking, G. 1982. *Race, Culture, and Evolution: Essays in the History of Anthropology*. Chicago: University of Chicago Press.
Stoller, P. 1997. *Sensuous Scholarship*. Philadelphia: University of Pennsylvania Press.
Strang, V. 1997. *Uncommon Ground*. Oxford: Berg.
Strathern, M. 1995. 'The Nice Thing about Culture is that Everyone Has It', in Strathern (ed.), *Shifting Contexts: Transformations in Anthropological Knowledge*. London and New York: Routledge.
Taussig, M. 1987. *Shamanism, Colonialism, and the Wild Man: A Study in Terror and Healing*. Chicago and London: University of Chicago Press.
Touraine, A. 1981. *The Voice and the Eye: An Analysis of Social Movements*, trans. Alan Duff. Cambridge: Cambridge University Press.
Tsing, A. 2000. 'The Global Situation', *Cultural Anthropology* 15(3): 327–60.
———. 2005. *Friction: An Ethnography of Global Connection*. Princeton, NJ: Princeton University Press.
Turner, V. 1957. *Schism and Continuity in an African Society: A Study of Ndembu Village Life*. Manchester: Manchester University Press.
———. 1967. *The Forest of Symbols*. Ithaca: Cornell University Press.
———. 1990. 'Are There Universals of Performance?', in R. Schechner and W. Appel (eds), *By Means of Performance: Intercultural Studies of Theatre and Ritual*. Cambridge: Cambridge University Press.
Wartofsky, M. W. 1979. *Models: Representation and the Scientific Understanding*. Dordecht, Netherlands: Reidel.
Williams, R. 1973. *The Country and the City*. London: Chatto and Windus.
Wolf, E. R. 1971. *Peasant Wars of the Twentieth Century*. London: Faber and Faber.
———. 1982. *Europe and the People without History*. Berkeley and Los Angeles: University of California Press.
Worsley, P. 1984. *The Three Worlds: Culture and World Development*. London: George Weidenfield and Nicolson.
Yang, M. M.-H. 1997. 'Mass Media and Transnational Subjectivity in Shanghai', in A. Ong and D. M. Nonini (eds), *Ungrounded Empires: The Cultural Politics of Modern Chinese Nationalism*. New York: Routledge.
Yates, F. A. 1966. *The Art of Memory*. London: Routledge and Kegan Paul.

Chapter 2
Against Space: Place, Movement, Knowledge

Tim Ingold

I wish to argue, in this chapter, against the notion of space. Of all the terms we use to describe the world we inhabit, it is the most abstract, the most empty, the most detached from the realities of life and experience. Consider the alternatives. Biologists say that living organisms inhabit *environments*, not space, and whatever else they may be, human beings are certainly organisms. Throughout history, whether as hunters and gatherers, farmers or herders of livestock, people have drawn a living from the *land*, not from space. Farmers plant their crops in the *earth*, not in space, and harvest them from *fields*, not from space. Their animals graze *pastures*, not space. Travellers make their way through the *country*, not through space, and as they walk or stand they plant their feet on the *ground*, not in space. Painters set up their easels in the *landscape*, not in space. When we are at home, we are *indoors*, not in space, and when we go outdoors we are in the *open*, not in space. Casting our eyes upwards, we see the *sky*, not space, and on a windy day we feel the *air*, not space. Space is nothing, and because it is nothing it cannot truly be inhabited at all.

How have we arrived at such an abstract and rarefied concept to describe the world in which we live? My contention is that it results from the operation of a particular logic that has a central place in the structure of modern thought. I call this the logic of inversion (Ingold 1993). What it does, in a nutshell, is to turn the pathways along which life is lived into boundaries within which it is enclosed. Life, according to this logic, is reduced to an internal property of things that occupy the world but which do not, strictly speaking, inhabit it. A world that is occupied but not inhabited, that is filled with existing things rather than woven from the strands of their coming-into-being, is a world of space. In what follows I shall show how the logic of inversion transforms our understanding, first, of place; secondly, of movement; and, thirdly, of knowledge. Emplacement becomes enclosure, travelling becomes transport, and ways of knowing become transmitted culture. Putting all these together, we are led to that peculiarly modular conception of being that is such a striking feature of modernity, and of which the concept of space is the logical corollary.

Place

I have nothing against the idea of place. I do, however, think there is something wrong with the notion that places exist *in space*. The persistent habit of counterposing space and place, as Doreen Massey complains, leads us to imagine that life is lived at the base of a vortex, from which the only escape is to lift off from the ground of real experience, upwards and outwards, towards ever higher levels of abstraction (Massey 2005: 183). Time and again, philosophers have assured us that as earthbound beings, we can only live, and know, *in* places (e.g., Casey 1996: 18). I do not live, however, in the sitting room of my house. Any ordinary day sees me wandering around between the sitting room, dining room, kitchen, bathroom, bedroom, study and so on, as well as in the garden. Nor am I housebound, as I travel daily to my place of work, to the shops and to other places of business, while my children go to school. To this, philosophers of place respond that, of course, places exist like Russian dolls on many levels in a nested series, and that at whatever level we may select, a place is liable both to contain a number of lower-level places and to be contained, alongside other places at that level, within a higher-level one. Thus my house, as a place, contains the smaller places comprised of the rooms and garden, and is contained within the larger places of my neighbourhood and home town. As J. E. Malpas writes, 'places always open up to disclose other places within them …, while from within any particular place one can always look outwards to find oneself within some much larger expanse (as one can look from the room in which one sits to the house in which one lives)' (1999: 170–71).

Only a philosopher could look from his sitting room and see his whole house! For its ordinary residents, the house or apartment is disclosed processionally, as a temporal series of vistas, occlusions, and transitions unfolding along the myriad pathways they take, from room to room and in and out of doors, as they go about their daily tasks. Malpas, however, writes of leaving his room for his apartment, his apartment for the building, and the building for the neighbourhood and city in which he lives, as though each step along the way were a movement not along but *upwards*, from level to level, from smaller, more exclusive places to larger, more inclusive ones. And the higher he climbs, the further removed he feels from the groundedness of *place*, and the more drawn to an abstract sense of *space*. Conversely, the return trip homeward takes him on a downward movement, through the levels, from space back to place (1999: 171). Each level, here, is like one line on an address that enables the postman eventually to deliver the letter into the lowest-level container within which the recipient is supposed to lie ensconced. When the letter drops through the philosopher's front door it is as if it also drops *down* one level, from street to house. And when he picks it up and takes it through to his living room (rather than, say, the kitchen), it drops another level still. Although, in reality, the letter comes into his hands through having been relayed along a number of paths that have touched one another at various places along the way, such as the letter box, the sorting office, and so on, the impression is conveyed that it has come 'down' to him through a progressive refinement of spatial scale, from everywhere to somewhere, or from space to place.

Opening the letter in his living-room, he might pause to reflect on how the concepts of 'life' and 'room' have come to be conjoined in the denomination of this area of his house. In vernacular English the word 'room', in this context, simply means an interior part of the building enclosed by walls, floor, and ceiling. And 'living' covers a suite of common indoor activities that would be undertaken by the occupants of this particular room. But as Kenneth Olwig has pointed out, when 'life' and 'room' are joined in German they yield an entirely different concept, namely '*lebensraum*' (Olwig 2002: 3). Here, the meaning of life comes closer to what the philosopher Martin Heidegger identified as the foundational sense of dwelling: not the occupation of a world already built but the very process of inhabiting the earth. Life, in this sense, is lived in the open, rather than being contained within the structures of the built environment (Heidegger 1971). Hence, too, the 'room' of '*lebensraum*' is not an enclosure but an opening, one that affords scope for growth and movement. It has no walls, only the horizons progressively disclosed to the traveller as he passes along a trail; no floor, only the ground beneath his feet; no ceiling, only the sky arching overhead.

My reason for digressing on the significance of 'room' is to address a peculiar problem of translation. The German '*raum*', or its cognate '*rum*' in the Scandinavian languages, is nowadays the accepted equivalent of the Anglo-American concept of space. Yet their connotations are far from identical. In English, 'space' and 'room' are quite distinct, with 'room' conceived as a highly localized, life-containing compartment within the boundless totality of space. It appears, however, that in its translation as 'space', '*raum*'/'*rum*' never entirely lost the sense of containment or enclosure that currently attaches to the notion of place. Perhaps that is why, as Olwig suggests, a geography that has its roots in the intellectual traditions of Germany and the Nordic countries so often rolls together space and place. For, in the modern concept of '*raum*'/'*rum*', it seems that the two contradictory connotations of openness and closure, of 'absolute space and confined room' (Olwig 2002: 7), are conflated. It was this duplicity that allowed Nazi propagandists, in the run-up to the Second World War, to seize upon the notion of '*lebensraum*' as justification at once for unlimited expansion and for the bounded self-sufficiency of the German nation.

Even Heidegger, himself somewhat complicit in this enterprise, thought of '*raum*' as a clearing for life that was nevertheless bounded. But he promptly went on to explain that this boundary was not a border but a horizon, 'not that at which something stops but … that from which something begins its presencing' (Heidegger 1971: 154). It seems that in the transition from its ancient sense of a clearing, opening or 'way through' to the modern oxymoron of 'space and place', the concept of 'room' has been called upon to perform the trick of inversion, turning the affordances for dwelling opened up along a path of movement into an enclosed capsule for life suspended in the void. The idea that places are situated in space is the product of this inversion, and is not given prior to it. In other words, far from being applied to two opposed yet complementary aspects of reality, space and place, the concept of 'room' is centrally implicated in setting up the distinction between them. It is not a distinction that is immediately given to our experience which, as I shall now argue, is drawn from lives that are never exclusively here or there, lived in this place or that, but always on the way from one place to another.

Let me introduce the argument by way of a simple experiment. Take a piece of plain paper and a pencil, and draw a rough circle. It might look something like this:

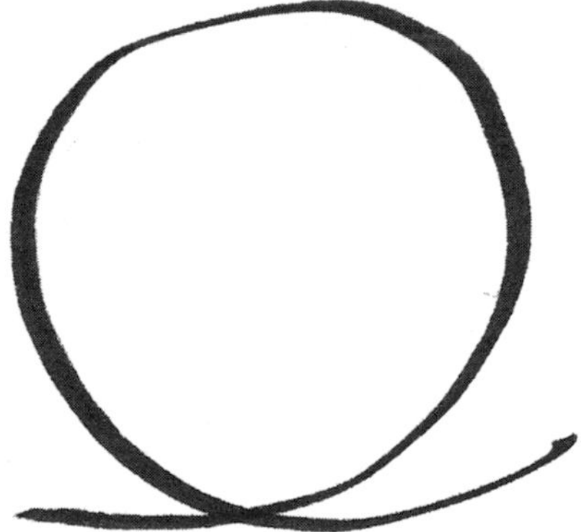

How should we interpret this line? Strictly speaking, it is the trace left by the gesture of your hand as, holding the pencil, it alighted on the paper and took a turn around before continuing on its way to wherever it would go and whatever it would do next. However, viewing the line as a totality, ready-drawn on the page, we might be more inclined to interpret it quite differently – not as a trajectory of movement but as a static perimeter, delineating the figure of the circle against the ground of an otherwise empty plane. In just the same way we tend to identify traces of the circumambulatory movements that bring a place into being as boundaries that demarcate the place from its surrounding space. Whether on paper or on the ground, the pathways or trails along which movement proceeds are perceived as limits within which it is contained. Both cases exemplify the logic of inversion at work, turning the 'way through' of the trail into the containment of the place-in-space. This is illustrated below.

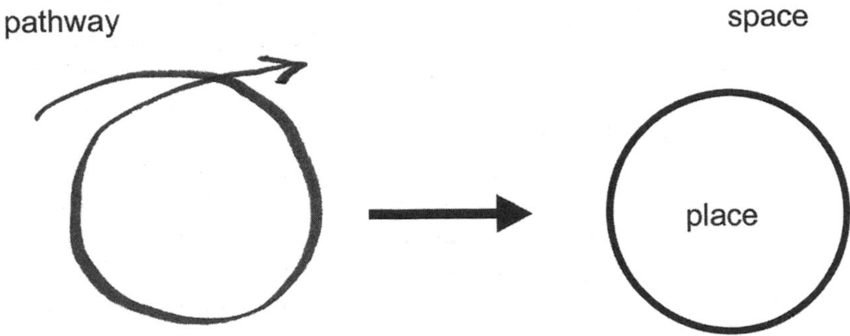

My contention is that lives are led not inside places but through, around, to and from them, from and to places elsewhere (Ingold 2000: 229). I shall use the term *wayfaring* to describe the embodied experience of this perambulatory movement. It is as wayfarers, then, that human beings inhabit the earth. But by the same token, human existence is not fundamentally place-*bound*, as Christopher Tilley (1994: 25) maintains, but place-*binding*. It unfolds not in places but along paths. Proceeding along a path, every inhabitant lays a trail. Where inhabitants meet, trails are entwined, as the life of each becomes bound up with the other. Every entwining is a knot, and the more that life-lines are entwined, the greater the density of the knot.

Places, then, are like knots, and the threads from which they are tied are lines of wayfaring. A house, for example, is a place where the lines of its residents are tightly knotted together. But these lines are no more contained within the house than are threads contained within a knot. Rather, they trail beyond it, only to become caught up with other lines in other places, as are threads in other knots.

Together they make up what I shall call a *meshwork*. I borrow the term from Henri Lefebvre, who speaks of 'the reticular patterns left by animals, both wild and domestic, and by people (in and around the houses of village or small town, as in the town's immediate environs)', together making up the texture of the world. Caught up in these multiple entanglements, the built environment is more 'archi-textural' than architectural (Lefebvre 1991: 117–18).

Places, then, are delineated by movement, not by the outer limits to movement. Indeed, it is for just this reason that I have chosen to refer to people who frequent places as 'inhabitants' rather than 'locals', for it would be quite wrong to suppose that such people are confined within a particular place, or that their experience is circumscribed by the restricted horizons of a life lived only there. Inhabitants can indeed be widely travelled, as David Anderson, for example, found during fieldwork among Evenki reindeer herders in Siberia. When he questioned his hosts about the location of their original clan lands, he was told that in the past people travelled – and lived – not 'somewhere' but 'everywhere' (Anderson 2000: 133–35). This 'everywhere', however, is not 'nowhere'. Evenki herders did not formerly live in space rather than place. The illusion that they did is a product of our own cartographic conventions that lead us to imagine the surface of the earth divided into a mosaic of areas, each occupied by a named nation or ethnic group. On a map drawn according to these conventions, the few thousand Evenki appear to occupy an area almost twice the size of Europe! The Evenki people, however, did not occupy their country, they inhabited it. And whereas occupation is areal, habitation is lineal. That is to say, it takes people not *across* the land surface but *along* the paths that lead from place to place. From the perspective of inhabitants, therefore, 'everywhere' is not space. It is the entire meshwork of intertwined trails along which people carry on their lives. While on the trail one is always somewhere. But every 'somewhere' is on the way to somewhere else. This is an appropriate moment, therefore, to turn from place to movement. How has our understanding of movement been transformed by the logic of inversion?

Movement

In his contemplation on the Arctic, *Playing Dead* (1989), the Canadian writer Rudy Weibe compares native Inuit understandings of movement and travel over land or sea-ice with those of the sailors of the Royal Navy in their maritime search for the elusive Northwest Passage to the Orient. For the Inuit, *as soon as a person moves he becomes a line.* To hunt for an animal, or to find another human being who may be lost, you lay one line of tracks across the expanse, looking for signs of another line of motion that would lead to your objective. Thus the entire country is perceived as a mesh of lines rather than as a continuous surface. The British sailors, however, 'accustomed to the fluid, trackless seas, moved in terms of area' (1989: 16). The vessel, supplied for the voyage before setting sail, was conceived as a moving dot upon the surface of the sea, its position always located by latitude and longitude. We have already encountered this difference between lineal movement along paths of travel and lateral movement *across* a surface in our comparison of the respective 'everywheres' of habitation and occupation. I have referred to movement of the former kind as *wayfaring*. Movement of the latter kind, I call *transport*. I shall now show that the inversion that renders the inhabited world as space, also converts wayfaring into transport.

The wayfarer is continually on the move. More strictly, he *is* his movement. As with the Inuit in the example presented above, the wayfarer is instantiated in the world as a line of travel. It is a line that advances from the tip as he presses on in an ongoing process of growth and development, or of self-renewal. As he proceeds, however, the wayfarer has to sustain himself, both perceptually and materially, through an active engagement with the country that opens up along his path.[1] Though from time to time he must pause for rest, and may even return repeatedly to the same place to do so, each pause is a moment of tension that – like holding one's breath – becomes ever more intense and less sustainable the longer it lasts. Indeed, the wayfarer has no final destination, for wherever he is, and so long as life goes on, there is somewhere further he can go.

Transport, by contrast, is essentially destination-oriented (Wallace 1993: 65–66). It is not so much a development along a way of life as a carrying across, from location to location, of people and goods in such a way as to leave their basic natures unaffected. For in transport, the traveller does not himself move. Rather he is moved, becoming a passenger in his own body, if not in some vessel that can extend or replace the body's powers of propulsion. While in transit he remains encased within his vessel, drawing for sustenance on his own supplies and holding a predetermined course. Only upon reaching his destination, and when his means of transport come to a halt, does the traveller begin to move. But this movement, confined within a place, is concentrated in one spot. Thus the very places where the wayfaring inhabitant pauses for rest are, for the transported passenger, sites of occupation. In between sites, he barely skims the surface of the world.

A second experiment might serve to highlight the contrast. Take up your pencil once again and, this time, draw a continuous freehand line. Like the circle you drew before, the line remains as the trace of your manual gesture. In the memorable phrase of the painter, Paul Klee, your line has gone out for a walk (Klee 1961: 105).

1. Based on fieldwork among the Inuit of Igloolik, Claudio Aporta writes that travelling 'was not a transitional activity between one place and another, but a way of being … Other travellers are met, children are born, and hunting, fishing and other subsistence activities are performed' (Aporta 2004: 13).

But now I want you to draw a dotted line. To do this you have to bring the tip of your pencil into contact with the paper at a predetermined point, and then cause it to perform a little pirouette on that point so as to form a dot. All the energy, and all the movement, is focused down on the point, almost as though you were drilling a hole. Then you have to lift your pencil from the paper and carry it across to the next point where you do the same, and so on until you have marked the paper with a series of dots.

But where, in this series, is the line? It is not generated as a movement, or even as the trace of a movement, since all the movement is in the dots. Whatever movements you might make between drawing each dot serve merely to carry the pencil-tip from one point to the next, and are entirely incidental to the line itself. During these intervals the pencil is inactive, out of use. Indeed you could even rest it on your desk for any length of time before picking it up again and returning it to the paper surface.

The dotted line, in short, is defined not by a gesture but as a connected sequence of fixed points. Now, just as in drawing, where the line is traced by a movement of your hands, so the wayfarer in his perambulations lays a trail on the ground in the form of footprints, paths and tracks. Thus, writing of the Walbiri, an Aboriginal people of the Australian Central Desert, Roy Wagner notes that 'the life of a person is the sum of his tracks, the total inscription of his movements, something that can be traced out along the ground' (Wagner 1986: 21). The logic of inversion, however, converts every track or trail into the equivalent of a dotted line, first by dividing it into stages,

and then by rolling and packing each stage into the confines of a destination.

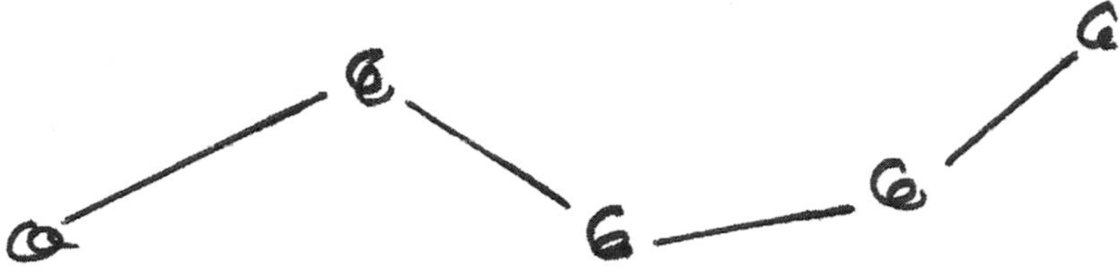

The lines linking these destinations, like those of an air or rail traffic map, are not traces of movement but point-to-point connectors. These are the lines of transport. And whereas the wayfarer signs his presence on the land as the ever-growing sum of his trails, the passenger carries his signature about with him as he is transported from place to place. Wherever he may be, he should be able to replicate this highly condensed, miniature gesture as a mark of his unique and unchanging identity. Once again we find the logic of inversion at work here, turning the paths along which people lead their lives into internal properties of self-contained, bounded individuals. Whenever the individual is required to sign on the dotted line, this inversion is re-enacted. An occupant of everywhere and an inhabitant or nowhere, the signatory declares by this act his allegiance to space.

As I have already suggested, occupation is areal whereas habitation is lineal. The various destinations to be linked in a system of transport are understood to be laid out upon an isotropic surface, each at a location specified by global co-ordinates. The lines connecting these destinations comprise a network that is spread across the surface, and 'pinned down' at each of its nodes. To the wayfarer, however, the world is not presented as a surface to be traversed. In his movements, he threads his way *through* this world rather than routing *across* it from point to point. Of course the wayfarer is a terrestrial being, and must perforce travel over the land. The surfaces of the land, however, are *in* the world, not *of* it (Ingold 2000: 241). And woven into the very texture of these surfaces are the lines of growth and movement of inhabitants. What they form, as we have already seen, is not a network of point-to-point connections but a tangled mesh of interwoven and complexly knotted strands. Every strand is a way of life, and every knot a place. Indeed the mesh is something like a net in its original sense of an openwork fabric of interlaced or knotted cords. But through its metaphorical extension to the realms of modern transport and communications, and especially information technology, the meaning of 'the net' has changed.[2] We are now more inclined to think of it as a complex of interconnected points than of interwoven lines. For this reason I find it necessary to distinguish between the *network* of transport and the *meshwork* of wayfaring. The key to this distinction is the recognition that the lines of the meshwork are not connectors. They are the paths *along* which life is lived. And it is in the binding together of lines, not in the connecting of points, that the mesh is constituted.

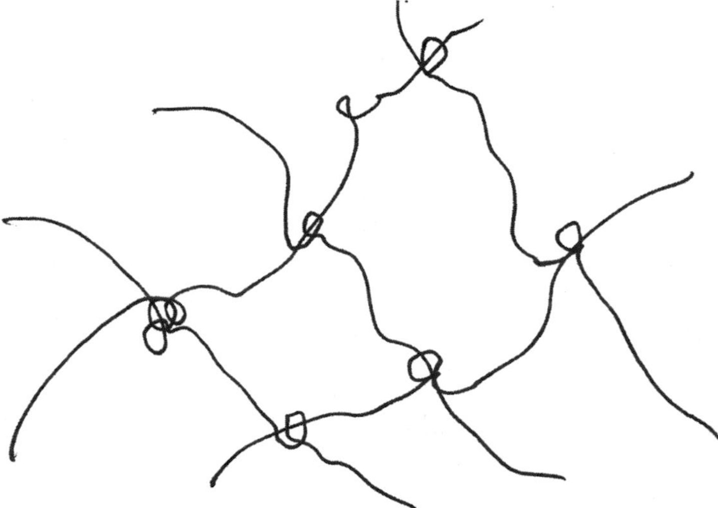

I have argued that wayfaring is our most fundamental mode of being in the world. Does this mean that the possibility of genuine transport is but a dream, on a par with the illusion that the places it connects are fixed in space? If so, then we must also acknowledge that modern metropolitan societies have done much to turn the dream into reality. They have created transport systems that span the globe in a vast network of destination-to-destination connections. And they have converted travel from an experience of movement in which action and perception are intimately coupled into one of enforced immobility and sensory deprivation. The passenger, strapped in his seat, no longer has the 'all around' perception of a land that stretches without interruption from the ground beneath

2. To me, as a relatively inexperienced user, navigating the Internet is a matter of activating a sequence of links that take me, almost instantaneously, from site to site. Each link is a connector, and the web itself is a network of interconnected sites. Travel through cyberspace thus resembles transport. Experienced users, however, tell me that, as they 'surf' the net, they follow trails like wayfarers, with no particular destination in mind. For them, the web may seem more like a mesh than a net. How, precisely, we should understand 'movement' through the Internet is an interesting question, but it is beyond the scope of this chapter, and most certainly beyond my own competence, to address it further here.

his feet towards the horizon. It rather appears as so much scenery projected onto vertical screens, more or less distant, that seem to slide past one another due to the operation of parallax. This flattening and layering of the landscape may, as Orvar Löfgren has observed (2000: 24), have more to do with the effects of travel at speed than with the anchoring of vision to a fixed location. Yet the essence of speed may lie less in the actual ratio of distance travelled to elapsed time than in the decoupling, in transport, of perception and motility.

Once this decoupling has been effected – once, that is, movement is reduced to sheer mechanical displacement – the speed of transport can, in principle, be increased indefinitely. Ideally it should take no time at all. This is because the lines of the transport network, criss-crossing the continuum of space, lack duration. By connecting points on a network, or 'joining the dots', the prospective traveller can *virtually* reach his destination even before setting out. As a cognitive artefact or assembly, the route plan pre-exists its physical enactment. Yet in practice it takes time to get there, even by the fastest means. Perfect transport is impossible for the same reason that one cannot be in two places, nor indeed everywhere, simultaneously. As all travel is movement in real time, a person can never be quite the same on arrival at a place as when he set out: some memory of the journey will remain, however attenuated, and will in turn condition his knowledge of the place. We might wish it were otherwise: thus scientific researchers are routinely advised not to allow the travails of gaining access to field sites to intrude upon their observations, lest this might distort the data collected and compromise their objectivity. But total objectivity is as impossible an ideal as is perfect transport. We cannot get from one place to another by leap-frogging the world. Or in the wise words of the nursery rhyme, *We're Going on a Bear Hunt*, 'We can't go over it, We can't go under it, Oh no! We've got to go through it'.

Knowledge

A team of scientists has set out to investigate changes in the ecology and hydrology of the arctic tundra in a particular region of the Russian North.[3] They wish to ascertain the major drivers of these changes, including global warming and industrial pollution. On a map of the region they have drawn a straight line of twenty dots, spaced out at equal intervals of one centimetre (corresponding to

3. The example that follows is loosely based on a project in which I was marginally involved. This was the EU-funded TUNDRA project (Tundra Degradation in the Russian Arctic), which ran for three years from 1998 to 2000, co-ordinated by the University of Lapland's Arctic Centre. The project set out to assess feedbacks from the Russian Arctic to the global climate system through changes in greenhouse gas emissions and in freshwater run-off, and to understand the relations between climate change, carbon and hydrological cycles, industrial pollution and social awareness. The study was carried out in the Usa river basin, in the north-eastern part of the territory of the Komi Republic, just to the west of the Ural Mountains.

fifty kilometres on the map). Each of these dots marks a site where the team intends to collect soil and water samples, to record the vegetation, and to take any necessary measurements, for example of the acidity of the soil or of background radiation. As overland travel is slow and hazardous in this region, which in summer is a maze of mosquito-infested swamps, aimlessly meandering rivers, and stagnant pools, the team will hire a helicopter to transport themselves and their equipment from one location to the next. In effect, these airborne trips re-enact at full scale the drawing of the dotted line on the map. Just as the tip of the pencil had been lowered at a succession of points in order to mark the paper surface of the map, so the helicopter with its burden of scientists and instruments will 'drop down' at site after site, enabling them to take their readings from the actual surface of the tundra. Though it might be otherwise for the pilot, who has to guide his machine to the right place and find a suitable spot to land, so far as the scientists are concerned their helicopter transport is wholly ancillary to the primary task of data collection. Indeed, while the pilot, an inhabitant of the region, is preoccupied with finding the way to the next landing place, the scientists have little to do but admire the view from the windows. Only when the pilot takes a break can the scientists get on with the job of making their observations.

In this example, data are being collected from a series of fixed locations. For the scientific team these locations comprise a thousand-kilometre transect that cuts across the surface of the earth. But the transect is not a pathway: it is not the trace of a movement but a chain of point-to-point connections. Held together by these connections, the constituent locations of the transect are – we could say – *laterally* integrated. But what of the data obtained from them? Every datum is a 'thing given', a fact. Though discovered among the contents of a site, *where* it is, or how it came to be there, forms no part of *what* it is. As a sample or specimen, each fact is deemed to be one of a kind. And its significance lies not in the story of its discovery but in its juxtaposition and comparison with facts of similar kind – or whose intrinsic properties can be measured by the same yardstick – collected from other sites. Thus once the season's fieldwork is completed, members of the team will send the data they have collected back to their respective laboratories, where it will be fed into a database that will, in turn, allow them to search for systematic correlations upon which could be built predictive models of ecosystemic and climatic change. The data, in effect, are passed 'upwards' for analysis, as they are fed into frameworks of progressively wider and ultimately universal scope. In the construction of the database, in their classification and tabulation, the scientists' findings – we could say – are *vertically* integrated. Through this process of integration, knowledge is produced.

In short, to the laterally integrated geography of locations there corresponds a vertically integrated classification of the things found in them. The former is held together by chains or networks of point-to-point connections, the latter by the taxonomic aggregations and divisions of the database. But what of the knowledge of inhabitants? How is *that* integrated? Consider the helicopter pilot in our example. He has accumulated a good deal of experience of flying in these parts. Unlike the visiting scientists, he knows the terrain, and how to find his way under variable weather conditions. But this knowledge is not derived from locations. It comes, rather, from a history of previous flights, of take-offs and landings, and of incidents and encounters en route. In other words it is forged in *movement*, 'in the passage from place to place and the changing horizons along the way' (Ingold 2000: 227). Thus, as an inhabitant, the pilot's geographic knowledge is not laterally integrated, since places for him are not spatial locations, nor are they held together by point-to-point connections. They are rather *topics*, joined in stories of journeys actually made. Nor is his knowledge of things vertically integrated. For the things the inhabitant knows are not facts. A fact simply exists. But for inhabitants, things do not so much exist as *occur*. Lying at the confluence of actions and responses, they are identified not by their intrinsic attributes but by the memories they call up. Thus things are not classified like facts, or tabulated like data, but narrated like stories. And every place, as a gathering of things, is a knot of stories.

Inhabitants, in short, know as they go, as they journey *through* the world *along* a path of travel. Far from being ancillary to the point-to-point collection of data to be passed up for subsequent processing into knowledge, movement is itself the inhabitant's way of knowing. I have trawled the vocabulary of English to find a word, grammatically equivalent to 'laterally' and 'vertically', that would convey this sense of knowing 'along', rather than 'across' or 'up'. But I have found nothing. I have therefore had to resort to an awkward neologism. Inhabitant knowledge – we could say – is integrated *alongly*. Thus instead of the complementarity of a vertically integrated science of nature and a laterally integrated geography of location, wayfaring yields an alongly integrated, practical understanding of the lifeworld. Such knowledge is neither classified nor networked but *meshworked*.

In reality, of course, scientists are human like everyone else. And so, like everyone else, they are also wayfarers. Thus the picture of scientific practice presented in the example above is somewhat idealized. It corresponds, if you will, to the 'official' view of what is supposed to happen. In the actual conduct of scientific investigation materials collected in the field are sent not 'up' but 'along' to the laboratory, which is, after all, just another place where the work goes on. Moreover, there is no unified framework within which observations of all kinds, from all contexts, can be accommodated. Much of the labour of science, it seems, lies in attempts to establish the commensurability and connectivity that would render procedures developed and results obtained in one place applicable in another. As the sociologist David Turnbull (1991) has shown, scientific knowledge is not integrated into one grand edifice but rather grows in a field of practices constituted by the movements of practitioners, devices, measures, and results from one laboratory to another. 'All knowing', Turnbull writes, 'is like travelling, like a journey between the parts of a matrix' (1991: 35). Thus, contrary to the official view, what goes for inhabitant knowledge also goes for science. In both cases, knowledge is integrated not through fitting local particulars into global abstractions, but in the movement from place to place, in wayfaring. Scientific practices have the same place-binding (but not place-bound) character as the practices of inhabitants. Science, too, is meshworked.

It is, of course, the logic of inversion that lays the epistemological foundations for official science by turning occurrences into discrete, self-contained facts and their taking place into the occupation of enclosed sites. The same logic, moreover, also underlies the orthodox view of inhabitant knowledge as a kind of 'upside down' science that works not through the *export*, from specific locales, of observational data for processing at higher levels, but through the *import*, into them, of a system of concepts and categories for ordering the data of experience. These concepts and categories, it is supposed, are not so much 'built up' as 'passed down', ready-made, as part of a received tradition. Thus as places are construed as containers for people, so these people – or rather their minds – come to be seen as containers for the elements of tradition that are passed on to them from their ancestors, and that they in turn will pass on to their descendants. That is why traditional knowledge is so often assumed to be local. It is knowledge in the heads of local – and hence *localized* – people (Ingold and Kurttila 2000: 194). Conventionally, this knowledge goes by the name of culture. It is conventional, too, to contrast culture to science, which – since it is founded on the export of data rather than the import of schemata for organizing them – claims a global reach, and appeals to principles of rational analysis of universal scope. Thus cultures appear to be in place, science in space. The same logical operation that bifurcates room into place and space also bifurcates knowledge into culture and science.

This operation, to conclude, converts the growth of inhabitants' knowledge along the manifold ways of the meshwork into a gradual filling up of the capacities of the mind with cultural content. The conversion is effected through the twin processes of what Paul Nadasdy (1999) has called 'distillation' and 'compartmentalization'. Distillation severs the links that bind every occurrence to its narrative context; compartmentalization inserts the entities and events thus isolated into the several divisions of a classification. In this way the alongly integrated knowledge of the wayfarer is forced into the mould of a vertically integrated system, turning the ways along which life is lived into categorical boundaries within which it is constrained. Stories become repositories of classified information; wayfaring becomes the application of a naïve science. I have argued, to the contrary, that inhabitant knowledge is forged not by fitting the data of observation into the compartments of a received classification but through histories of wayfaring. To unravel the meshwork, and to reassemble the resulting fragments on the basis of their intrinsic similarities and differences, is to destroy its very meaning and coherence. Rather than treating science and culture as equal and opposite, ranged on either side of an arbitrary division between space and place, and between reason and tradition, a better way forward – I suggest – would be to acknowledge that scientific knowledge, as much as the knowledge of inhabitants, is generated within the practices of wayfaring. For scientists are people too, and inhabit the same world as the rest of us.

References

Anderson, D. 2000. *Identity and Ecology in Arctic Siberia*. Oxford: Oxford University Press.

Aporta, C. 2004. 'Routes, Trails and Tracks: Trail Breaking among the Inuit of Igloolik', *Études/Inuit/Studies* 28(2): 9–38.

Casey, E. S. 1996. 'How to get from Space to Place in a Fairly Short Stretch of Time: Phenomenological Prolegomena', in S. Feld and K. H. Basso (eds), *Senses of Place*. Santa Fe, NM: School of American Research Press, pp. 13–52.

Heidegger, M. 1971. *Poetry, Language, Thought*, trans. A. Hofstadter. New York: Harper and Row.

Ingold, T. 1993. 'The Art of Translation in a Continuous World', in G. Pálsson (ed.), *Beyond Boundaries: Understanding, Translation and Anthropological Discourse*. Oxford: Berg, pp. 210–30.

———. *The Perception of the Environment: Essays on Livelihood, Dwelling and Skill*. London: Routledge.

Ingold, T. and T. Kurttila. 2000. 'Perceiving the Environment in Finnish Lapland', *Body and Society* 6: 193–96.

Klee, P. 1961. *Notebooks, Volume 1: The Thinking Eye*. London: Lund Humphries.

Lefebvre, H. 1991. *The Production of Space*, trans. D. Nicholson-Smith. Oxford: Blackwell.

Löfgren, O. 2000. 'Motion and Emotion: The Microphysics and Metaphysics of Landscape Experiences in Tourism', in A. Hornborg and G. Pálsson (eds), *Negotiating Nature: Culture, Power, and Environmental Argument*. Lund: Lund University Press, pp. 17–35.

Malpas, J. E. 1999. *Place and Experience: A Philosophical Topography*. Cambridge: Cambridge University Press.

Massey, D. 2005. *For Space*. London: Sage.

Nadasdy, P. 1999. 'The Politics of TEK: Power and the "Integration" of Knowledge', *Arctic Anthropology* 36: 1–18.

Olwig. K. R. 2002. 'The Duplicity of Space: Germanic "Raum" and Swedish "Rum" in English Language Geographical Discourse', *Geografiska Annaler* 84b(1): 1–17.

Tilley, C. 2004. *The Materiality of Stone: Explorations in Landscape Phenomenology*. Oxford: Berg.

Turnbull, D. 1991. *Mapping the World in the Mind: An Investigation of the Unwritten Knowledge of Micronesian Navigators*. Geelong: Deakin University Press.

Wagner, R. 1986. *Symbols that Stand for Themselves*. Chicago: University of Chicago Press.

Wallace, A. D. 1993. *Walking, Literature and English Culture*. Oxford: Clarendon.

Wiebe, R. 1989. *Playing Dead: A Contemplation Concerning the Arctic*. Edmonton, Canada: NeWest.

Chapter 3

Spatiality, Power, and State-Making in the Organization of Territory in Colonial South Asia: The Case of the Anglo–Gorkha Frontier, 1740–1816

Bernardo A. Michael

> *[T]he British possessions … classed by governments and revenue or judicial divisions, must be considered only* approximations to truth *on a subject, in its nature of great difficulty, and which has hitherto not received from the Indian authorities the degree of attention which its* practical value *and importance is entitled to.*
>
> John Crawfurd[1]

Introduction

The Anglo–Gorkha war (1814–16) vividly illustrates the territorial hubris and interpretive murk that can surround military conflict between very different societies in colonial settings. Historical writings on the war have narrated this event from divergent perspectives – military, diplomatic, and nationalist.[2] While these accounts of the war are not irrelevant, they are largely event-based accounts that have failed to undertake a detailed historical examination of the territorial disputes that led to the outbreak of war in 1814. Consequently, what remains obscured in these writings is the dynamic undercurrent of human movements and flows that were responsible for the organization of space (territory) along the Anglo–Gorkha frontier (see Map 3.1). This chapter,[3]

1. John Crawfurd, *Description of India*, 1822–23. IOR/Mss Eur D457a and 457b, APAC, BL. The quotation comes from D 457a, pp. 177–78. Emphasis mine.
2. Rana 1970; Husain 1970: 36; Regmi 1975; Shaha 1990: 108; Thapa 2048 BS [1991 CE], Pemble 1971; Khanduri 1997; Pant 2021BS [1963 CE], 2022BS [1964 CE], 2023BS [1965 CE].
3. This chapter has taken its present shape over a long period of time. The late Qeyamuddin Ahmad, Ian Barrow, Raymond Craib, Mary DesChene, Matthew Edney, Stewart Gordon, Peter Wynn Kirby, Sara Michael, Pratyoush Onta, the late Mahesh Regmi, and Phil Withington provided invaluable suggestions and advice. I am responsible for all errors. An earlier version of this chapter appeared in *Studies in Nepali History and Society*. Research for this chapter has been supported by a Junior Research Grant from the American Institute of Indian Studies and Scholarship Grants from Messiah College.

then, attempts to bridge this gap in the historical writings on the war by asserting that space is the product of constantly shifting social relations (but see Stiller 1976; Burghart 1984; DesChene 1991).

Space, in all its fluidity, is an important fourth variable that needs to be added to the existing complex of culture, power, and history that informs much contemporary social theorizing.[4] Space cannot be viewed as a static envelope or stage within which social life unfolds. Rather it is a dynamic entity constituted out of a shifting ensemble of meanings, practices, and interrelationships. The notion of space as deployed in this chapter refers to the layout and organization of territory produced by the ebb and flow of dynamic social forces. Such an understanding of space, as the product of social flux, echoes the concerns for studying movement in recent studies on state-making[5] State-making, or the study of state–society relationships, is a product of varied shifting historical forces and diffuse relationships of power. Such accounts of state-making and space can be further enriched by taking an ethnographic approach that generates 'thick descriptions' of culture, power, history, and space.[6] Such an interdisciplinary approach 'takes movement as its vehicle in analysing social experience of surroundings in politically laden contexts'.[7] This amounts to taking a processual approach to the study of the war where change rather than structure becomes the only constant informing the social relationships that organized territory.[8]

The specific questions of spatiality that I seek to address are those pertaining to the organization and transformation of administrative divisions along the Anglo–Gorkha frontier. The arrival of the English East India Company along this frontier in the eighteenth century resulted in the gradual insertion of a new spatial vision for the organization of a state's territories. This vision, which was operationalized through colonial wars, administrative fiat, and the use of modern cartography, ultimately resulted in the imposition of the geographical framework of the modern state, with its linear boundaries and neatly nesting internal divisions and sub-divisions.[9] In this sense, the Anglo–Gorkha War was 'diagnostic' of conflicting Anglo–Gorkhali understandings of their territorial

4. For recent emphasis on the study of culture, power, and history, see Dirks et al. (eds.), 1994.
5. See Sivaramakrishnan (1999) for such an account of state-making in colonial eastern India.
6. The term 'thick description', of course, is Geertz's (1973). For a timely caveat on writing 'thick descriptions', see Ortner (1995). For a rapprochement between ethnography and history sensitive to the flows and movements that animate social life see Cohn (1987), Comaroff and Comaroff (1992), Dening (1996), Dube (2004), Isaac (1984), Michael (2003), and Sivaramakrishnan (1993).
7. Kirby, Chapter One, this volume. For the anthropological significance of travel, movement, and continuity in social life, see Clifford (1997), Ingold (1994).
8. For more on processual analysis, see Moore (1975, 1987, 1994), Rosaldo (1989: 91–108). For more on the tensions of structure and agency, see Abrams (1982: ix–xv) and Bourdieu (1977).
9. See Kirby, Chapter One, this volume, for how European intellectual traditions produced distinct understandings of space. See also Edney (1997, 2003) for a discussion of the connections between European scientific culture and the cartographic projects of the English East India Company.

possessions as well as of wider territorial rearrangements that were initiated and sustained during the colonial period.[10] Unpacking the territorial disputes that led to the war helps us to map questions of spatiality, or territorial organization, prior to the actual implementation of the East India Company's cartographic projects of the nineteenth century. Such a theoretical move also registers a more faithful account of the fluidity, movement, and change that characterized the sticky materiality of everyday governance along this frontier.[11] In the sections that follow, I will first examine the territorial disputes surrounding the administrative division of Rautahat and then those involving twenty-two villages along the Champaran-Tarriani section of the Anglo–Gorkha frontier. Special attention will be given to those highly localized relationships pertaining to land tenure, taxation, and tribute that produced the mobile and shifting administrative spaces that made up this frontier.[12]

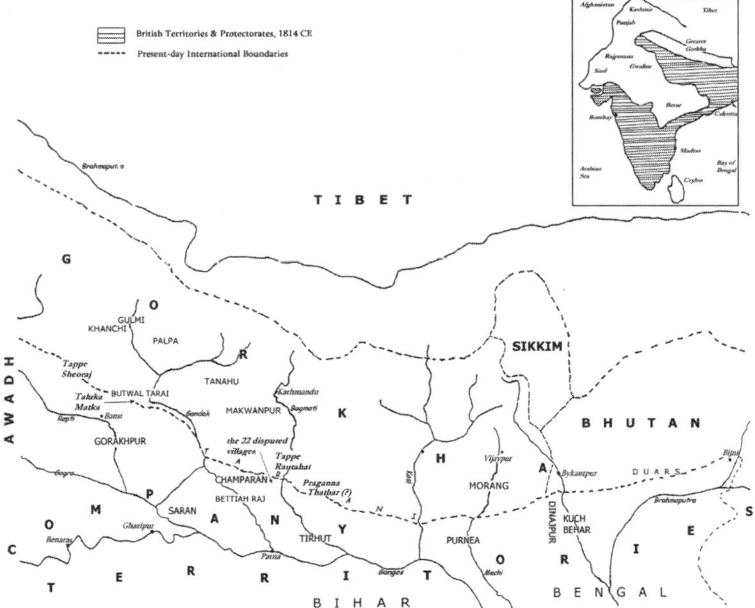

Map 1. The Champaran-Tarriani Frontier, 1814 CE. Mapwork by Saramma & Sharon Michael. This map is not drawn to scale. The location and boundaries of pargana, tappas and villages are approximate.

10. My treatment of the war as a 'diagnostic event' echoes the argument of anthropologist Sally Falk Moore (1987). For Moore, such events are diagnostic of the ongoing (re)ordering of social orders.
11. See Tsing (2004) for more about the texture of everyday life.
12. Such a historical project locates itself at the intersections of cultural anthropology and cultural geography and in this sense my efforts here echo the Nepali historian Pratyoush Onta's call for 'greater pluralism in [Nepali] history writing practices' (Onta 1994: 1–43).

The Production of Space on the Anglo–Gorkha Frontier

Anglo–Gorkhali relations between 1765 and 1814 were marked by a number of territorial disputes along their common frontier,[13] which may have involved as many as two hundred villages. I focus primarily on the territorial disputes that arose on the Champaran-Tarriani section of the Anglo–Gorkha frontier. The Champaran-Tarriani section of the Anglo–Gorkha frontier formed a critical arena for processes of state-making (see Map 3.2), and a variety of ecological and social factors had rendered its governance problematic for both states. Historically, dense malarial forests, recalcitrant little kingdoms and landed magnates, and a scarce supply of labour had always rendered the frontier an illegible space that opposed the centralizing thrusts of political regimes. Consequently, by 1814, both the English East India Company and Gorkha's rulers were struggling to secure these areas and acquire accurate knowledge to put in place institutional arrangements for the efficient collection of revenue. The situation was exacerbated by the presence of ill-defined and shifting administrative divisions that lay along this frontier. The *pargana* of (Gadh) Simraon is a fine example of these spatial dynamics (see Map 3.3).

Map 2. Little Kingdoms, *Parganas*, and Tappas on the Chaparan-Tarriani Frontier, 1814 CE. Mapwork by Bernardo A. Michael & Sharon Michael.

13. For fuller treatments of some of these disputes, see Michael (2001).

The Space of *Pargana* (Gadh) Simraon

The *pargana* of (Gadh) Simraon was made up of two sub-divisions or *tappas* – Rautahat and Nannor. In 1812 the Gorkhalis and the Company were embroiled in a dispute involving twenty-two villages lying along this section of the Anglo–Gorkha frontier. Unpacking these disputes reveals a complex web of entitlements concerning agrarian tenures and taxation rights. Such rights to property, taxation, and tribute remained unstable as they negotiated the vagaries of power. Between 1742 and 1783, such shifting relationships left their fingerprints on the body of the *pargana* and its dependent *tappas*, leaving it inconstant in its organization, layout, and boundaries. These merit further investigation.

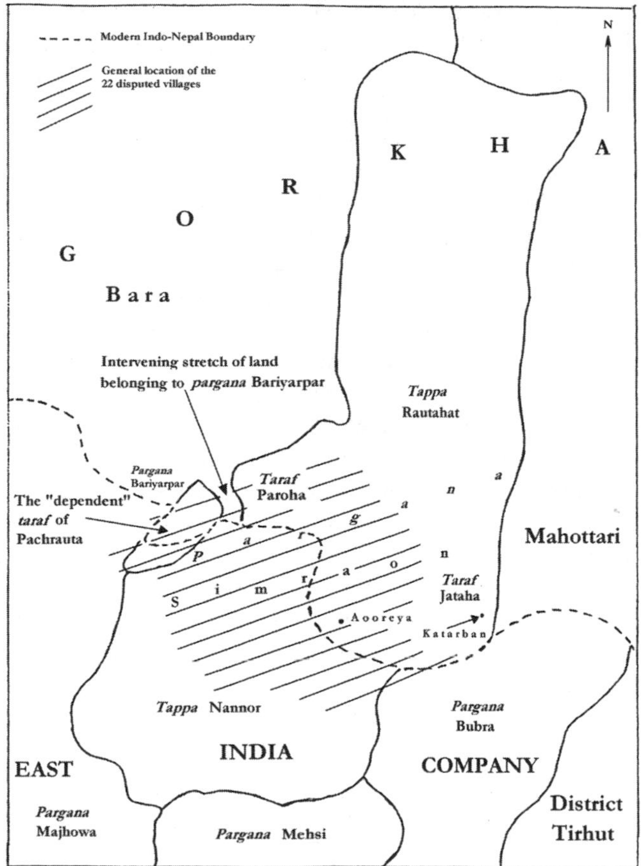

Map 3. Location and internal divisions of *Pargana* Simraon, 1814 CE. Mapwork by Bernardo A. Michael. This map is not drawn to scale. The location and boundaries of pargana, tappas and villages are approximate.

States, Little Kingdoms, Landed Magnates and the Question of tappa Rautahat

In the early eighteenth century, the *tappa* of Rautahat appears to have formed a part of the Tarriani possessions of the hill-kingdom of Makwanpur. The conquest of Makwanpur by Gorkha in 1762 rendered problematic the ownership of *tappa* Rautahat and its detached, but dependent, *taraf* of Pachrauta.[14] The *tappa* was claimed by a number of competing parties: Bir Kishor Singh, the raja of the neighbouring little kingdom of Bettiah, a local landed magnate by the name of Mirza Abdulla Beg, and the raja of Gorkha. While Bir Kishor argued that *tappa* Rautahat was an integral part of his kingdom, the Mirza claimed the *tappa* on the basis of a *birta* grant (land that is inheritable and tax-free) given to his maternal grandfather, Qulb Ali Beg, by Hem Karna Sen, the erstwhile raja of the hill-kingdom of Makwanpur. The year was 1743.

From 1743 to 1783, the status of *tappa* Rautahat underwent further changes. From the very outset, the raja of Bettiah disputed Mirza Abdulla Beg's ancestral claim to Rautahat. This dispute continued until 1753/54 when the Beg's family – probably unable to ignore the power of the Bettiah raja – obtained a royal decree (*sanad*) from the erstwhile Bettiah raja himself (Dhrub Singh, 1715–62). This *sanad* confirmed the former's right to Rautahat. But there was one crucial difference. While the Bettiah raja reconfirmed the rights of the Beg family's rights to Rautahat, he did not confirm its tax-free and inheritable clauses. Rather, he renewed the grant as a *jagir* grant (land held by government officials in lieu of a cash salary) that was non-heritable and that would revert back to the rajas of Bettiah whenever they chose to rescind the grant. In this manner, the Bettiah raja seems to have consolidated his tenurial claim to the *tappa* of Rautahat. These moves by the raja of Bettiah are revealing in two respects. For one, the conferral and renewal of land grants needs to be understood within a fluid context of shifting meanings. Any attempt to write ethnographies of state-making needs to map the 'webs of significance' and flows of power that contextualized such practices. Next, such shifts in meaning and practice had spatial effects as well. When the tenurial right to administrative divisions (such as *tappa* Rautahat) was altered these divisions would get detached from one kingdom or overlord (the kingdom of Makwanpur) and attached to new sources of authority (in this case the kingdom of Bettiah). That is, power struggles caused shifts within existing hierarchies of property rights that in turn resulted in entire administrative divisions (or bits and pieces of them) moving between diverse sources of authority.

14. A *taraf* is fiscal sub-division belonging to a pargana or tappa and includes several villages.

Between 1760 and 1764, Ali Quli Khan and his family obtained official orders (*parwana*) from various political authorities (local officials, petty chieftains and regional overlords, and an English East India Company official) lying south of Rautahat. These *parwanas* confirmed their inalienable rights to the *tappa* of Rautahat and Pachrauta made the observation that these divisions were struck off the records (*kharij*) of the accountants of the province of Bihar.[15] Some time later, Jugal Kishor, the raja of Bettiah (1762–83) seized control of *tappa* Rautahat and its dependency of Pachrauta. This is important and deserves further comment. In contemporary revenue discourse, terms such as *kharij* were commonly used to indicate that some item had been struck off from a particular heading in the accounts. Often this could refer to the status of rent-free lands. Since such lands were not expected to remit revenue to government they were struck off the account registers recording the details of revenue-yielding lands. Spatio-politically, this meant that an administrative unit such as Rautahat could belong to the revenue-yielding lands of a province or district at one time, only to be taken out of it at another. In this fashion, bits and pieces of a *tappa* or *pargana* could be separated from the revenue accounts without any consideration for preserving the territorial coherence or continuity of a district. In this instance, the Beg's consideration of his lands being considered rent-free and separate from the revenue accounts of Rautahat was lost on previous scholars of the Anglo–Gorkha war. Precolonial territories were often shaped by such dynamic flows and movements that left them irregular in their layout and internal organization. It is only by being alert to questions of spatiality, meaning, power, and history that it becomes possible to write a historical geography of moving state spaces.

It is clear that Company officials possessed a notion of territory as a fixed geographical container. They were always suspicious of distinctions between rent-free and tax-yielding lands and considered both as subject to their authority. By the beginning of the nineteenth century, Company officials were beginning to insist on the preservation of the spatial integrity of an administrative division and were averse to admitting any territorial claims that violated this. Indigenous landholders, for their part, felt such distinctions were critical (irrespective of their spatial implications) because they were legitimate entitlements derived from older arrangements. An instance of this occurred on the Gorakhpur–Butwal frontier. In 1812 the Gorkhalis would lay claim to half of *tappa* Mirchwar (*pargana* Binayakpur, in Gorakhpur district) on the grounds that the concerned lands had been given on a rent-free tenure by the nawab of Awadh to the raja of Butwal. Since the Butwal raj had been incorporated into

15. For details, see the *Monckton Report* (1814); PGGCB, 28 September, 1781, Consl. 1–3, WBSA; PGGCB, 1781. Press List Index, vol. 9, 6 March–18 December 1781, pp. 111–12, WBSA.

Gorkha in 1804, the Gorkhalis now claimed these lands. The Gorkhalis, while admitting the right of the Company to collect revenue from the *pargana* of Binayakpur, felt that this right did not extend to the rent-free lands of the Butwal rajas, which had been separated from the revenue-yielding accounts of the *pargana*. This came as a rude shock to Company authorities, who claimed the entire *pargana* (that is, all its lands), as it belonged to the ceded district of Gorakhpur. They were unwilling to recognize any Gorkhali claims to bits and pieces of it.

But to return to *tappa* Rautahat, even in 1765, as the Beg's family was seeking to assert its claims to Rautahat, the *tappa* continued to fluctuate in its layout. In 1765, we know that the Beg's family had rented ten villages in *tappa* Nannor (lying on its common border with *tappa* Rautahat) from Jugal Kishor Singh, the raja of Bettiah. In 1767, following Jugal Kishor's expulsion from the region by British forces, the Beg's family quietly added these ten villages to the *tappa* of Rautahat.[16] Such practices of sequestering villages from one *tappa* to another have tremendous spatial implications, especially if the villages concerned are not contiguous to each other. When such non-contiguous villages were added to the fiscal resources of a division then the contours of that division could be rendered spatially discontinuous on the ground (or a map as the case might be). Or, as British officials would frequently put it, it would give rise to the phenomenon of 'intermixture'. And such spatial discontinuity or 'intermixture' was invariably generated by the practices of various agents who were jockeying for positions of resource control. The presence of a new source of authority, such as the Gorkhalis, could only have further aggravated the situation. When *tappa* Rautahat was given to Gorkha in 1783, these ten villages also fell into Gorkhali hands and continued to be sequestered from the *tappa* of Nannor. Given these territorial dynamics, precolonial administrative divisions displayed a marked fluidity in their layout and organization.

But there is more to this complicated story. It appears that, some time between 1762 and 1781, the Beg's family got their claim to *tappa* Rautahat confirmed by the Gorkhali government. In 1813, during the course of the Company's investigations into the disputes in this area, Gorkhali officials would assert that following the Gorkhali conquest of the hill-kingdom of Makwanpur in 1762, Mirza Abdulla Beg the '*jagirdar*' of Rautahat got his *jagir* confirmed by authorities at Kathmandu.[17] If this account is correct, then the

16. See 'List of the villages in the Tuppeh of Nunnour, Purgunnah Simraon, Surcar Chumparun as taken from a document under the seal of Cazee Noorulhuk, 1173 Fuslee, being 48 years old' in Paris Bradshaw, Political Agent on the Nepal Frontier, *FP*, Procs. 25 March 1814, pp. 625–31, *NAI*.

17. See the statements of officials like *Kaji* Randip Singh and *sardar* Parshuram Thapa (see *Monckton Report*, pp. 272–74).

Beg might have got his right confirmed by Gorkha, following very close on the heels of the fall of Makwanpur. And this by itself is not implausible. It was an established custom that those having rights in landed resources got their grants reconfirmed by the new authority in the area. The tendency of local magnates such as the Beg to get their grants confirmed by various authorities clearly displays the accommodations they invariably had to make with diffuse and shifting fields of power. What is intriguing is why Mirza Abdulla Beg turned against Gorkha, especially if he had already got his grant confirmed? What events transpired between 1762 and 1781 that brought about this change in the Beg's loyalties? We know that between 1763 and 1770 the Beg made every effort to represent Rautahat as being fiscally separated from the accounts of Bihar. We also know that in 1778 a *parwana* was issued by the court at Saran commanding the Mirza's officers to be more careful in preventing *ryots* (cultivators) from deserting his *jagir* and taking refuge in the villages of Barwa and Bijay.[18]

This, in itself, is an important development. Bijay and Burwa were villages occupied by Gorkha. In fact, at Bijay a Gorkhali thana, or police post, had been built. Why were the ryots leaving the Beg's lands for a Gorkhali outpost? It is very possible that Gorkhali officials may have induced this flight, to secure labour that was always in short supply for purposes of cultivation. In fact, such acts were widely practiced along this frontier and even sanctioned by the authorities at Kathmandu.[19] Thus the scattered evidence seems to suggest that by 1780 Mirza Abdulla Beg's tenurial rights to Rautahat and Pachrauta were being subject to increasing pressure from powerful forces beyond his control, in this case the Gorkhalis. Hence his desire to get his rights to *tappa* Rautahat reconfirmed by Gorkhali authorities. I have not come across any further evidence that might clarify the issue at this level and reveal to us the world as the Beg meaningfully perceived it. Various authorities were claiming Rautahat and collecting revenue from it. A local Tharu leader, Bikha Chaudhari, noted that between 1766 and 1770 Gorkhali officials were collecting revenue in this area with Mirza Abdulla Beg being referred to as the *jagirdar* of Rautahat from 1770 to 1782. Witnesses from the Bettiah raja's side, too, would confirm that the Beg was the jagirdar of Rautahat, confirming the claim of the Bettiah raja that the Beg, being his dependent, was granted Rautahat in *jagir* by the Bettiah raja, Dhrub Singh.[20]

18. See John Young, Acting Magistrate of Saran district, to W. Leycester, Magistrate of Saran; Leycester to N. B. Edmonstone; and Edmonstone to Leycester, in FP Procs. 4 September 1812, nos. 50, 51 and 52, *NAI*.
19. Shortages of labour have a long history on the Champaran-Tarriani frontier, and predate and persist long before and after the Anglo–Gorkha war (e.g., RRS 16 (May 1984): 78–79; Mishra 1978: 60, 131, 268).
20. See deposition of Sheikh Ziauddin, *malguzar* of Mahsoonda, in *Monckton Report*, 1814.

Examining the intricacies of land-granting clearly suggests that this is not an innocent practice devoid of serious socio-spatial consequences. It is clear that the very act of granting land was capable of constituting and reconstituting social and spatial relationships. As a practice it was highly performative, productive of conflict and ambiguity, and sedimented with both the symbolic and the material – the very stuff of any ethnography of state-making. And given the number of times Mirza Beg's family got their claims processed by various authorities – at least seven times between the years 1743 and 1783 – the amount of semantic, spatial, and social rearranging that must have followed from this entire corpus of practices would have rendered the fiscal space of the *tappa* of Rautahat and its dependent *taraf* of Pachrauta extremely illegible – shot through with disputed claims and difficult for central authorities (both Gorkhali and British) to govern. *Tappa* Rautahat and Pachrauta became mobile spaces produced out of shifting and contested social relationships.

However, by 1781 the Beg was trying to manoeuvre himself into a position that would dissolve any ties of dependency on Gorkha. In 1783 Mirza Abdulla Beg would maintain that the Gorkha raja's claim that Rautahat and its dependency belonged to Gorkha, by virtue of the conquest of Makawanpur in 1762, was a weak one. Gorkhali officials, for their part, insisted that the conquest of Makwanpur entitled them to possession of its dependencies, such as Rautahat, lying in the plains. The Beg's counter-argument was revealing for its spatial implications. He noted that the Gorkha raja had no right to resume the *tappa* 'which had … for many years before his conquest remained *kharige* [*kharij*] or separate from it'. Rautahat had become detached from the revenue-yielding territories of Makwanpur by virtue of it being granted to the Beg's family.[21] I have already discussed the spatial implications of such an argument in an earlier paragraph. What becomes increasingly apparent from all this is that the Beg saw his territorial possession of Rautahat as being detached from the dominions of Makwanpur and Gorkha ever since the original grant was made in 1743. But then who was he attached to, especially if he seems to have made a number of attempts to sequester his possessions from both the provinces of Bihar and the kingdom of Gorkha? We know that between 1763 and 1770 he considered his possessions separate from the province of Bihar. This undoubtedly would have protected him from the demands of revenue administrators in Bihar in general and in particular from the influence of the Bettiah raja, his most powerful local competitor. This might have simultaneously led him to seek a closer connection with Gorkha, a relationship that must have soured, forcing him to resituate himself. Thus, between 1781 and 1783 he might have tried to steer away from the influence of Gorkha by making the claim that *tappa* Rautahat had been separated from Makwanpur as

21. See *PGGCB* (Revenue Department), Procs. 3 June, 1783, nos. 1–7, *WBSA*.

far back as 1743. In 1783 we find him claiming to be a subject of the East India Company and therefore claiming its protection in preserving his claim to *tappa* Rautahat. Clearly, the Beg was seeking to manoeuvre himself into a favourable position – either as independent landholder or as a dependant of a patron who would offer him the maximum benefit. And he sought to do this at a time of political uncertainty, the region being buffeted by many powerful political forces, from within and beyond.

Here, to open another strand of analysis, it is possible that factional struggles in Kathmandu might have had something to do with the attempts to oust the Beg from Rautahat. Between 1777 and 1785, when the Gorkahli raja Ran Bahadur Shah was a minor, the ebbs and flows of politics in Kathmandu coalesced around the manoeuvrings of a number of factions within the ruling elite. It is possible that these factions were competing to enhance their symbolic and material capital by gaining control of the rich and newly opened resources of the Makwani Tarai.[22] On the other hand, and at more local level, it is also possible that Gorkha's revenue and military personnel stationed in Rautahat might have developed an interest in this *tappa*. For instance, it was alleged that high-ranking Gorkhali officials had even tried to bribe local officials to give evidence that would support the Gorkhali claim to the *tappa* of Rautahat.[23] While it is difficult to verify this statement, the practice of bribe-giving was a common one, and many fiscal arrangements in this period (and probably earlier as well) were arrived at through this established practice. Whatever the case might have been, the Gorkhalis (or at least a dominant faction within the ruling elite) were decided about one thing – the Beg would have to relinquish his right to *tappa* Rautahat and its dependent *taraf* of Pachrauta.[24] Wresting control of *tappa* Rautahat would not only have meant access to and control over the agrarian and forest resources of the Rautahat *tarai*, but it would also have meant considerable prestige for the victorious faction.[25]

22. The recursive relationship existing between the availability of land and potential for military expansion always meant that there was a constant quest for fresh lands to conquer, in order to maintain a large standing army. This intricate land–military relationship might also have induced such claims on the part of Gorkha's ruling elite. For details on the 'land–military complex', see Stiller (1973: 277–94).
23. See 'Deposition of Sheikh Ziauddin', witness produced by the Bettiah raja Bir Kishor Singh, Monckton Report, 1814.
24. See 'Letter of raja Ran Bahadur Shah to Bahadur Shah', March 1783, Historical Letters, Kausi Tosakhana Collection, no. 85, NAN.
25. And there is evidence to suggest that there were at least two competing factions in Kathmandu jockeying for control during this period, their spokesmen being Dinanath Upadhyaya and one Bhavnanni Shah (an agent of Bahadur Shah, a son of Prithvinarayan Shah). See 'Letter from raja Ran Bahadur Shah to Bahadur Shah', January 1782, Historical Letters, Kausi Tosakhana Collection, no. 91, NAN; Letter from Ran Bahadur Shah to Bahadur Shah, March 1783, Historical Letters, Kausi Tosakhana Collection, no. 86, NAN.

Processes of state-making on the Champaran-Tarriani frontier unfolded precisely at the sites of such complex negotiations between multiple actors located at many levels. From the late eighteenth century, the English East India Company was increasingly drawn into the logic of these disputes unfolding along their common frontier with Gorkha. From 1781 the Governor-General-in-Council (Revenue Department) began to examine the claims of Mirza Abdulla Beg over Rautahat. On 28 September 1781, the Governor-General-in-Council (Revenue Department) decided to accept the Beg's claim. But then historically contingent forces intervened. The Council's decision of 28 September was never conveyed to local officials due to distractions that came in the form of a rebellion by one Chait Singh, the raja of Banaras. Consequently, Company officials in Patna remained oblivious of this decision. On 20 February 1782, William Brooke, the English Revenue Chief at Patna issued a *parwana* to the Gorkhalis recognizing their claim over Rautahat.[26] On the strength of this *parwana* the Gorkhalis now claimed Rautahat, something the Beg resisted.

Meanwhile the case dragged on and the Gorkhalis sent delegations to meet with the English Governor-General, Warren Hastings. They promised to help him quell Chait Singh's rebellion and in return asked that their claims to Rautahat be respected.[27] In October 1783, following prolonged discussions among Company officials, the Governor-General, Warren Hastings, summed up his opinion on the issue of *tappa* Rautahat:

> Whatever may be the right of Mirza Abdulla Beg and however unjust the conduct of the Raja of Nepal in depriving him of his Jagheer, it is a point not cognizable by this Government, since the lands comprising it do not appertain to our jurisdiction. I therefore recommend that the orders of 28 September 1781 and 25 February 1783 be repealed, our sepoys recalled, and Mirza Abdulla left to the mercy or Justice of his own Sovereign.[28]

What is intriguing about this minute is its spatial ambiguity. What exactly did Hastings mean by 'the lands comprising it do not appertain to our jurisdiction', especially given the fact that he did not possess any accurate maps of the frontier? It is doubtful that he was aware of the spatial implications of such territorial disputes. For instance, when the Beg noted that *tappa* Rautahat was separated from Makwanpur, he was using a fiscal idiom that recognized that

26. See, *PGGCB* (Revenue Department), Procs. 3 June 1783, nos. 1–7, WBSA.
27. For details see *Papers Respecting the Nepaul War* (PRNW), 2: 371; Naraharinath 2022 BS [1966 CE].: 10.
28. *PGGCB* (Revenue Department), 11 November 1783, no. 56, *WBSA*, emphasis mine.

patches of land could be attached or separated from fiscal units on the basis of their obligation to pay (or not to pay) revenue.[29] Such representations and practices were common in precolonial north India and they took place without any consideration of the spatial integrity or compactness of the territory in question. Hastings's inability to recognize this subtle point and its spatio-political ramifications – namely of its inability to generate coherent and compact territories – seems to reflect the confusion and ambiguity the early Company officials displayed in their attempts to understand the production of precolonial fiscal divisions. Company officials displayed a somewhat panoptical vision of state spaces – that is, they were made up of coherent, bounded , territorial divisions that could be plainly discerned through surveys and represented on maps. That is, states were territorially coherent entities, occupying definite portions of the earth's surface, and made visible through maps. The body of the state was further divided and sub-divided into non-overlapping divisions, implying surveillance from above (cf. Foucault 1979; cf. Kaplan 1995). Such a vision of territory found its best expression in modern maps where the entire body of the state (along with its internal divisions clearly marked) could be displayed for purposes of control and manipulation. This is clearly evident in territorial representations of the state produced by Company surveyors and cartographers of this period. For instance, James Rennell's maps of the kingdom of Bengal, prepared in 1768, clearly show the divisions and sub-divisions of the province marked off from one another by distinct linear boundaries. It is obvious that this was not the spatial reality that existed on the ground, and Rennell himself may have been aware of this when he inserted these imaginary boundaries.[30] Rennell's practices reveal, more than anything else, what Company officials wanted to see, because that was the only way they were able to grasp or 'know' the space of the state. It was much later, through the revenue surveys of the nineteenth century, that Company surveyors would succeed in mapping precolonial fiscal divisions such as *tappas* and *parganas*. And it is through these revenue survey maps that we get the first images of the intermixed and discontinuous bodies of these divisions.[31]

In this section, I have attempted to reconstruct the fluctuating tenurial status of fiscal divisions such as *tappa* Rautahat. *Tappa* Rautahat, like almost every other fiscal division on the Anglo–Gorkha frontier, was a site of conflicting territorial disputes involving states, both petty and large. Various factors such as recurrent warfare, unsettled political conditions, and the emergence of new political formations (such as Gorkha and the Company after

29. See Burghart 1987: 259.
30. See 'A Map of the Kingdom of Bengal', by James Rennell, 1768, IOR X\1018, *APAC* Map Collection, *BL*.
31. More details about these revenue surveys can be found in Michael (2007).

1765) involving a range of human actors (state officials, little kings, landed magnates, cultivating groups, and agricultural labour) intervened to bring about a number of rearrangements and realignments within this layer of rights. These fiscal, and subsequently political, rearrangements and realignments produced mobile fiscal divisions possessed of fluid boundaries and changing, even perforated, bodies. Between 1742 and 1783 *tappa* Rautahat had shifted back and forth between Makwanpur, Bettiah, Bengal, the Company state and Gorkha. And, even in its spatial layout, this *tappa* does not seem to have been a coherent whole, with its *taraf* of Pachrauta lying separated from it (see Map 3.2).[32] In the Company's official discourse, Pachrauta is always referred to as a 'dependent' *taraf*, 'dependent' on *tappa* Rautahat. In fact, terms such as 'attached', 'separated', and 'dependent' recur in the Company state's official discourses and often encoded shifting tenurial connections and relationships that joined and separated patches of territory in a highly irregular and discontinuous fashion. While such spatial characteristics may not have posed any dilemmas for indigenous authorities, they caused considerable anxiety for colonial officials. Hasting's decision concerning Rautahat in 1783 only provided a temporary resolution to such spatial dilemmas. Indeed, they persisted all along the Company state's frontiers. Along the Anglo–Gorkha frontier, they cropped up again in the first decade of the nineteenth century along the Champaran-Tarriani section of the frontier, especially along the common boundary of the *tappas* of Rautahat and Nannor.

Local Agency and the Production of Territory along the Edges of *tappas* Rautahat and Nannor

Thus, in 1783, *pargana* (Gadh) Simraon was broken up with one of its constituent *tappas* (Rautahat) being handed over to the Gorkhalis while *tappa* Nannor remained in the hands of the raja of Bettiah, a subject of the English East India Company. However, information about the internal resources, actual extent and boundaries of these divisions was still unavailable. In short, while Company officials gave away an administrative unit called '*tappa* Rautahat' to Gorkha, its ontology remained an epistemological and spatial enigma that would complicate Anglo–Gorkha relations in the decades to come. Consequently, by 1814 the two states were confronted with a new set of

32. This becomes evident from a preliminary examination of an 1820 map of this frontier where the *taraf* of Pachrauta appears cut off from the main body of *tappa* Rautahat by an intervening stretch of territory formed by the *pargana* of Bariyarpar. See 'Sketch of the line of boundary between the Nipaul Terriani and the Zillah Sarun', prepared for the information of Government and reduced from the original survey by Lt. J. Pickersgill, 1822, IOR/X/2994, APAC Map Collection, *BL*.

conflicts, this time pertaining to their rights to twenty-two villages that straddled the common boundary of *tappas* Rautahat and Nannor.[33] Gorkhali officials would maintain that these twenty-two villages belonged to *tappa* Rautahat, while the Bettiah raja Bir Kishor Singh and his agents would argue that they belonged to the neighbouring *tappa* of Nannor.[34] Company officials were drawn into this dispute since the raja of Bettiah was a Company subject. In 1811, the disputes took a violent turn when the Gorkhali *subba* of Rautahat, Laxman Giri, was allegedly attacked and killed by the supporters of the Bettiah raja.[35] Between 1813 and 1814, this dispute became the subject of a number of official investigations on both sides.[36]

Most accounts of the Anglo–Gorkha war treat the disputes over these twenty-two villages as an inter-state affair. Relatively little agency has been granted to local forces – such as cultivating groups, local landed magnates, and elites and their contested relationships involving the rights to hold land, collect taxes, and tribute. Examining district records in north India clearly reveals that local forces played a formative role in these inter-state territorial disputes. These frequent struggles gave rise to considerable ambiguity concerning the demarcation of territory along this frontier. Examining the ensuing negotiations between the Gorkhalis and the English officials bears this out. An analysis of the depositions of fifteen witnesses taken during John Young's investigation in 1812, and the various lists of disputed villages drawn up by Company officials, proves to be revealing. For one, the Bettiah raja's witnesses

33. There is some confusion surrounding the actual number of villages that became the cause of dispute between the two governments in 1814. A comparison of the lists prepared by John Young, John Monckton and Paris Bradshaw reveals discrepancies in both the number and place names of the villages in question. Most discernable are at least ten new villages in Monckton's list that do not appear in Young's list. Similarly, Bradshaw while claiming that twenty-four and a half villages (and not twenty-two) were disputed, supplies the names of only sixteen villages. I would like to suggest that the number 'twenty-two' not be taken literally, but rather as a shorthand to indicate the presence of a large number of disputed villages that lay all along the Anglo–Gorkha frontier.
34. See letter from W. Leycester, Magst. of Saran to J. Adam, Secretary to Government, 5 January 1816, FS Consl. 3 February, 1816, no. 21, NAI. See depositions of Bassun Raut and Sheikh Ziauddin, *Monckton Report, 1814*.
35. Details in RRC 40: 54–58, and 194. See also the *Monckton report*.
36. See 'Report on the enquiry into the disputes between the Nepalese and the raja of Bettiah concerning the lands on the frontier of Zillah Sarun in the dominions of the Honourable Company', FS Procs. 26 March 1813, Consl. no. 36, NAI (hereafter the *Young Report*); see also the series of dispatches between Lt. Col. Paris Bradshaw and Government, FP Procs. 25 March 1814, nos. 25–34, pp. 547–635, *NAI* (hereafter the *Bradshaw Report*); and *Monckton Report, 1814*. On the Gorkhali side see the following among others – '*subbas* and other officials of Bara-Parsa and Rautahat directed to provide necessary help to Ramjit Bhandari and Mir Munshi Raza Khan in settling Border Disputes, 1810 A.D.', *RRC* 39: 165; '*guru* (Ranganath Pandit) authorized to demarcate Nepal–India border with *amil* (*amin*?) from India, in Butwal and elsewhere, 1813 A.D.', *RRC* 39: 557.

seemed to have been more coherent and unanimous in their arguments, especially when it came to reiterating the fact that the twenty-two villages belonged to Bettiah and not to Gorkha. But this by itself would not have meant that their claims were genuine. We need to bear in mind that investigations such as those conducted by the Company's officials, with their peculiar questions about linear boundaries, issues of possession, objectification of rights, and their quest for principles of right, justice, reason, and precedent, were details that the raja of Bettiah and his supporters, following nearly fifty years of colonial rule, may have become quite skilled in negotiating. Accordingly, the raja of Bettiah would have schooled his witnesses in British procedures and expectations. Undoubtedly the Gorkhalis might have instructed their witnesses as well, but these witnesses seem to have had little idea about the topo-political particulars (establishment of firm linear boundaries and compact territories) that the British investigating officers were trying to determine. Thus, Bassun Raut, leader of the Ahir cultivators and key Gorkhali witness, would make potentially damaging statements claiming that the disputed twenty-two villages had, since 1791, been under the charge of the Bettiah raja, Bir Kishor Singh. He would further clarify that of the twenty-two villages, seven had, of old, belonged to the English government, while the remaining fifteen had been recovered from a state of barrenness and brought under cultivation under the English government. Such statements would undoubtedly have convinced British officers of the legitimacy of their own claims.[37] Another instance of ambiguity can be seen in the fact that while Gorkhali witnesses found it difficult to delineate the boundary that separated the possessions of Gorkha from those of the Company, the witnesses from Bettiah were able to do this without much difficulty, clearly tracing the linear run of the boundary. Indeed, it is intriguing that people sharing a common frontier could display such dissimilar spatial imaginations. One possible explanation for this is that the witnesses brought forward by the raja of Bettiah might have been instructed to convey information in this manner, rather than to possess any real knowledge of when, how, and by whom such a linear boundary might have been constituted in the first place.

Other details, especially those concerning trends in revenue collection, emerge clearly through the epistemological fog of such investigations. Gorkhali witnesses in particular are clear about one fact: that the rights to collect revenue from these twenty-two villages were constantly fluctuating between various parties, never remaining the sole monopoly of a single authority. The depositions of witnesses such as Bikha Chaudhari, Bassun Raut and Girdhari Lal clearly reveal that different parties were collecting revenues from these villages. And these collecting agents included Gorkhali officials

37. For Bassun Raut's deposition, see *Monckton Report*, 1814.

(1766–70; 1782–85), Mirza Abdulla Beg (1770–82), and Bir Kishor Singh, the raja of Bettiah (from 1790 onwards).[38]

Given these frequent shifts in the arrangements for the collection of revenue, all that mattered to headmen like Bassun Raut was paying revenue to the concerned authority when the time arrived. Further examples of such shifting agrarian rights abound, one such being the case of *gosain* Hait Giri. In 1799, he obtained a deed for a ten-year contract for the collection of revenue for the village of Ghewra from the Gorkha raja.[39] This village lay close to the Rautahat–Nannor boundary and Hait Giri began to collect customary forest dues from the local populace. The raja of Bettiah who had collected such dues in the past opposed the Giri's collections. Despite this dispute, Hait Giri continued to collect these dues until, in 1804, he was forcibly dispossessed of his lands by Gorkhali officials stationed in the area.[40] Hait Giri's account maps the conflicts between local officialdom and small landholders for the control of the agrarian resources along the Champaran-Tarriani sections of the Anglo–Gorkha frontier. For Company officials, the situation of fluctuating rights to landholding and revenue collection was perplexing. They tried to discern some continuity in patterns of landholding and revenue collection. Such continuity was the only way to establish stable, coherent, and well-defined territories that were free from disputes. Again, the evidence provided by the examples of Bassun Raut and Hait Giri quickly dispelled such aspirations. Such shifting and contested claims to land rights and tax collection paid little respect to maintaining the spatial integrity of the administrative units to which they belonged (*mauzas*, *tappas*, *parganas*). Consequently, administrative divisions such as *parganas* and *tappas* (either in whole or in part) could shift back and forth between different collecting authorities, leaving their bodies discontinuous, dispersed, and intermixed in many places. This kind of dispersal of land, taxation, and tribute collection rights was widespread all along the Anglo–Gorkha frontier.

Such a study of shifting relationships admits of the formative role of power in the organization of territory. The complicated and multi-cornered disputes taking place along the Anglo–Gorkha frontier resist a neat conception of state power flowing outwards from the centre. Rather, they admit to the discontinuities, contradictions and multi-directional flows that were energized by the role of local agents. These multi-cornered contests coalesced around rather unstable alignments

38. The dates are as given by Bikha Chaudhari and, even though they might be speculative, they do clearly show that between 1743 and 1814 the collection of revenue on the Champaran-Tarriani frontier was never resolved in favour of one party for any length of time. See depositions of Bikha Chaudhari, Bassun Raut and Girdhari Lal, *Monckton Report, 1814*.

39. See letter from P. Bradshaw to J. Adam, 6 July 1814, *KRR*, microfilm reel IOR 2, part 2, pp. 35–38, NAN. (Hereafter referred to as *Hait Giri's Account, 1814*.)

40. See *Hait Giri's Account*.

among these actors. Such alliances often spilled over into the spaces of neighbouring states to produce their intermixed territories (or at least that is how they appeared to central authorities). The variations, contingencies and randomness of such strategies of resource control constitute the critical ingredients needed for reconstructing processes of state-making on the Anglo–Gorkha frontier. Such local manoeuvring left fluid the institutional arrangements established by both states to administer the collection of revenue. As central authorities belonging to both states became increasingly drawn into the dynamics of these local conflicts, the disputes were rearticulated in the form of formal inter-state disputes.[41] The arrival of the Gorkhali *subba* Laxman Giri seems to have only drawn him into the prevailing relationships of dispute that then underwent further alignments and realignments. His death has to be understood against this background of local initiative and struggle. The varied practices of local kings, landlords, officials, headmen, and cultivators also point to the creativity human agents bring to bear on existing arrangements for the organization and appropriation of landed resources, rendering them flexible and open-ended. Given this scenario, these actors had little concern for their physical location within the territories of a state, or for preserving the integrity of a linear boundary, or even the connectedness of territory. What mattered most to them was securing control over various kinds of agrarian rights and resources and payment of taxes or tribute to their immediate superiors. This required these human agents to make situational adjustments within shifting contexts of culture, power, and history, which left their fingerprints on the organization of territory or space.[42]

Conclusion

This chapter is an ethnographic history of how shifting social relations produced moving state spaces along a colonial frontier. It argues that previous accounts of the Anglo–Gorkha war need to be unpacked to reveal the fluid relationships that produced the intermixed and mobile geographies of precolonial states. It examined those aspects of agrarian governance concerning a hierarchy of land, taxation, and tribute collection rights that informed the territorial disputes between the British and the Gorkhalis in the decades leading up to the outbreak of war in 1814. Shifts in cultivation patterns and

42. I have adapted the term 'situational adjustments' from the work of Sally Falk Moore (cited in Turner 1985: 153 but see also Sally F. Moore (1975)). I take 'situational adjustments' to mean those practices through which persons either arrange their immediate situations by exploiting the indeterminacies of the context they are placed in, or generate indeterminacies by redefining the rules and their roles within these historically configured contexts.

41. See reports of John Young, John Monckton, and Paris Bradshaw. For a map of pargana Simraon that helps somewhat in locating the disputed villages, see *Map of pargana Semrown, District Sarun* by Alex Wyatt (Wyatt 1847).

political hierarchies produced commensurate movements in this hierarchy of rights and claims. This inquiry was supported by careful, detailed accounts of those conflicts that helped capture the rich socio-spatial significance of colonial encounters along the Anglo–Gorkha frontier. Consequently, this frontier became a mobile zone marked by unstable and frequently changing social relationships. These, in turn, left their impression on the organization and knowledge of precolonial territorial divisions. The fluctuating histories of property rights, taxation and tribute collection claims that peppered the frontier strained against the territorial structure of the region, producing administrative divisions marked by movement, fluidity, improvisation, and change. These caused patches of territory to intermix and overlap, leaving behind discontinuous bodies and boundaries that would confound the British.

In the diplomatic exchanges that took place between the two states prior to the war, each accused the other of complicity and intransigence, encoding critical questions about spatiality, which was in the final analysis the referent in question. The discourse of conflict couched in tropes such as 'the predatory system of the Goorkhas', or the machinations of the Company's petty *zamindars* 'ill-disposed' towards Gorkha, revolved around the organization and knowledge of space. But in the abrasive interfacing of two semantic worlds, at a critical moment of cross-cultural encounter, issues of spatiality eluded the vision of officials belonging to both the states and were instead recoded in terms of political and territorial rights. While both contested their rights to specific territories, they did so with the deeply held conviction that their contest was a morally defensible one. In retrospect, it becomes clear that the war was fought over the right to mark, define, and bound space that was, in reality, always in motion. The victory of the Company meant that their spatial visions would be imposed on the Gorkhalis and, over time, on much of south Asia. It should come as no surprise that the most significant result of the war was the formal demarcation of the Anglo–Gorkha boundary by Company officials. This boundary was to be linear, marked by permanent posts, clearly demarcating the territories of the two states along their common border. Further surveying and map-making operations conducted by the colonial state in the nineteenth and twentieth centuries would generate a fixed cartographic framework that hid from view the constant entropy in environmental, social, spatial, political, and resource relations. This would create a new geographical template for the modern state in south Asia – occupying a definite portion of the earth's surface and divided and sub-divided into non-overlapping divisions and sub-divisions. Modern cartography fetishizes the state as an abstract space, a container within which action unfolds, hiding from clear view the boundless social worlds we all ultimately occupy.[43]

43. During the colonial period (1765–1947) the older administrative divisions such as the *tappa* and the *pargana* would be surveyed, mapped, reorganized and ultimately dissolved across much of south Asia.

Abbreviations

BL	British Library, London
BSA	Bihar State Archives
Coll.	Collector
Consl.	Consultation
FS	Foreign Secret
KRR	Kathmandu Residency Records
Magst.	Magistrate
NAI	National Archives of India, Delhi
NAN	National Archives of Nepal, Kathmandu
OIOC	Oriental and India Office Collections
PGGCB	Proceedings of the Governor-General-in-Council in Bengal
Procs.	Proceedings
RRC	Regmi Research Collection
RRS	Regmi Research Series
WBSA	West Bengal State Archives, Calcutta

Glossary

birta	Tax-free grants made by the state to individuals, usually on an inheritable basis
B.S.	Bikram Sambat calendar which is approximately arrived at by adding fifty-seven to the Gregorian calendar
ijara	A contract for the collection of revenue
jagir	Land assigned to government employees, usually in lieu of cash salary
kaji	A senior member of Gorkha's ruling elite, higher in rank than a *sardar* and in charge of civil and military affairs
malguzar	A person paying revenues to a government
nankar	Rights to lands enjoyed by officials such as *quanungoyes* in north India as their emoluments
pargana/praganna	Fiscal division in north India which could be further subdivided into *tappas* or *mauzas* (villages)
quanungo/-goye	Record-keeper
sardar	A high ranking civil and military officer
subba	Chief provincial administrator, usually in charge of a district in Gorkha
syahamohar	Historical documents belonging to the Sen rajas, bearing a black seal

tappa/tappe A small tract or division of country, smaller than a *pargana*, comprised of a number of villages
taraf A fiscal sub-division including several villages

References

Abrams, P. 1982. *Historical Sociology*. London: Open Books.

Bourdieu, P. 1977. *An Outline of a Theory of Practice*. Cambridge: Cambridge University Press.

Burghart, R. 1984. 'The Formation of the Concept of the Nation-State in Nepal', *Journal of Asian Studies* 44(1): 101–26.

———. 1987. 'Gifts to the Gods: Power, Property, and Ceremonial in Nepal', in D. Cannadine and S. Price (eds.), *Rituals of Royalty: Power and Ceremonial in Traditional Societies*. Cambridge: Cambridge University Press, pp. 237–70.

Chaudhuri, K. C. 1960. *Anglo–Nepalese Relations*. Calcutta: Firma K. L. Mukhopadyaya.

Clifford, J. 1997. *Routes: Travel and Translation in the Late Twentieth Century*. Cambridge: Harvard University Press.

Cohn, B. S. 1987. *An Anthropologist amongst the Historians and Other Essays*. New Delhi: Oxford University Press.

Comaroff, J. L. and J. Comaroff. 1992. *Ethnography and the Historical Imagination*. Boulder: Westview Press.

Craib, R. 2004. *Cartographic Mexico: A History of State Fixations and Fugitive Landscapes*. Durham: Duke University Press.

Dening, G. 1996. *Performances*. Chicago: University of Chicago Press.

DesChene, M. K. F. 1991. 'Relics of Empire: A Cultural History of the Gurkhas, 1816–1987', Ph.D. dissertation. Palo Alto, CA: Stanford University.

Dirks, N. B., G. Eley, and S. Ortner (eds). 1994. *Culture/Power/History: A Reader in Contemporary Social Theory*. Princeton: Princeton University Press.

Dube, S. (ed.). 2004. *Postcolonial Passages: Contemporary History Writing in India*. Delhi: Oxford University Press.

Edney, M. 1997. *Mapping an Empire: The Geographical Construction of British India, 1765–1843*. Chicago: University of Chicago Press.

———. 2003. 'Bringing India to Hand: Mapping an Empire, Denying Space', in F. Nussbaum (ed.), *The Global Eighteenth Century*. Baltimore: Johns Hopkins University Press, pp. 65–78.

Foucault, M. 1979. *Discipline and Punish: The Birth of the Prison*. New York: Vintage.

———. 1980, *Power/Knowledge: Selected Interviews and Other Writings, 1972–1977*. C. Gordon (ed.). New York: Pantheon Books.

Geertz, C. 1973. *The Interpretation of Culture*. New York: Basic Books.

Gupta, A. and J. Ferguson. 1997. 'Beyond "Culture": Space, Identity and the Politics of Difference', in Gupta and Ferguson (eds), *Culture, Power, Place: Explorations in Critical Anthropology*. Durham: Duke University Press, pp. 33–51.

Husain, A. 1970. *British India's Relations with the Kingdom of Nepal, 1857–1947*. Oxford: Clarendon Press.

Ingold, T. 1994. 'The Art of Translation in a Continuous World', in G. Pálsson and J. Gledhill (eds), *Beyond Boundaries: Understanding Translation and Anthropological Discourse*. Oxford: Berg Publishers, pp. 210–48.

Isaac, R. 1984. *The Transformation of Virginia, 1740–1790*. Chapel Hill: University of North Carolina Press.

Jarrett, H. S. 1949. *Ain-i-Akbari*, trans. Col. H. S. Jarrett. Calcutta: Asiatic Society of Bengal.
Kaplan, M. 1995. 'Panopticon in Poona: An Essay on Foucault and Colonialism', *Cultural Anthropology* 10(1): 85–98.
Khanduri, C. 1997. *Re-Discovered History of Gorkhas*. Delhi: Gyan Sagar Publications.
Lefebvre, H. 1991. *The Production of Space*. London: Blackwell.
Massey, D. 2005. *For Space*. London: Sage.
Michael, B. A. 2001. 'Separating the Yam from the Boulder: Statemaking, Space, and the Causes of the Anglo–Gorkha War of 1814–1816', Ph.D. dissertation. Manoa: University of Hawaii at Manoa.
———. 2003. 'When Soldiers and Statesmen Meet: "Ethnographic Moments" on the Frontiers of Empire', in S. Gordon (ed.), *Robes of Honour: Khil'at in Pre-Colonial and Colonial India*. Oxford University Press, pp. 80–94.
———. 2007. 'Making Territory Visible: The Revenue Surveys of Colonial South Asia', *Imago Mundi: Journal for the International History of Cartography* 59(1): 78–95.
Mishra, G. 1978. *Agrarian Problems of Permanent Settlement: A Case Study of Champaran*. New Delhi: Peoples Publishing House.
Mojumdar, K. 1973. *Anglo–Nepalese Relations in the Nineteenth Century*. Calcutta: Firma K. L. Mukhopadhyaya.
Moore, S. F. 1975. 'Epilogue', in S. F. Moore and B. Meyerhof (eds), *Symbol and Politics in Communal Ideologies*. Ithaca: Cornell University Press, pp. 210–39.
———. 1987. 'Explaining the Present: Theoretical Dilemmas in Processual Anthropology', *American Ethnologist* 14(4): 727–36.
———. 1994. 'The Ethnography of the Present and the Analysis of Process', in R. Brodsky (ed.), *Assessing Cultural Anthropology*. New York: McGraw Hill, pp. 362–76.
Naraharinath, Y. 2022 B.S. [1966 CE]. *Itihasaprakashma Sandhipatrasamgraha*. Dang.
Onta, P. 1994. 'Rich Possibilities: Notes on Social History in Nepal', *CNS* 21(1): 1–43.
Ortner, S. 1995. 'Resistance and the Problem of Ethnographic Refusal', *CSSH* 37(1): 173–93.
Pant, M. R. 2021 B.S. [1963 CE]. '1871–72 Ko Nepal Angrez Yuddhama Nepal le Harnema Euta Thulo Karan', *Purnima* 1(1): 47–58.
———. 2022 B.S. [1964 CE]. 'Nepal Angrez Yuddha: Nepal Angrez Yuddhako Ghoshana Nahundai Angrezle Gareko Yuddhako Taiyari', *Purnima* 5, 2(1): 54–62.
———. 2023 B.S. [1965 CE]. 'Nepalsang Ladai Khelnuaghi Angrezharule Gupt Bheshma Gareko Nepal-Bhotbhraman', *Purnima* 26, 7(2): 67–100.
Pemble, J. 1971. *The Invasion of Nepal: John Company at War*. Oxford: Clarendon Press.
Rana, N. R. L. 1970. *The Anglo–Gorkha War of 1814–1816*. Kathmandu: Jore Ganesh Press.
Regmi, D. R. 1975. *Modern Nepal. Vol. 1: Rise and Growth in the Eighteenth Century*. Calcutta: Firma K. L. Mukhopadhyaya.
Sanwal, B. D. 1965. *Nepal and the East India Company*. Bombay: Asia Publishing House.
Schendel, W. V. 2002. 'Stateless in South Asia: The Making of the India–Bangladesh Enclaves', *Journal of Asian Studies* 61(1): 115–48.
Scott, J. C. 1998. *Seeing Like a State: How Certain Schemes to Improve the Human Condition Have Failed*. New Haven: Yale University Press.
Shaha, R. 1990. *Modern Nepal: A Political History, 1769–1885, Vol. 1*. Delhi: Manohar.
Sivaramakrishnan, K. 1993. 'Unpacking Colonial Discourse: Using the Anthropology of Tribal India for an Ethnography of the State', *Yale Graduate Journal of Anthropology* 5: 57–66.
———. 1999. *Modern Forests: Statemaking and Environmental Change in Colonial Eastern India*. Stanford: Stanford University Press.
Soja, E. 1989. *Postmodern Geographies: The Reassertion of Space in Contemporary Social Thought*. London: Verso.
Stiller, L. 1973. *The Rise of the House of Gorkha*. Delhi: Manjushri.

———. 1976. *The Silent Cry: The People of Nepal, 1816–1839*. Kathmandu: Sahayogi Prakashan.

Thapa, S. B. 2048 B. S. [1991 CE]. *Sugauli Sandhi ke ho*. Kathmandu: Shamsher Bahadur Thapa.

Thongchai, W. 1994. *Siam Mapped: The History of the Geo-Body of a Nation*. Honolulu: University of Hawaii Press.

Thrift, N. 2003. 'Space: The Fundamental Stuff of Human Geography', in S. L. Holloway, S. P. Rice and G. Valentine (eds), *Key Concepts in Geography*. London: Sage, pp. 95–107.

Tsing, A. 2004. *Friction*. Princeton: Princeton University Press.

Wyatt, A. 1847. *Statistics of the Districts of Sarun, Consisting of the Sircars of Sarun and Chumparun*. Calcutta: Military Orphan Press.

Yang, A. A. 1989. *The Limited Raj: Agrarian Relations in Colonial India, Saran District, 1793–1920*. Berkeley: University of California Press.

Chapter 4
Embodying Spaces of Violence: Narratives of Israeli Soldiers in the Occupied Palestinian Territories

Richard Clarke

The British Army calls it 'Fighting in Built-Up Areas' or FIBUA. The US Army calls it 'Military Operations in Urban Terrain', or MOUT. It has other names, too, such as 'conventional warfare in an urban environment'. Most straightforwardly of all, it is sometimes called 'street fighting'.

Dewar (1992: 7)

Introduction

In the late summer of 1999, as part of field research on the interrelationship between space, violence, movement, and knowledge in Israel/Palestine, I visited the occupied Palestinian territories with a number of Israelis: retired soldiers, those between periods of *miluim* reserve duty,[1] and a handful of those who, for political reasons, now refused to serve in the territories.

This chapter is based on their evocative and careful narratives, as they sought to explain how it felt to them to be returning to what they saw as the violent landscape of the territories, and to spaces that they had first encountered as occupying soldiers. I argue – borrowing from the theoretical approach of Bourdieu – that the process of habituating young Israelis to soldiering is fundamentally a dialectic between visceral, bodily experiences and the context of particular discourses about particular places.

At one level, of course, my informants were seeking to possess and control the spaces around them. When they returned to the particular places they had occupied, however, it became clear that they themselves had been possessed by them – their reaction to the phenomena they had experienced had become embodied through a concrete process of habituation.

But it was also clear, in speaking to the soldiers afterwards, that it was the process of movement, the interaction between the body and spaces, and their experience of moving through the places they had occupied that had been at the

1. Except where indicated, all italicized terms in the text are Hebrew.

heart of their experiences. It had been the political and military operational tool of 'the patrol' that had marked the territory as 'occupied' and it had been patrolling that had constituted by far the most marked period of danger for the soldiers.

After illustrating this briefly through descriptions of how the individuals' narratives changed when they went back to the territories after their military service, I conclude by discussing some of the implications of my analysis for those seeking to understand recent events in Israel/Palestine and, by implication, the current situation in Iraq.

However, it should be noted that at its heart, this chapter - the fieldwork for which was carried out only five years ago - is historical. It is based on the words of a small number of Israelis – mainly young men – who, in the (now) extraordinary and rare calm of the late summer of 1999, chose to travel the short physical distance back to the areas over which they had fought years before.

Context: the Six Day War and the Discursive Creation of the 'Territories'

In the Israeli 'popular imagination', the Six Day War of June 1967 has become a totem of national pride and military prowess (Cohen 1994). Following a build-up of military tension for weeks, culminating in a pre-emptive Israeli strike on the Egyptian air-force, the Israel Defence Forces (IDF) captured land on the West bank of the Jordan River, the Golan Heights, and the Gaza Strip. These areas – quickly dubbed 'the territories' (*hashtachim*)[2] – contained a large number of Palestinian Arab refugees who had fled the fighting that had established the State in 1948 and they now saw an influx of more refugees who were accommodated in United Nations camps. For years, the situation in the territories remained at an impasse, with Israel building large Jewish settlements in key strategic locations and refusing to countenance the return of the land without recognition from the surrounding Arab nations. By 1987, the Palestinian population had grown in number and anger and exploded in a political uprising, the Intifada (in Arabic, literally 'the throwing off'). Israeli

2. Various labels can be used to describe the areas of land captured by Israel during the Six Day War of June 1967 (the West Bank of the Jordan River, the Gaza Strip and the Golan Heights). The least politically problematic term seems to me to be 'the Occupied Territories' or 'the Occupied Palestinian Territories'. I use the emic term 'territories' as a literal translation of the Hebrew '*shtachim*', the word most commonly used by the 'Dovish', liberal Israelis with whom I worked. Simply describing them as 'Palestine' seems to me politically problematic and misleading, until a viable Palestinian state is established there (if ever). Other terms, such as Judea-Samaria (*Yehuda-Shomron* in Hebrew – sometimes combined with *Azza* (Gaza) and shortened to *Yesha*) are used by religious Jews, settlers and many Israelis to the right of the political centre (and is still used in much official Israeli documentation). The implication of the term is that the area was always part of *Eretz Yisrael*, the Land of Israel.

troops were poured into the territories in increasing numbers; a young Israeli man growing up in the 1980s could expect to serve a period of military service in the burning refugee camps of the West Bank and Gaza. The Intifada also fundamentally altered Israeli public perceptions of safety in relation to travelling in the territories. The West Bank and Gaza became places travelled to almost entirely by soldiers and settlers.

In 1993, as part of the Oslo Agreement, Israel allowed Yasser Arafat's Palestine Liberation Organization to establish an autonomous 'government' – the Palestinian National Authority (PNA) – in small enclaves in the West Bank and Gaza. Bypass roads were built to carry Israeli traffic to Israeli settlements while avoiding the PNA areas. Israeli civilians continued to stay away from the territories but they were now joined by soldiers who were withdrawn from their bases in the Palestinian cities. Stories about the territories fell away from newspapers and the television. As far as most Israelis were concerned, the occupation was over. More than at any other period in Israeli history, Palestinians had become marginalized. An Israeli could drive from Tel Aviv, through Jerusalem, and on to the large settlement of Kiryat Arba, just outside Hebron, and only pass small Palestinian villages en route. Israelis were, to borrow Bourdieu's (1977) powerful descriptor, caught in what I have elsewhere called a 'habitus of avoidance' (Clarke 2001). Almost without being aware of it, Israelis in the late 1990s had become habituated into physically, emotionally, and politically avoiding the West Bank and Gaza.

There is an apparent anthropological irony at the heart of this. Israeli public discourse is centred on the notion of settlement, of the static and autochthonous relationship between the Jewish people and the land of Israel. Yet the creation and maintenance of the State as a discrete space, at least since 1967, has been about movement and (as the introductory chapter to this volume notes is often the case) the curtailment of movement (both of the Self and the Other). This is not restricted to the obvious – the creation of the networks of roads and settlements that keep the populations apart and yet mingled (like the parallel movements of bloodstreams that never mix), on the one hand, and the creation of the large security barrier that runs through the territories, on the other – but extends to the practice of control.

The notion of the geographical 'matrix of control' (Halper 2000) has become familiar in Israeli social science in recent years – it describes the web of roads, buildings, homes, surveillance points, and, crucially, restricted movement provisions that execute a wealth of carefully controlled political practices that between them create the ongoing occupation. These practices were diverse and often attributed to particular local contexts – the city of Hebron, for example, undoubtedly the most stark example of a divided West Bank place, was regularly the subject of curfews in which the movement of the overwhelmingly Palestinian population was curtailed while the comparatively small Israeli Jewish population was able to walk throughout the city in what settlers there explicitly described as a form of marking their territory.

The relatively small geographical size of the territories and their close proximity to Israel, something that never fails to strike visitors, bizarrely meant that, at least for soldiers serving their *miluim* in the West Bank, the option was open to commute to their reserve duties. This context, on which my broader research has focused (Clarke 2001, 2003), is seemingly as postmodern as it is possible to be. Yet it is, at best, a very particular version of postmodernity; while other parts of the world enjoy a seemingly exponentially increasing ability to move, communicate, and interact, Israelis and Palestinians, in the late 1990s, were circumscribed in their movements, on the one hand by a discourse of fear and separation and on the other by mechanisms and provisions of control (cf. Clarke 2001).

But the voices and experiences of those who, over time, built this matrix of control from 1967 onwards (for this is not exclusively a post-Oslo structure or practice) have been comparatively absent from anthropological discussions of the West Bank and Gaza. This chapter seeks to play a small part in addressing that gap. It emphasizes the sense in which occupying a space, at least in military terms, is all too often about movement, especially patrolling and locating; settlements, locations and places are created and maintained by people and the complex web of movements across spaces that they operate. Seeking to understand their movement, however, will be unsuccessful unless it appreciates the visceral, bodily characteristic of moving through what the soldiers themselves saw as spaces of violence.

Protest and Challenge

By the late 1990s, a small number of Israeli activists had become increasingly angered by the situation of 'detachment' from the territories. They argued (and continue to argue) that the occupation of most of the territories has continued and that Palestinians are now trapped in, at best, semi-autonomous cantons and, at worst, Bantustans. They believe that the territories must be held in front of the Israeli general public, to remind them of the situation there. It was the work of these individuals on which my research focused and it was through the range of activities they organized – from visiting those whose homes had been demolished by the Israeli army, to attending 'peace tours' of the territories – that I met those whom I interviewed for this chapter.[3] Although I have changed their names, I include a brief biography of each below.

3. My research focused on Israeli public knowledge of the territories (Clarke 2001). I would like to thank all those individuals with whom I worked while in the field, particularly Jeff Halper, Yossi Klein Halevi, Eyal Ben-Ari and Dani Rabinowitz. Special thanks to Yael Navaro-Yashin.

'Uri' is a student, in his early twenties. He served as an administrative officer in Hebron and travelled to Ramallah soon afterwards. 'Moshe' is an American-born Israeli student in his mid-twenties who served with an infantry unit, also in Hebron. He travelled to the West Bank with friends and dialogue projects. 'Ben', also in his mid-twenties, served with a paratrooper unit in Gaza during the final days of the Intifada. He is now involved in politics and dialogue. 'Dan' is an academic in his forties. He spent some of his reserve duty serving in Nablus and Hebron during the Intifada and travelled to Ramallah with a Palestinian friend in 1999. 'Yitzhak', in his thirties, moved to Israel in the late 1980s. After serving in Southern Lebanon and Gaza as a paratrooper, he became increasingly uncomfortable with the IDF and left the army. He is now the director of a dialogue project and travelled frequently in the territories. 'Yoram' is an American-born businessman who served in the army during the Intifada. He attended a 'peace tour' to Nablus. 'Oren' is a journalist and writer who has lived in Israel for over twenty years. He served in Gaza and Ramallah during the Intifada and has travelled in the territories since then as part of his work and in dialogue contexts.[4]

Embodying Spaces of Violence: Creating the Israeli Soldier

> *You're not the symbol, you're the* embodiment *of everything that's gone wrong in these people's lives.*
>
> Oren

The Israeli response to the Intifada represented a process both of penetration and protection. At its heart were Israeli soldiers patrolling spaces transformed by conflict.[5] My analysis below focuses on the day-to-day experiences of these individuals, something that has often been left out of general treatments of 'war',[6] and presents them as intensely embodied, spatial practices. I argue that the process of 'policing' the Intifada involved soldiers being trained into a particular habitus, much of which, as Bourdieu has argued, involves practices of the body (e.g., 1977: 87–95). The subsequent sensations of being in the territories, as a soldier, were also fundamentally physical. They were centred on fears of attacks which were related to spaces and occupying (in both the physical and political

4. I would like to thank all those Israeli soldiers whose words appear in this paper for agreeing to speak to me. I would especially like to thank Dan, for reasons that will be obvious to him.
5. The border guards of the *magav* (*hamishmar hagvul*) also played a key role in Israel's Intifada strategy. They are not covered here because of constraints of space and data (none of the individuals with whom I worked had served in the *magav*).
6. Prof. J.A. Cook (personal communication).

senses) particular terrains of violence. The body was simultaneously the subject through which events were experienced, the object onto which violence could take place (and from which it had to be protected) and the device through which the occupation was enacted. Bodies, both Israeli and Palestinian, became both the subjects and the objects of political actions (Feldman 1991).

Israeli units sent to the territories rapidly developed techniques, adopted from urban combat procedures, to balance their need to quell the uprising and also to protect themselves as they did so. After it became clear that the Intifada would not simply be a passing disturbance, the soldiers began to settle into a rhythm of patrolling the towns and villages of the West Bank and Gaza.[7] Dewar, in his discussion of the British Army in Northern Ireland, presents foot patrols as a means of 'dominating the cities' (1992: 158). Halevi echoes this in his Intifada diary, when he writes of the official importance of 'demonstrating a presence' (1991a: 22).

This concept of patrolling is presented as primarily operational but is deeply political (in the richest sense) and harks back to 'pioneering' Israeli notions of making spaces by walking or taking a hike (*tiyul*) through them. As Ben-David (1997) notes in his rich treatment of this powerful concept, *tiyul* became a form of 'consecration', a way of marking and remarking territory. It is no coincidence that, soon after the end of the 1967 war, groups of Israelis began consciously to 'hike' through the West Bank.

The patrols, and the individual soldiers who formed them, moved through hostile spaces – if the soldiers' patrolling was a piece of political movement, so the increasingly ritualized hurling of stones at patrols became a piece of parallel political theatre on the part of Palestinian youths. Although comparatively few Israeli soldiers were killed or wounded during the uprising, the length of time that units spent in the field meant that they were almost continually exposed to danger. The boredom of military service was punctuated by occasional attacks, against which the soldiers sought to protect themselves. The nature of patrolling towns and cities, however, and the particular characteristics of the urban spaces of the West Bank and Gaza, meant different spaces and particular places were associated with specific threats. The town of Nablus, for example, was seen as especially dangerous because of its tight, winding streets and

7. Moshe noted that 'The first day you walk through *Chevron* (Hebron), you're scared. And then the second day, you're a little scared. And by the third day, it's very, very boring'. Dan said, 'I was very worried before going to Hebron, because we'd seen all the violence on television and so on. But the minute you're there, there are some tough times but it's not as frightening as it's made out on television. There's a certain rhythm'. Ben-Ari quotes from a soldier who had served as a company commander in Hebron: 'It looked very violent, very difficult. That's what they showed on television. … I came with a lot of apprehension, and I couldn't imagine how we would grapple with this thing with all that we saw in the media. And after a week, I think, we settled into the routine there. Within a week, you already understand what's going on …' (1998: 72).

confined *qasbah* (marketplace area): 'From what I remember, Nablus and Hebron were really the worst, in terms of the *qasbot*, the two *qasbahs*' (Dan).

Spaces became defined, and moved through, according to their tactical significance. Narrow, covered areas presented the danger of ambushes, while moving in crowds exposed soldiers to stabbings. Jeeps could be stranded and attacked by Molotov cocktails. Individual soldiers could be kidnapped or shot by a sniper.

The protection of soldiers therefore quickly became a concern for the IDF. Frankel (1994: 75) argues that the first wave of soldiers sent into the territories lacked the necessary skills:

> In the early weeks of the intifada soldiers felt trapped when confronted by stone-throwing youths. They had no training in riot control and no feel for the streets of the cities and villages they patrolled or for the people who confronted them.

The new training emphasized the importance of continual vigilance and protection and focused both on the body and on the new spaces the soldiers needed to patrol. Instructions were embodied through repeated physical instructions, something to which I shall return in the next section, and highlighted the importance of protecting the bodies of the men. Bourdieu, in his analysis of the embodied enculturation of Kabyle children, presents the internalization of the habitus as a bodily process (1977: 87–95). Mauss had earlier argued that the learning of cultural elements, such as posture, was achieved through the positioning of the body in different ways, which become 'natural' to the individual (1973). The process of being trained as a soldier, I would argue, is one of embodying a style of behaviour, a way of using one's body. For Bourdieu this process of embodiment among the Kabyle is exemplified in '*the dialectical relationship between the body and a space* structured according to the mythico-ritual oppositions' (1977: 89, emphasis mine). This constitutes: 'the form par excellence of the structural apprenticeship which leads to the em-bodying of the structures of the world' (ibid.: 89).

The structured embodying of the soldier of the Intifada, I would argue, was not only a strategy of protection from harm, however. It was constituted through those trained actions that internalized dispositions towards particular spaces. Soldiers were not simply told to avoid crowded, covered areas – their training embodied these sentiments, through '*structural exercises* tending to transmit this or that form of practical mastery' (ibid.: 88, original emphasis).[8]

8. Connerton summarizes the notion of bodily memory well: 'By exercise the body comes to co-ordinate an increasing range of muscular activities in an increasingly automatic way, until awareness retreats, the movement flows 'involuntarily', and there occurs a firm and practised sequence of events which take their fluent course' (1989: 94).

Through imitating the actions of others (officers in the field and during training), the men embodied their training. They became soldiers rather than men acting in a conscious manner. Again, Bourdieu on Kabyle children becomes an important reference for understanding this aspect of the embodiment of the habitus:

> The child [soldier] imitates not 'models' but other people's actions. Body *hexis* speaks directly to the motor function, in the form of a pattern of postures that is both individual and systematic, because linked to a whole system of techniques involving the body and tools [weapons, protective gear] (ibid.: 87, original emphasis).

Certain areas, I shall argue in the next section, become powerfully, subconsciously associated with danger, fear, and (automatic) responses. The soldier's body becomes habitually postured according to the internalized, constructed logic of these places. The soldiers whom I interviewed remembered this experience clearly. Some of it took place during basic training:

> I went into the army. After basic training, I went to a combat unit … as a young person, it was very, very difficult … We were really very young soldiers … [After training], we knew how to do everything, to be a real fighter, how to identify the enemy (Ben).

However, training continued with experience as the soldiers began to work in the territories and became more familiar with the terrain. Instructions were given as they patrolled the new spaces. The officers reiterated the importance of the soldiers protecting their bodies and being continually alert (as well as presenting guides to be imitated):

> I was with the company commander, and we were in the *qasbah*, and he was the first who said to me 'Put your back against the wall'. 'Keep your finger not on the trigger'. 'Be always on the lookout' (Dan).

Units on patrol moved slowly, often with one soldier walking backwards to protect the others from attacks from behind. Whenever the patrol stopped moving, however, the soldiers would each take cover against walls or in doorways. Ben-Ari quotes from a platoon commander, interviewed in the Israeli newspaper, *Davar*:

> It was a dangerous game. In the alleys we were scared of a knife; someone pulling us into an enclosure and knifing us. We used to go in

> the street in groups of six with the person bringing up the rear wearing a bullet-proof vest against a knifing or a shot (1998: 81–82).

The training embodied the importance of defence against ambushes. The danger of an exposed back is one that many of my informants remembered being highlighted: 'Don't present, physically, an exposed back. That's ground into me ...' (Yitzhak).

Ground into him, physically, continually emphasized. The back was an obvious danger area, but so was the head. Rocks were often aimed at soldiers' heads or dropped from above:

> 'Keep together, look up'. Gaza, when we were doing the *miluim*, in that period, there were two main tactics. There were hit and run drivers and there were *blockim* [large bricks] being thrown. So you look to the road and you look up (Oren).
>
> [T]hey put up a position there, because it's where you see everything. You can see if anybody is sitting on any of the rooftops who's going to throw a big boulder on somebody's head while you're walking down the *simta* [alley] (Moshe).
>
> We scan the rooftops for falling cinder blocks, intersections for flying stones (Halevi 1991a: 22).

A participant in an Israeli–Palestinian dialogue group in Gaza told me that Palestinians would sometimes drop refrigerators from windows onto the soldiers below.

Patrols were mobile sites of continual tension.[9] They were also, as was the presence of the army more broadly, a paradoxical combination of distance and presence. The army had to show a visible occupancy but separate itself from the 'locals'. As Oren notes:

> The message was delivered very clearly, and very sensibly I think – 'Don't have anything to do with the local population. You don't buy from them, you don't socialize with them'. You could be lulled into a trap. That was the rationale.

Many of the soldiers with whom I spoke constructed this aspect of the Intifada in contrast to the situation faced by Israeli troops in the territories before 1987.

9. Writing on the First World War, Fussell notes that '[t]he presence of the enemy off on the borders of awareness feeds anxiety in the manner of the dropping-off places of medieval maps' (1975: 76). Cf. Bourne's analysis of the stresses experienced by a US Special Forces unit in Vietnam: 'Men frequently express the wish that the enemy would make an all-out attack and relieve the tension of constant anticipation' (1970: 114).

While there were clearly some dangers then, the day-to-day practices of dealing with Palestinians seem to have been considerably more relaxed. Dan described one of his earliest reserve duties:

> I was stationed in the occupied territories with a paratrooper unit '74 to '75 for a year … and we used to go up to Jenin and Nablus all the time. We used to buy meat, for barbecuing, in uniform.

These kinds of interactions were presented by Oren in contrast to his experiences in the 1980s:

> In the old days, before the Intifada, the soldiers used to wander in and buy cigarettes, hummus …[10] but the army that I knew – I became a soldier after the start of the Intifada – the whole civilian population was off limits, the whole civilian population hates you.

The metaphor of the separate bloodstreams seems powerful once again. Two distinct but interwoven and overlaid topologies were at work throughout the occupation and this is perhaps the greatest irony of Israel's attempt to assert sovereignty and not just political or military control over the spaces of the West Bank and Gaza. Again, nowhere is this more stark that in Hebron, where tours for Israelis and foreign visitors sometimes cross each other while following entirely different routes and 'marking out' entirely different spaces (Clarke 2000).

With the entire population seen as constituting a potential threat, each space becomes a hostile landscape. Dewar evokes this powerfully in his presentation of British troops in Northern Ireland:

> [they] run zigzagging out of the gate [of the base]. They are instantly 'on patrol', away from the comparative safety of the company base where, even if they can be mortared, they at least cannot be shot at (1992: 162).

Patrol commanders, he writes, 'will be looking into every window and doorway, every street corner and hedgerow for a possible telltale sign of an ambush' (ibid.: 164). More common in the Intifada than the ambushes, stabbings, and shootings, however, were the hails of stones. 'Someone tried to kill me', said one of the soldiers interviewed by Liebes and Blum-Kulka:

> He stood above me, with a rock and if this rock had hit me … He was on the roof and I pointed my gun at him and told him, in Arabic, that I would

10. An Arab dish made from chickpeas.

> … shoot him. He said: 'Shoot me, I don't care'. He aimed and threw the rock at me … I jumped to one side … escaping the stone (1994: 57).

There seems to have been a visceral, immediate quality to rocks that all of my interviewees mentioned at some point. Their impact came from their intensity. Many of the people I interviewed spoke in terms of 'showers' or 'hails' of rocks:

> We were on a roof for about a week, guarding some *Shin Bet* [Israeli internal security service] people … There were a few of us and we couldn't go downstairs. Any time you tried to go down, you got a barrage of rocks. People tried to throw rocks up to the fifth floor roof, where we were stationed. So you can't go anywhere (Oren).
>
> The worst that happened is that I went with the commander of company C. We became good friends … and we really got stuck in a village, driving somewhere … you couldn't get out of the jeep and they were throwing a lot of stones … There were three of us, the guy who was in charge of communications, this guy and myself. And then he fired one rubber bullet … And then 'voom', it just quietened down. And by this time, he'd radioed for some help from his unit (Dan).

The rocks also became seen as manifestations of hatred.[11] Oren captures this feeling well:

> I got hit in the head with a rock during that reserve duty and I remember the feeling was … not pain or hurt, it was outrage, it was this feeling of being violated, having this intimate connection with hatred, that these people hate me so much, they don't know who I am, they just hate me so much, that somebody's really going to take the trouble to try to [laughs, pauses] to hurt me. It's silly, it's all silly, because I was a soldier, but that'll give you an idea of what went on in our heads.[12]

These kinds of events were also individualized, physical enactments, microcosms of the occupation. Israeli control of the West Bank and Gaza frequently came down

11. Kaufman quotes from Knesset Member Michael Bar Zohar: 'The revolt of 1987 troubled us deeply by suddenly exposing this intense hatred that had been simmering in the hearts of the Palestinian people' (1991: 22)
12. 'I was very interested in the graffiti. One of the things that really stuck in my mind, the horror of the place, was these walls that were just covered with graffiti against you. You are the demon of Palestine. You are responsible for these people being thrown out of their homes, thrown into refugee camps and not being allowed to go back … So, you are like a Nazi … For these people, there's nothing worse than you … This scream, this hatred … I am their German … The unease was being in a place where you're not just the enemy, you're the *devil*. (Oren)

to an individual Palestinian facing an individual Israeli. Both the Self and the Other became radically depersonalized. Oren remembered Sari Nusseibeh, the Palestinian academic and politician, emerging from an office in Ramallah while he was patrolling. For a moment, he became excited, and the journalist in him was about to try to secure an interview. He checked himself, however – 'I'm not a journalist and he's not Sari Nusseibeh. I'm an Israeli soldier and he's a Palestinian'.

As I will go on to expand below, the experience of serving in the territories as a soldier was intensely bodily but it was linked to particular spaces. A jolt in either could shatter the apparently solid experience of the soldiers – either, as above, because a person or experience reached to the non-soldier within them while soldiering or because, while apparently far from the soldier in their experience, they were confronted by a reminder that forced a recreating of a bodily praxis that had lain dormant.

The 'barrages' of rocks on the streets meant that protective vehicles became more widely used, separating the bodies of the men, as much as possible, from the street:

> After a very short while, you had these *rechavim hamegunim* [shielded vehicles] which were very much used. You're moving in these cocoons (Dan).

Patrols began increasingly to travel in jeeps and protected vehicles. If attacked, soldiers would often abandon them and chase stone-throwing youths down side streets (Cohen 1994). The effect was of suddenly being 'on the ground', 'in the thick of it'.[13] Chasing Palestinians, however, also meant exposing the bodies of the soldiers to potential ambushes, dangers, and traps. Etgar Kerrett's (1996) short story, 'Cocked and Locked', presents a brief battle of wills between a Palestinian and an Israeli soldier. The Palestinian mocks the Israeli by highlighting the recent death of a soldier who had exposed himself to attack after chasing him down a side street:

> I saw how they had to bring in a helicobter [sic] to take him, how he run after me. A half street he runs after me like a beast and in the end? Boom, his head exblode [sic] like a watermelon (ibid.: 202).[14]

13. A parallel situation can be found in Northern Ireland. Some sections of Armagh – 'bandit country' – were seen by the military as too dangerous even for protected vehicles. Soldiers were moved by helicopter and then dropped at patrol points. The 'on patrol' feelings presented by Dewar above are felt even more intensely in these situations. For another discussion of being dropped suddenly into a combat environment, see Bourne (1970: 83–102) on medical evacuation pilots in Vietnam.
14. Kerrett's use of 'b' instead of 'p' is a reference to the difficulty that Israelis often feel Palestinians have in pronouncing the letter.

Becoming suddenly exposed was also a more general concern in the Intifada. Partly because of the sheer size of the areas being patrolled, units often ended up operating seemingly 'on their own':

> It should be noted that in the *intifada*, small units assigned to do policing jobs, are spread out over a large area, often with no higher ranking officers on the spot. ... Special standards of behavior can develop within these units – which Martin Van Krefeld calls 'gangs' – *who often feel left on their own, without 'backing from above'* (Liebes and Blum-Kulka 1994: 58–59, emphasis mine).

Although reinforcements could often be brought in quickly, the danger of being suddenly caught up in unanticipated violence (or the threat of it) was very real:

> [A]nd then we came walking back and we saw this mob of people screaming. At that point there were about ten of them [Palestinians] and there were two of us and two others [Israeli soldiers] ... so, anyway, at this point we came back and they just got in our faces, which is very dangerous ... suddenly you have ten Palestinians screaming in your face ... One guy stuck his gun in somebody's face (Moshe).

Moshe used this event to highlight what he felt had been symptomatic of his time in Hebron, namely that there was always the potential for conflict and that events could get out of hand very fast:

> These [Palestinians] are people you see every day, you have this sort of very normal relationship and then suddenly someone gets pissed off and 'boom' it all blows up and that's beneath the surface.

The fear of becoming trapped in confined spaces was inverted in the IDF's attempts to control the uprising through house searches.[15] These penetrations of domestic, private spaces, which have also been a key feature of British control in Northern Ireland (Feldman 1991; Aretxaga 1997), are often highlighted by Israeli soldiers as occasions when they felt physically uncomfortable – 'in control', but invasive. The same can be said of observation

15. The issue of intrusion here parallels Feldman's discussion of the fear with which security personnel in Northern Ireland associate being photographed. Their concern, he argues, relates to the danger that they will be attacked while off-duty. 'Republican paramilitaries', he writes, 'relish such attacks as eloquent inversions of the mutations of their own homes into war zones by these same representatives of the state' (2000: 47).

posts established on the roofs of buildings. Ben, Oren, and Moshe all independently described what might be seen as a kind of 'de-civilizing' process that they had undergone:

> To knock on a family's door, at three in the morning, because someone in the family is wanted … You know, there were a lot of times when we were observing on the roof of a house and sometimes my food fell down, my cocoa and my bread, and [the children below] took it like it was gold or something (Ben).
>
> It sucks if you're the guys living in that house [with an observation post on its roof] because first of all, you don't want Israeli soldiers on your roof at all but on top of that there's a ladder and every time they go up their gun bangs against the ladder at two in the morning. Every twenty minutes, somebody's making noise. A guy up there, he's got to take a leak, he takes a leak on the roof of your house and it stinks or they leave food up there (Moshe).
>
> There's no bathroom. There's a little alcove, a little room, on this roof and that's where you relieve yourself. And at first, when I got up to the roof, I said, 'This can't be, it's an apartment building. What are we doing? We're shitting on people's heads here?' And the first day, I couldn't do it, the second day it felt really uncomfortable and by the end of the week you don't think anything of it. That's what you do (Oren).

This notion of erosion, of 'gradual coarsening' as one of the soldiers put it, was also a theme frequently highlighted in the interviews and in other discussions of Israeli reactions to the Intifada:

> An air force colonel, temporarily assigned to Ramallah, described to Abraham Rabinovich of the Jerusalem Post how he felt about conducting house-to-house searches. The first night, he recalled, soldiers threw property around and arrested a teenaged boy whose mother burst out crying. 'I felt terrible. How could I participate in something like this? The next night we did the same thing. This time I said to myself, "Well, what do you expect?" … The third night it was already routine and when the woman starts to cry you say, "Oh God, is that wailing beginning again?" The fourth night you're shouting at the woman, "*Uskut*! Shut up!" I felt us hardening from day to day' (Frankel 1994: 86).
>
> [W]hen a soldier arrests somebody and he [the Palestinian] says: 'Leave me alone, I haven't done anything' and the soldier hits him in the face … The first week it shocked me and I fought all the time with

> everyone. But after a while … you have to remind yourself that it's not right. Otherwise you don't feel it (Liebes and Blum-Kulka 1994: 65).[16]
>
> They understood it gradually. … After we were there for a month already … they realised it wasn't just brutality, without reason. … After being there for some time, bombarded with curses and stones … In the beginning, they thought that … the soldiers really became … corrupt. Then they say, it happens to everyone (ibid.: 55).

Moshe, who had emphasized that events could get out of hand rapidly, nonetheless spoke of the mundane quality of much of daily life as a soldier:

> It wasn't a war. I have this image of going to Beirut. Going to Beirut is walking through an enormous civil war, that's my image of it. I've been to Ramallah and Chevron and I realized that there's no civil war. People walk around, live their lives and do their thing (Moshe).

However, this 'normality' of events is frequently interrupted by the surreal, the unusual. 'It was like a play', said Dan. Oren remembered the odd sensation of running through a crowd of Palestinians living their lives 'normally':

> It was a very bizarre mix of normal life and people throwing things at each other and shooting. It was like a kind of surreal dream and you're being chased or you're chasing somebody and everybody else is just going about their daily business.

'The soldier's gaze' is specific and scopic (Feldman 2000). As a leading Israeli Human Rights lawyer argued:

> Many Israelis go into the West Bank and Gaza as soldiers and so … they are socialized to look at Palestinians through the eyes of a soldier and not feel safe without having a gun.[17]

The soldier's view of the local population was intensified by the marginalization of the territories, an idea that I introduced above. All the soldiers described their shock on first arriving in the West Bank or Gaza: 'I

16. Ben's commanding officer had advised him: 'All the time, don't forget that you are a human being'. For more general discussions of Israeli soldiers considering challenging orders that they see as immoral, see Linn (1996a; 1996b; 1999), Liebes and Blum-Kulka (1994) and Kidron (1996).
17. It is important to note here that Moshe argued that his knowledge of the territories had been improved by his period of army service there: 'Having spent that time in the territories made me more comfortable … I knew it was just a place. Ok, sure, I was sitting on a roof with a gun but I watched people live their lives'.

knew, yes I knew, the Intifada was over three years old, so I shouldn't have been shocked' (Oren).

Uri described his arrival in Hebron, on his first day as part of the IDF presence there. He caught a bus from Jerusalem, with bullet-proof glass and mesh over the windows, and finally arrived in the centre of town. As the bus left, he said, he felt as if he had 'been dumped in another world'.[18] The effect was deeper because of the comparatively brief journey that the bus had taken. Ben described similar feelings:

> I saw things that I didn't believe. I saw in the media that they throw stones and the soldiers shoot back, that's it. I said to myself, this is one hour from my house, from my school, the background in which I was educated. I didn't see the spirit of God there, really. People living in great poverty and in a way that you just don't know how to look in peoples' eyes.

He captured the idea powerfully when discussing house searches:

> I have a little brother, he was twelve years old. I sat and I tried to compare it – this Palestinian is one hour's drive away from him and in Israel now, he's in school, he'll be back after school, he'll have his lunch, he can go to play on his computer and these kids will not. Cannot and never.

However, many of the soldiers also spoke of a fascination with being a part of something as large and powerful as the occupation, crystallized into their personal, day-to-day experiences (cf. Ben-Ari 1998: 74). 'You really learn a lot in the *shuq* [market]', said Moshe.[19] Particular images became embedded in the soldiers' memories:

> I try to remember all the pictures that I saw there, in Gaza especially. The children most of all, the people that were … getting up every morning at 3 A.M. to try to go to Israel, leaving their families to try to get some money for food. … To look in their eyes. I'm not such an emotional person but these are very emotional memories (Ben).

18. Citing John Brophy, Fussell describes the trenches as 'the world which might have been another planet' (1975: 65).
19. 'I remember once I stopped this guy with a Jaguar. In the middle of Hebron, who's got a Jaguar? So I stopped him and I said, "Who are you?" and he's from Argentina. So I talked to him for 15 minutes after that. I always talk to Palestinian Authority guys because I want to talk to them. One time, I stopped this guy and I wanted to talk politics to him. … At first he thought he had to say nice stuff, so I'd let him go, so he was like, "Yes, we have to live in peace" and stuff like that and then I gave him back his stuff and I said, "Yeah, but what about this" and then he realized I just wanted to talk to him and then he took off' (Moshe).

'There [was] a certain way of relating to people, to a population', Yitzhak said. 'There was a way that people spoke.' Even now that he is no longer in that social context, he sometimes becomes too relaxed and allows himself to underestimate the impact that the Intifada had on both him and the Palestinian co-director of the dialogue group for which he works. One morning, he said, the door to their office had stuck. '*Ifta! Jaish!*' ('Open! Army!' in Arabic), he shouted as a joke while banging on it:

> You step into a joking mode but ... then you slip into a situation where actually we've both been there, and it's not such a joke. I actually have spoken like that and I've been in houses and spoken like that ... and he's been on the other side (Yitzhak).

'Our few Arabic phrases are all imperatives', notes Halevi (1991a: 22).

As their periods of service or *miluim* came to an end, the soldiers were pleased to leave. 'I took a Palestinian flag and a stone that was thrown at me', Dan remembered. Many returned for further *miluim* as the Intifada wore on. With the end of the uprising, however, most Israeli soldiers undoubtedly felt pleased that they would never have to return to the areas in which they had risked their lives. However, in the period after Oslo, some chose to return to these embodied places of violence.

Revisiting and Remembering: 'Knowledge' and Embodiment

> *Fourteen years after the war J.R. Ackerley was wandering through an unfrequented part of a town in India. 'The streets became narrower and narrower as I turned and turned', he writes, 'until I felt I was back in the trenches'.*
>
> Fussell (1975: 51)

It was some time after the end of the Intifada and the signing of the Oslo Accords before any of the individuals whom I interviewed travelled back to the territories. They did so for a variety of reasons (curiosity, work, to attend a dialogue meeting) and in different ways (with a friend, with a group of Palestinians). However, in speaking with them I was struck by the fact that they all stressed the ways in which their experience of entering Palestinian spaces again had been a markedly bodily experience, at least at first. Following on from my earlier presentation of Bourdieu's image of the way in which embodied memories speak 'directly to the motor function' (1977: 87), I believe that the ways in which the bodies of the men had been formed by the spatial habitus of the territories resurfaced when they returned.

The clearest indication of this comes in the narratives of arrival, in the ways in which the men described the initial stages of returning. The first time he walked through Ramallah, Uri said, he had been aware of repeatedly reaching for his gun. Travel to, and through, the territories had become fundamentally bound up with soldiering. The first time Dan's Palestinian friend had asked him if he would like to visit Ramallah, he told me, he had replied: 'Ramallah? With an APC [Armoured Personnel Carrier]?' I reminded him of this when I interviewed him:

> Yes. I thought, you know, that's the way you go, but no ... cognitively, I was aware of the fact that you can go there and Israelis go there and so on,[20] it was emotionally the problem of getting myself motivated to go (Dan).

'I was interested in going to Ramallah', he said, 'and [being asked if he wanted to go] was a good opportunity'. However, as with all of the men I spoke with, his training 'kicked in' without him noticing. The comment I cited above from the dialogue participant, when he mentioned people dropping refrigerators, had been elicited from the fact that he had been very nervous when we walked through Gaza City with our Palestinian hosts. He seemed to be continually checking the upper stories of buildings and was happier when we were away from confined, small alleyways. Dan had been walking for some time, he said, before he noticed that he had been standing with his back to the walls every time he and his friend had stopped to look at a new building or a view. He was not on patrol but his embodied memories were sufficiently powerful that he subconsciously behaved as if he was.

Other people I spoke with were more consciously aware of their feelings, but were able to trace them to their experiences in the territories as a soldier. Oren returned to Ramallah, where he had spent a month on a rooftop. 'I was interested. I'm interested to see the stores, the people, how they dress', he said. Despite the very visible changes, however, the place still had the feel of being threatening:

> I felt very edgy, I felt that I was on enemy ground, definitely. When you've experienced that kind of hatred (I'm not saying it's justified or not justified, I'm just speaking in an emotional way).

Gaza had the same effect but intensified:

20. When I interviewed Dan, in the late summer of 1999, some Israelis had just begun to start visiting Ramallah in the evenings. It was becoming, as an Israeli friend put it to me, 'the Tel Aviv of the Palestinians'.

> [I felt] very edgy. I went back last week to Nusseirat, this refugee camp where I got a rock on my head. That was interesting. There I really felt … that I was on enemy ground.

Yitzhak argued that this difference came from the unique character of Gaza:

> Gaza's even stranger, because Gaza's really like a [hits hand with fist], especially during the Intifada, it was a trip. That was mind-blowing. Things that were done in Gaza, during army service and the Intifada … that was a very powerful experience and going back was a lot more powerful.

As with Dan and Uri, he was also aware, eventually, of reflex actions:

> Even today, if you dropped me in the middle of Bethlehem … I've still got this caution, this Intifada experience, like a *large group* will suddenly see me and see me as an Israeli. I've still got that caution … there's some funny things, like birds, birds in the sky. There was something about serving in the territories, there were so many stones and so many things being thrown at you. If my field of vision catches anything in the air, immediately I'll be avoiding it.

As the American journalist Glenn Frankel wrote, 'the commanders could remove a unit from the West Bank, but they could not always remove the West Bank from the unit' (1994: 79). Yoram described his visits to Jerusalem's Old City:

> I like the Old City. I love walking through the Old City … I've walked through the Old City during the Intifada too. I'm a little bit more nervous – I don't know if *nervous* is the right word – but I'm more careful because you're cognizant of the fact that someone could just come out a side alley and stab you and you don't want that to happen.

In all these cases, however, a heightened sense of awareness is fixed to a particular kind of location. Yitzhak does not duck in Tel Aviv or Haifa, he said. This spatial dynamic, which is prompted not by types of spaces (such as being suddenly confined in a lift) but by the specific places (Ramallah, Nablus, etc.) seems to be different to accounts of US soldiers returning from Vietnam and suddenly 'flashing back' to their time during the war. It also offers a practical insight into the theoretical distinction between space (conceived as an area of land) and place (as a particular space imbued with specific characteristics). Research from Vietnam – and indeed the quotation from the top of this section from the First World War – tends to concentrate on experiences that are linked to spaces, rather than specific places. This is, of course, partly due to the practical and personal difficulties many soldiers face in returning to the specific battlefields of their youths.

However, Frankel quotes from an Israeli soldier whom he interviewed and who did seem to fit this kind of model:

> Sometimes when strolling through Tel Aviv [he] found himself scanning the rooftops, looking for snipers and rock throwers as if he were still in Balata. The intifada was a memory he could not erase and could hardly explain (1994: 87).

With those, however, for whom memory is so specifically tied to places, the body becomes once more the site through which past experiences are relived. Dan was driven into Ramallah in a Volvo. The impact of leaving this 'cocoon', like the protected vehicles of his army service, was clear from his description:

> You go in a Volvo, which is rather protective. It's a stronger car than usual and you're ensconced in this shell and then 'voom', you're out, you breathe the air. I remember walking from the car to the restaurant and [there was] no Hebrew lettering anywhere … which added to this impression that it's a foreign country.

Bodily experiences and positions also construct particular images. As soldiers patrolled the towns and cities of the territories, their views and perspectives were dictated by where and how they moved. The view from a jeep, a patrol or an observation post, combined with orders that emphasized the importance of not talking casually with Palestinians,[21] will inherently produce a distanced, separated view of the local population. Soldiers view specific images as a result of their position within spaces and power relationships.[22] These images then produce particular 'knowledges' of the local population and the act of returning once more to the places prompted a reflexive presentation of this contextual positioning:

> In the army, there was a big distance. I couldn't think of any Palestinian that I knew or I'd spoken to (Yitzhak).

An occupation puts you in the situation where ultimately you *can't* treat the occupied as full human beings. That is the nature of occupation, because your job does not make it possible. Your presence, their hatred, your inability to function normally in that society – it's a cycle (Oren).

21. These orders, it should be pointed out, were not always followed.
22. For discussion of perspectival images from observation posts in Hebron, see my paper on political tourism (Clarke 2000).

Conclusions: the Body, Space, and Power

Part of the aim of this volume is to interrogate the relationship between movement and power. What can the experience of Israeli soldiers returning to the territories tell us about this complex dialectic?

At one level, it helps to remind us – if a reminder is needed in the context of the postmodern milieu – of the intensely physical nature of the interweaving of space, violence, power, fear, and knowledge. In this sense, as I have argued above, Israeli soldiers are merely the most conspicuous microcosm of the wider experience of occupation and power. Israeli soldiers, like their counterparts in Iraq, Northern Ireland and elsewhere, move through contested territory as a mark of control and ownership. Occupation, as we can see from above, is seldom merely about stasis and the corralled; though the fence constructed recently to separate the territories from Israel is a powerful emblem, the real presence and power of occupation frequently stems from patrolling and marking territory through sustained movement.

The bodily nature of encountering violent spaces and the way that it maps directly onto the experience and 'knowledge' of places is also a powerful evocation of the play of forces on bodies. As much as Israeli soldiers move through the territories to mark and make spaces of occupation, so occupying the territories shapes their bodies as they do so. Individual soldiers who felt – both literally and metaphorically – that they had left Gaza and the West Bank behind when they finished their tours of duty there were transported back seemingly instantly when they revisited the places once again. This physical version of Proust's madeleine cakes (cf. Connerton 1989) is fascinating partly because it is so intimately tied to space and landscape. It was the places of the territories that evoked the sensations, again, of being attacked, hated, and feared and, pace Mauss, inspired an innate revocation of the actions of occupation – reaching for a gun, standing against a wall. The experience of occupation becomes so marked on the body that it seems etched almost permanently.

However, what is more interesting, in the context of the pieces in this volume and my Bourdieu-inspired theoretical approach, is whether the experience of travelling can affect individuals and effect a change in their habitus. Elsewhere (Clarke 2003), I have argued that political protests in Israel can be most effective when they serve as innovative interpellatory devices, sudden interruptions that disrupt and jar the habitus of those at whom they are directed. Young Israelis leaving a bar on a warm afternoon do not expect to see films of beatings being broadcasted in the streets or to be handed a leaflet reminding them of their close proximity to a prison where Israeli human rights activists believe Palestinians are being tortured. For such activists, interpellation is powerful because it forces individuals to confront the context in which they live. It may be fleeting and ineffective against the 'ingrained' power of a habitus of avoidance but it can begin slowly to alter perceptions (cf. Cohen 2001).

However, not all activities, I believe, are qualitatively of the same order when it comes to experiences that unsettle and challenge the habitus (Clarke 2001; Clarke 2003). All of the Israeli soldiers with whom I spoke described the act of travelling back to the territories, of moving through the spaces once again, as being more powerful than potentially similar experiences, such as meeting young Palestinians inside Israel or witnessing televised images from the West Bank and Gaza. Crucially, when striving to understand the relationship between space and the habitus, many of the soldiers reported, reflexively, a real questioning of their previously held views on the territories and the position of Palestinians. Many (though by no means all) of those who returned to the places they had patrolled did so because they were curious to see Palestinian life under the PNA and/or because they wanted to meet and speak to Palestinians. In interviews afterwards, they reported that it was the experience of actually being in the places – Ramallah, Nablus, Gaza – that was central to the power of the trip. For some, reflexivity flowed from their sudden awareness of their training (prompted by their moving through space), their associated perceptions of 'the Other' and, from there, slowly towards a more nuanced understanding of their position within a complex discourse of power relations. This was by no means the experience of all those with whom I worked but it was a significant part of the narratives of several – movement, if done in the right way, can perhaps genuinely be transgressive.

Conclusions: Distance and the Habitus of Avoidance

The relationship between space, memory, knowledge, and power in Israel/Palestine deserves a more detailed treatment than I can offer in this chapter but I believe that the words of the soldiers above help to shed some light on to the interweaving of landscape and the variously constituted habitus of 'the Israeli' and 'the Israeli soldier'.[23] I mentioned above Oren's story of having seen Sari Nusseibeh and instinctively wanting to ask him for an interview. Both he and Nusseibeh, however, rapidly fell back into the prescribed social roles (in his mind) which had been laid down by what I have called the habitus of the Israeli soldier. He was not Oren, but 'an Israeli soldier'; he was not Sari Nusseibeh, but 'a Palestinian'.

In his discussion of images of 'the enemy' in the IDF, Ben-Ari (1998) cites Rieber and Kelly's psychological model of double dehumanization. On the one hand, soldiers (along with doctors and other professionals working in high-stress environments) dehumanize themselves by distancing themselves from

23. See Clarke 2001.

the situation in which they work. At the same time, they dehumanize the people with whom they work; a patient becomes an object to be treated. This process, they argue, allows individuals to cope with the strains of dealing with what would otherwise be potentially horrifying situations – ruminating on the 'humanness' of a patient, for example, might render the doctor potentially unable to carry out his/her work.

However, in relation to soldiering, this process is taken one stage further. As Rieber and Kelly argue:

> Object dehumanization, the other side of self-dehumanization, describes the process and dynamics whereby the individual depersonalizes the other; enemification takes the process one step further and reduces the other to a 'thing' that is potentially dangerous (cited in ibid.: 87).

In contrast to studies of US troops in Vietnam or the Pacific War, Ben-Ari argues, Israeli soldiers do not regularly, and are not encouraged to, demonize their enemies. Instead, their images are constructed around a central 'machine analogy' that they apply to both themselves and their enemies. Palestinians (at least in the Intifada) become objects within a particular space to be moved or cleared, rather than animals or monsters to be destroyed. They also become, like the soldier in the battalion, part of a broader unit. It is this gathering of individuals that poses the greatest threat. Hence, Palestinians become objectified and distanced from the Israeli soldiers. The entire civilian population becomes a potential threat; each individual Palestinian, however, is not demonized but is, rather, dehumanized and lost in the collective, potentially threatening body of 'the Palestinians'. When this is tied to the situation that I described, in which soldiers are discouraged from forming contacts with the local population, we can see the emergence of a specific kind of 'knowledge' of the territories, tied to the constructed habitus of the soldier.

If this argument was important when I first spoke to the individuals whose words appear above, it has become even more so since. Almost as soon as I left the field, the situation in Israel/Palestine deteriorated markedly and the last five years have seen a second Intifada, a reoccupation of swathes of the territories, the election of Ariel Sharon as Israeli Prime Minister, several peace plans, the construction of the 'security fence', the attacks on America in September 2001, and the ensuing creation of the US political discourse of 'the war on terror' and the invasion of Iraq. Both in the territories and in Iraq, as I write, individual Palestinians and Iraqis are becoming lost in the comfortable media rhetoric of crowds of stone-throwing youths. Hence the shocking power, of course, of the images of prisoner abuse; they suddenly shatter this collective into a series of individuals.

In Israel/Palestine, the security fence and the closure of the territories has made the projects with which I worked, and the experiences they sought to offer Israelis, all but impossible. They sought to challenge Israelis through the kinds of unsettling experiences only really possible by visiting the territories. The activists who organized the trips refused to allow for the spaces of denial that the Israeli habitus of avoidance creates, but most of the projects have now ended their activities, something many of the activists feel they have been forced into by the level of violence in the West Bank and Gaza. More interesting, analytically, however, is the sense in which the security fence and the enforced military closure of areas are merely the culmination of the broader habitus of avoidance and separation, on the part of Israelis, abstracted from the specific experience of the soldier up to the broader spatial dynamics of the Israeli collective and its complex relationship with the spaces of the West Bank and Gaza that I have discussed above. The territories are, once again, covered intensely by the Western and Israeli media but distanced, avoided, and, in the sense that they are hidden behind media frames and a habitus of avoidance, ignored by Israelis on the streets of Tel Aviv.

References

Alcalay, A. 1993. *After Jews and Arabs: Remaking Levantine Culture*, Minneapolis. MN: Minnesota University Press.

Aretxaga, B. 1997. *Shattering Silence: Women, Nationalism and Political Subjectivity in Northern Ireland*. Princeton, NJ: Princeton University Press.

Ben-Ari, E. 1998. *Mastering Soldiers: Conflict, Emotion and the Enemy in an Israeli Military Unit*. Oxford: Berghahn Books.

Ben-David, O. 1997. '*Tiyul* as an Act of Consecration of Space', in E. Ben-Ari and Y. Bilu (ed.), *Grasping Land: Space and Place in Contemporary Israeli Discourse and Experience*. Albany: State University of New York Press.

Bourdieu, P. 1977. *Outline of a Theory of Practice*. Cambridge: Cambridge University Press.

Bourne, P. 1970. *Men, Stress and Vietnam*. Boston: Little, Brown and Co.

Clarke, R. 2000. 'Self-Presentation in a Contested City: Palestinian and Israeli Political Tourism in Hebron', *Anthropology Today* 16(5): 12–18.

———. 2001. 'The Politics of Knowledge: "Understanding", Reflexivity and Engagement on the Israeli-Palestinian Frontier', Ph.D. dissertation. Cambridge: University of Cambridge.

———. 2003. 'Voices from the Margins: Knowledge and Interpellation in Israeli Human Rights Protests', in R. A. Wilson and J. P. Mitchell (eds), *Human Rights Protests in Global Perspective: Anthropological Studies of Rights, Claims and Entitlements*. London: Routledge.

Cohen, S. 2001. *States of Denial: Knowing about Atrocities and Suffering*. Cambridge: Polity.

Cohen, S. 1994. 'How Did the Intifada Affect the IDF?', *Conflict Quarterly* 14(3): 7–22.

Connerton, P. 1989. *How Societies Remember*. Cambridge: Cambridge University Press.

Dewar, M. 1992. *War in the Streets: The Story of Urban Combat from Calais to Khafji*. Newton Abbot: David and Charles.

Feldman, A. 1991. *Formations of Violence: The Narrative of the Body and Political Terror in Northern Ireland*. Chicago: Chicago University Press.

———. 2000. 'Violence and Vision: The Prosthetics and Aesthetics of Terror', in V. Das et al. (eds), *Violence and Subjectivity*. Berkeley: University of California Press.

Frankel, G. 1994. *Beyond the Promised Land: Jews and Arabs on a Hard Road to a New Israel*. New York: Simon and Schuster.

Fussell, P. 1975. *The Great War and Modern Memory*. Oxford: Oxford University Press.

Halevi, Y. K. 1991a. 'Notes from a Reservist's Diary: Part One', in *The Jerusalem Report* 24 October 1991, p. 22.

———. 1991b. 'Notes from a Reservist's Diary: Part Two', in *The Jerusalem Report* 31 October 1991, p. 18.

Halper, J. 2000. 'The 94 Percent Solution: A Matrix of Control', in *Middle East Report* 216.

Kaufman, E. 1991. 'Israeli Perceptions of the Palestinians', in *Terrorism and Political Violence* 3(4): 1–38.

Kerrett, E. 1996. 'Cocked and Locked', in M. Gluzman and M. Seidman (eds), *Israel: A Traveller's Literary Companion*. San Francisco: Whereabouts Press.

Kidron, P. 1996. 'Selective Refusal', *The Palestine-Israel Journal* 3(4): 129–37.

Liebes, T. and S. Blum-Kulka. 1994. 'Managing a Moral Dilemma: Israeli Soldiers in the Intifada', *Armed Forces and Society* 21(1): 45–68.

Linn, R. 1996a. *Conscience at War: The Israeli Soldier as Moral Critic*. Albany: State University of New York Press.

———. 1996b. 'When the Individual Soldier Says "No" to War: A Look at Selective Refusal during the Intifada', *Journal of Peace Research* 33(4): 421–31.

———. 1999. 'In the Name of the Holocaust: Fears and Hopes among Israeli Soldiers and Palestinians', *Journal of Genocide Research* 1(3): 439–53.

Mauss, M. 1973. 'Techniques of the Body', *Economy and Society* 2: 1–35.

Chapter 5
This Circle of Kings: Modern Tibetan Visions of World Peace

Martin Mills

On 3 May 1999, His Holiness the Fourteenth Dalai Lama, spiritual leader of the exiled Tibetan government, inaugurated a new Peace Garden in London, sited in the grounds of the Imperial War Museum. The garden, sponsored by the Tibet Foundation, was centred around a two-metre-wide Kilkenny-stone dais holding a bronze relief of the Kalacakra mandala, a representation of the divine palace of the tantric Buddha Kalacakra ('Wheel of Time'). The dais was immediately surrounded by a ring of eight stone seats – set aside for 'personal contemplation' – and then by a series of large stone carvings depicting the principal elements of Tibetan cosmology – earth, water, wind, fire, and space. The entrance to this enclosure was via a pathway, leading towards the museum, that was itself heralded by a three-metre-high 'Language Pillar', on which was carved a 'message of World Peace' from the Dalai Lama on each of its four faces, in (respectively) Tibetan, English, Hindi, and Chinese. Based on the Shol pillar in the Tibetan capital Lhasa – which outlined the royal proclamation of peace between China and Tibet by the eighth century Tibetan king Trisong Detsen – the message on the London Language Pillar read:

> We human beings are passing through a crucial period in our development. Conflicts and mistrust have plagued the past century, which has brought immeasurable human suffering and environmental destruction. It is in the interests of all of us on this planet that we make a joint effort to turn the next century into an era of peace and harmony. May this peace garden become a monument to the courage of the Tibetan people and their commitment to peace. May it remain as a symbol to remind us that human survival depends on living in harmony and always choosing the path of non-violence in resolving our differences.

The message of the Language Pillar – emphasizing the present historical necessity of a commitment to non-violence, peace, and the reversal of environmental destruction – marks it as a component of the central plank of His Holiness's international political profile: the discourse of World Peace (in

Tibetan, *dzamling zhi-de*). It is this discourse and the images and precedents it evokes – not in Western audiences, but amongst its Tibetan originators – that is the subject of this paper.

'An Innocent Abroad'

Whilst the notion of World Peace has a Buddhist provenance on the international scene that long precedes its rhetorical adoption by the Tibetan government-in-exile (see Lopez 1996: 199; Huber 2001), its adoption within the milieu of Tibetan exiled politics has been systemic and, with certain crucial exceptions, relatively unified (see Mills 2003b). On the international stage, most attention has been given to His Holiness's speeches on the topic, which contain two core themes; firstly, the concept of Tibet as a 'Zone of Peace'. This idea was first put forward in its full form to the US Congressional Human Rights Caucus in 1987, and later revised for its presentation as the so-called Strasbourg Proposal (see Shiromany 1996a: 156–62, 163–67). In this proposal, the Dalai Lama presented a vision of Tibet as a 'neutral demilitarized Zone of Peace where people live in harmony with nature. I call this a Zone of Peace, or Ahimsa' (Shiromany 1996: 334). He views this vision of national autonomy for Tibet as the basis for a general vision of world peace:

> It is my dream that the entire Tibetan Plateau should be a free refuge where humanity and nature can live in peace and in harmonious balance. It would be a place where people from all over the world could come to seek the true meaning of peace within themselves, away from the tensions and pressures of much of the rest of the world. Tibet could indeed become a creative centre for the promotion and development of peace. The Tibetan Plateau would be transformed into the world's largest natural park or biosphere (Dalai Lama 1991: 18, cited in Lopez 1996: 205).

Whilst the Strasbourg Proposal itself was withdrawn as the basis for negotiations with China in September 1991, its impact as a general vision for Tibet is still widely accepted within the Tibetan government-in-exile and the Tibetan refugee communities.

The second element of the Dalai Lama's World Peace rhetoric is the assertion that peace on the international stage derives from a groundwork of internal mental peace within individual leaders, politicians, and citizens; that 'world peace' derives from 'inner peace'. This specifically rejects the notion that there is a general political morality that is separate in any fundamental way from a bedrock of personal morality:

> True peace, the peace within, has to be cultivated. Internal peace is an essential first step to achieving peace in the world, true and lasting

> peace. How do you cultivate it? It's very simple. In the first place, by realising clearly that all mankind is one, that human beings in every country are members of one and the same family. In other words, all these quarrels between countries and blocs are family quarrels and should not go beyond certain limits. Just as there can be friction, disputes between man and wife in a union, but within specific limits, as each party knows deep down in the heart that they are bound together by a far more important sentiment. Next, it is important to grasp the real meaning of this brotherhood based on love and kindness (cited in Shiromany 1996: 79).

This rejection of national identity as a basis for ultimate political difference is mirrored by his emphasis on inter-religious dialogue, both within the various orders of Tibetan Buddhism, and between wider religious traditions. In this regard, the Dalai Lama has persistently emphasized the requirement for religious communities to be involved in continuous and deep dialogue, and has spoken out against the tendency by religious movements (whether Buddhist or otherwise) to emphasize conversion.

It would be understating the issue to observe that the Dalai Lama's vision of World Peace has often been treated as naïve and idealistic within the arena of modern politics: perhaps because of his persistent opposition to violent resistance to Chinese rule in Tibet; or because of the apparent utopianism of his notion of Tibet as a 'zone of peace'; or maybe because his ultimate rejection of national political identities and borders as the basis for the promotion of peace all place him at odds with the entire precedent of twentieth-century political thought (including the very idea behind the modern United Nations). In many regards, his pronouncements on World Peace have been seen as in some sense non-political or sub-political, to be treated with symbolic respect but not practical urgency by modern politicians, as the actions of 'an innocent abroad' (*The Scotsman*, 8 November 2003). For all of these reasons and more, his pronouncements have led him to be embraced by that large, counter-cultural (and middle-class) constituency within the West which sees itself as both disenchanted and disenfranchised from modern politics, and whose dream of peace is that of a social and territorial space beyond the hegemony of political powers and religious sectarianism. In this regard, His Holiness – as a political leader forcibly divested of political power, and a religious leader apparently divest of religious dogmatism – seems the ideal spokesman.

How realistic, however, is this picture? While Rupert Murdoch's famous description of the Dalai Lama as 'a very political monk shuffling about in Gucci shoes' may well be apocryphal, overly cynical, and factually inaccurate in footwear terms, His Holiness's popular image in the West fairly obviously elides his clear position as head of an extremely active exiled government, and heir to a lineage of rulers whose throne straddled the heartlands of Asia. Many have argued, indeed, that the projection of a rather precious and apolitical image of His Holiness (and of Tibetans as a whole) by supporters of the Tibetan cause is not only misleading, but counter-productive.

Rather, it is the argument of this paper that whilst Tibetan lamas and their Western followers may well be voicing the same words in their chorus of world peace, they are singing to entirely different tunes: that, by reducing the Tibetan articulation of *dzamling zhi-de* to a depoliticized prop for the West's own growing sense of anomie, we fail to recognize the older, but no less compelling, kingly politics of old Tibet as it reaches across the postmodern world.

World Peace Projects Worldwide

Within the Tibetan political milieu, the concept of World Peace, or *dzamling zhi-de*, has been adopted by a variety of factions. Whilst there is no space to precisely enumerate them here (see Mills 2003b), it suffices to say that the most influential of these are those associated with His Holiness the Fourteenth Dalai Lama and his government-in-exile in Dharamsala, north India. Much of the widespread authority of this movement within the wider Buddhist world derives from His Holiness's emphasis on a *ri-mé*, or non-sectarian, approach to Tibetan Buddhism (Samuel 1993: ch. 27). His Holiness's position is not uncontroversial within the often sectarian world of Tibetan religious politics, but has nonetheless served to bring together a powerful coalition of important religious leaders from all the principal Tibetan religious schools. Despite the prevalence of the Dalai Lama's rhetorical message within the international media, however, the World Peace rubric within Tibetan affairs has been dominated not by political speeches and policies, but by ritual action within a Buddhist framework, of which the Tibetan Peace Garden is an iconic (if peripheral) example.

In the decades following the diaspora from Chinese-occupied Tibet in 1959, the performance of Tibetan Buddhist ceremonial on the 'global stage' has intensified markedly, with monastic masked dances, sand mandala rites, and elaborate tantric initiations carried out by prominent religious leaders in places as diverse as Mongolia, London, Tokyo, and Madison Square Gardens. For the purposes of this chapter, I would like to concentrate on four principal ritual projects either carried out by the Fourteenth Dalai Lama, or by senior Tibetan lamas closely allied to the interests and intentions of His Holiness's exiled government, under the World Peace rubric. These include:

1. The Kalacakra Initiations for World Peace performed by the Dalai Lama from the 1980s onwards. Public tantric empowerments into the ritual practices associated with the Buddha Kalacakra – or

'Wheel of Time', a core tutelary deity (or *yidam*) within the Tibetan Buddhist pantheon – the tradition itself is strongly associated with a millenarian myth concerning a final great battle between the forces of good and evil, which will centre round the mythical Buddhist kingdom of Shambhala, wherein initiates into the Kalacakra are destined to be reborn at the appropriate time (Dalai Lama and Hopkins 1985; Lopez 1996: 181–82). The present Dalai Lama has performed the ceremony almost thirty times in eight countries across the world, far exceeding all thirteen of his predecessors in both the frequency and geographical diversity of his performance of this complex and lengthy ritual, and often attracting in excess of 100,000 initiands.

2. The World Peace Ceremonies, performed under the auspices of Tarthang Tulku in India and Nepal from 1989 onwards. Initially carried out by the Nyingmapa school of Tibetan Buddhism at Bodhgaya – the site of Buddha Sakyamuni's enlightenment 2,500 years ago in Bihar, North India – these ceremonies now include large scale prayers for World Peace at four principal pilgrimage sites associated with the Buddha's life, hosted by each of Tibetan Buddhism's four main orders during the Tibetan New Year (Yeshe De 1994).

3. The World Peace Vase Project, carried out under the auspices of Dilgo Khyentse Rinpoche and Dzongsar Khyentse Rinpoche since 1987. Possibly the most conceptually ambitious of the World Peace projects, the World Peace Vase project involved the consecration of 6,200 'peace vases' in Bhutan, designed to be buried across the globe at astrologically and geomantically-determined sites of (i) major mountain ranges and water bodies, (ii) sites of conflict and warfare, (iii) sites of environmental fragility and destruction, and (iv) principal human capitals and indigenously-recognized 'power-places'.

4. Stupas for World Peace, constructed under the auspices of Akong Tulku Rinpoche and Penor Rinpoche (amongst others) since 1990. Placed at specific spots close to Tibetan monasteries, these elegant reliquary monuments are seen as representations of the mind of the Buddha, and are held to 'bring peace' to their immediate environment and the world as a whole. Erected in both India and near various Tibetan religious establishments around the world, their action is often seen as ritually 'binding down' the negative

> forces of a place, by equalizing unbalanced elemental constituents.[1] The stupas placed around the world were seen as part of a similar project to rebuild certain important stupas within Tibet, which had either degraded due to neglect or been destroyed during the fifty years since the Chinese invasion.

Although presented under the rubric of promoting world peace, the wider trend of global Tibetan ritual practice has been read by Western scholars in terms of the articulation of ethnicity and the continuity of religious culture: a 'theatre' that ritually re-enacts a lost culture of a dispossessed group before a caring, but ultimately uninvolved, Western audience (Korom 1997; McLagan 1997; see also Lopez 1996: 199). Whilst this may well be true of the manner in which such activities have been understood from the Western end of this inter-cultural dialogue, such an interpretation elides their historical place and significance within pre-1959 Tibetan systems of theocratic statecraft. Such evocations, I would argue, cross-cut Western understandings of political action and territorial statehood, as well as challenging the validity of increasingly popular postmodern renditions of Otherness.

Bringing Peace – Buddhist Rites and the Ritualized Landscape of the World

While the Tibetan adoption of the World Peace vocabulary appears to be a relatively recent development, they have nonetheless applied it reasonably consistently to certain long established facets of Buddhist ritual practice. Specifically, most high lamas associated with the various World Peace projects assert the capacity of specific rituals to positively influence the moral and geomantic environment in which they are performed.

This is perhaps clearest in the case of the World Peace Vase Project, where medicinal vases were placed at specific sites in order to ameliorate conflict, disease, and environmental damage. Filled with precious medicinal substances and a mandala (a symbolic depiction of a divine palace), their impact is deemed to be both global and site-specific, both transcendent (in the sense of promoting religion) and worldly (in the sense of promoting health and

1. Thus, on the inauguration of the first Stupa for World Peace in Scotland, Samye Ling's retreat master, Lama Yeshe Losal, explained: 'We would be the happiest, healthiest human beings – but we are not. Why are we unhappy? Because the earth is not happy. What are the symptoms of unhappiness? The way the elements are manifesting in the world, you see it every day, every year, how much harm they are doing all over the world. *The whole purpose of the Stupa is to balance the elements.* If its location is the right one the elements or energies of the world are channelled by it and according to the location it will bring more or less nourishment and energy'

wealth). Dilgo Khyentse Rinpoche, originator and principal consecrator, explains their influence:

> According to the main treasure text [from which the vase tradition derives], if the vase is made properly and according to the instructions, there will be long life, free from illness, [Buddhist teaching] lineages and family lineages will increase as will the power of the wealth of the [Buddhist teachings] and worldly good fortune. The whole earth will be made auspicious with the luxuriant growth of animals, plants, forests, harvests, medicines, water and wind. All will increase and all will attain well-being and happiness as in the perfect acorn, and all the universe and beings will be sublimely perfect.
>
> If it is hidden in the centre of a house, that dwelling will gain auspicious good fortune, wealth and fortune. If it is placed in the middle of a kitchen or on the hearth, one will gain food, provisions and wealth. If it is buried in a fertile field, the harvest will become bounteous. If it is buried in a mountain in front of a spring, rain and water will be plentiful. If it is buried in the manger of horse and cattle, it will prevent the loss of livestock. If this local deity heart treasure vase is buried on top of a high mountain above a village and cities then, in that it will be as medicine to dispel their illness, their limbs will be restored and it will be medicine which pacifies their suffering. The vases also contain mantras to pacify opposing enemies in this time of strife and misery in the world.[2]

For Dilgo Khyentse Rinpoche, the primary purpose of the peace vases was the healing and pacification of local spirits of the landscape, seen as responsible for health, wealth, and fertility, as well as hailstorms, earthquakes and disease. This follows a reasonably well-established precedent in Tibetan Buddhist ritual life, where consecrated vases – sometimes filled with precious substances to promote wealth, sometimes with medicines to promote healing and prevent natural calamities – were planted in the ground as gifts to local area deities and spirits (Atisha 1991).

Other lamas involved in the World Peace projects also asserted this kind of ritual influence on the landscape. Thus, Akong Tulku Rinpoche, abbot of Samye Ling Tibetan Buddhist centre in Scotland, argues that the Stupas for World Peace to be built at Samye Ling and their coastal retreat island would automatically generate peace both within the landscape and within people, in the immediate area and in the wider world:

2. Retrieved 13 July 2001 from http://www.siddharthasintent.org/shhi/peace/rinpoche.html. Also Glen Fawcett (World Peace Vase co-ordinator), interview with author, Delhi, 21 June, 2003.

> Within the [stupa] are many kinds of mantras and mandalas with many different powers, to overcome thunder and lightning, to prevent bad crops, earthquakes and – on another level – to overcome people's negativities, to purify past and future faults which we have made.[3]
>
> Wherever a stupa is built it gives peace; and wherever the wind blows [from it], it carries peace … it benefits all races and all species such as birds, animals and insects. The influence of a stupa is natural, like the rain, and influences regardless of belief.[4]

While such assertions can arguably be read as borrowed elements of new age discourse (see for example Huber and Pedersen 1996; Huber 2001), to do so would be to ignore the clear continuities that they have with traditional Tibetan interpretations of ritual practice. Structures such as stupas have long been used as *khak-non*, geomantic structures intended to influence the features of the landscape in order to avert disasters such as earthquakes, landslides, and hail storms (Mills 2003: 149; Stutchbury 1994; see also Mumford 1989).

A similar kind of influence was asserted for the Kalacakra initiations by the Dalai Lama. When asked about the capacity of the public Kalacakra initiations to promote World Peace, he commented:

> We believe that the Kalacakra ceremony is very good for eliminating negative forces [such as] warfare. So, the Kalacakra is something useful for peace. [Moreover] while I don't know what the real reason for this is, whenever the Kalacakra is performed and people sit together and develop good motivation and meditate for a few hours, that produces some kind of unified energy that helps not only the individual, but also the environment, the area.[5]

All of these projects mark their impact on the landscape primarily through the symbolic device of the mandala – the divine tantric circle – which acts to ritually inscribe the presence of particular Buddhas within the lived landscape (see also Mills 2003: 122–23). In the Kalacakra initiations themselves, the place where the mandala – a complex geometric object about two metres across, comprised most usually of coloured sands – is to be placed must first be exorcized of 'hindering spirits' (*gyeg*) before being 'nailed-down' by ritual daggers (each representing Buddhist protective deities). Following this, the mandala is constructed and the 'mind' of the Buddha Kalacakra summoned

3. Akong Tulku Rinpoche, talk to Stupa Committee, 21 February 1998. Samye Ling Stupa Office records, Samye Ling, Scotland.
4. Akong Tulku rinpoche, public fund-raising speech, March 1998. Samye Ling Stupa Office records, Samye Ling, Scotland.
5. Public interview at Kalacakra initiations given at Tabu, Spiti, north India, 1996.

down into it. In this sense, ritual practice was primarily performative rather than merely expressive: it served to create a set of ritually subjugated domains.

Here, a series of interlocking symbolic and religious metaphors were evoked, metaphors that linked together: (i) the formation of ritual relations with local deities and spirits associated with particular places; (ii) the symbolic balancing of elemental constituents; and (iii) the further central image of the enlightened mind (*changchub-kyi-sems*) as a ritual fulcrum. These three metaphors are not as incongruous as they may appear: the symbolism of the Buddhist stupa, for example, contains within it all three components. Thus, it is at once a symbolic representation of the mind of the Buddha, as well as being designed – through its combination of geometric shapes – to represent the perfect hierarchical balance of the elements of earth, water, air, fire, and space. At the same time, the ritual presence of an enlightened mind is also seen as the natural pinnacle of the hierarchy of numinous forces in the landscape: beneath the axis of each stupa is a box given over to the *naga* earth spirits, and Tibetan hagiography and Buddhist literature as a whole are replete with tales of the magical mastery that enlightened Buddhist virtuosi have gained over terrestrial gods. At the same time, however, this is a set of metaphors with a distinctly medical flavour: the lived landscape is seen within Tibetan religious culture as like the human body, deriving its health and wealth from the balancing of these forces.

This Circle of Kings: Tibetan Antecedents to the World Peace Traditions

While such rituals may aim at apparently apolitical processes – such as the 'balancing of elements' and the 'bringing of peace' – their practice involves a gulf of meaning between the Western interpretation of peace as the absence of power and sovereignty, and the Tibetan practice of such rites as moments of ritual suzerainty. In particular, the organization of the World Peace rites demonstrates a marked hierarchical centralization. In one way or another, these practices all evoke 'world peace' as part of a ritualized 'galactic polity' (Tambiah 1980; Samuel 1993), whose nexus is Tibet as a central sacred enclosure constituted through elite Buddhist ritual practice.

Such practices are centralized in three ways. Firstly, all Buddhist ritual – most particularly the tantric classes of rites described above – cannot be performed ex nihilo, but require an authorizing religious lineage, one that in this case is embodied in the presence of authorized Tibetan incarnate lamas, who are seen as representing the very Buddhas whose ritual presence they evoke. The various projects are thus seen as deriving their authority and efficacy across the world from the fact that they are consecrated by a series of elite Tibetan religious virtuosi. Secondly, most of these ritual practices are 'empowered' by relics from the Tibetan region itself. Consecrated texts, priestly clothes, ritual implements, even the ashes of high Buddhist teachers, had been relocated and placed within the stupas and vases of the various World Peace projects in order to ensure their ritual power.[6]

Whilst these facets of the organization of Tibetan World Peace rites clearly create lineages of presence that lead back to an authoritative Tibetan sacred centre, they could certainly be dismissed as the secondary by-products of an entirely standard Buddhist emphasis on lineage. That the World Peace paradigm is more actively constructed according to models of centralized ritual power can be seen more clearly in the precise ritual precedents they draw upon from Tibetan history, most commonly the life-events surrounding the early 'religion kings' (*chogyal*) of Tibet, Srongtsen Gampo and his great-nephew, Trisong Detsen, both credited with establishing Buddhism in Tibet under the Yarlung dynasty. The fourteenth-century 'revealed' scripture, the Mani Kambum, describes how the aggressive tendencies of the seventh-century Yarlung Kings of Central Tibet brought their forces into contact with China to the west, and Nepal to the south. In order to halt their military incursions on Chinese and Nepalese territory, King Srongtsen Gampo – depicted as the earthly manifestation of Tibet's patron deity, Chenresig – was offered by way of conciliation a bride each from the courts of T'ang China and Kathmandu.

The Chinese Princess, Wengchen Kongjo, travelling over the western mountains of China in *c.*650 AD, brought with her a statue of the Buddha Sakyamuni called the Jobo ('Lord') in a chariot. However, the new arrival did not come unopposed: whilst approaching Lhasa, the Tibetan capital, an earthquake occurred, causing the chariot's wheels to sink into the ground. No amount of effort could release it, but the princess was well-versed in geomancy, and consulted a geomantic chart given to her as a parting gift by her father, in order to discover the nature of the obstruction. She found that the land of Tibet was a maelstrom of negative geomantic elements, arranged like a she-demon lying on her back, thrashing her arms and legs to repel the new arrival. More specifically, the Plain of Milk where the capital city lay was the palace of the king of the *naga* water spirits, and the lake at its centre was the heart-blood of the demoness. Such malignant forces, she determined, accounted for 'the evil behaviour [of the Tibetans] including brigandage' (Aris 1980: 13).

To counteract these negative influences, Kongjo and Srongtsen Gampo built a series of twelve temples on the various *me-tsa* ('fire veins', a term borrowed from the medical term for moxibustion points in Tibetan acupuncture) of the Tibetan landscape in three huge concentric squares crossing the entirety of central Tibet, with each temple constructed around a 'nail' designed to bind down respectively the hips, shoulders, knees, elbows,

6. Akong Tulku Rinpoche, interview, August 2002; Glen Fawcett, interview, June 2003.

hands, and feet of the demoness (Stein 1972: 38–39; Aris 1980: 14–15). These were the necessary preliminaries to finally filling in the lake near Lhasa and building the new Jokhang shrine – which was to house the Buddha-statue – on top of it. In the fourteenth-century royal genealogy, the Gyalrab Salwa'i Melong, the author Sakyapa Sonam Gyaltsen (1312–75) describes this ritual suppression of the land of Tibet as turning the Tibetans against warfare and towards religion. Following this, Srongtsen Gampo enacted rites designed to bring wealth, fertility, and peace to Tibet, through the burying of symbolic items within the ground near the central temples at Lhasa:

> Gold, silver and other valuables were placed in precious vessels, wrapped in various kinds of fine silk, and concealed in the *tsen*-shrine, the *naga*-shrine and the inner circle of the [main] shrine to ensure that the land remains lush, that rain falls in season, that the various grains ripen, that drought, frosts, hail, blight, famine, disease, pestilence and damage by foreign armies are averted, to render all times and places auspicious and to spread virtue and happiness over everything (Gyaltsen 1996: 194).

Srongtsen Gampo's descendent, King Trisong Detsen, also sought to advance the Buddhist doctrine within Tibet. Much of Trisong Detsan's life is discussed in the widely-read Padma Kat'ang, the Tibetan *namt'ar* (or 'history of liberation') of the tantric yogin Guru Rinpoche, a semi-mythic figure often credited with finally converting Tibet to Buddhism. In his attempts to secure Buddhism in Tibet, Trisrong Detsen ordered the founding of Tibet's first monastery at Samye near Lhasa. Initially, the king himself oversaw the building work, but he was met with resistance: what the king's builders erected in the day, earthquakes destroyed the following night. Consulting his astrologers, the king was told that the local spirits of Tibet were inimical to the new monastery, and thus would destroy whatever was built. Unable to continue, the king summoned the renowned tantric exorcist Guru Rinpoche to overcome the recalcitrant deities. Guru Rinpoche – a married Buddhist yogin and exorcist from the Swat Valley in Southern Afghanistan, depicted in many subsequent texts as the Second Buddha – accepted the call, and began his journey across the Himalaya to Samye. Using his tantric powers, the exorcist travelled throughout Tibet, challenging the local gods and spirits of each region to magical battle. Systematically, he brought the local gods of each region to their knees, threatening them with destruction, and binding them to renounce their previous demands for human and blood sacrifice, to accept vegetarian offerings instead, and to protect Buddhism; to each he gave a series of treasures to be hidden until a future time when the Buddhist doctrine would fall into darkness. By the time he arrived at Samye, the whole of Tibet was subjugated. The exorcist then performed a dance, called a Cham, at the site of the future monastery, using his esoteric powers to summon up all the divine local powers he had mastered, not simply to protect the monastery from them, but also to invoke their protection of the new institution. From that point, the Padma Kat'ang records, the building of the monastery continued unhindered.

The actions of both of these royal forebears are explicitly taken as precedents for at least two of the World Peace projects. Thus, the World Peace Vase Project organizers asserted that the project's lineage descends from Guru Rinpoche himself (whom they identify as having buried 'peace' vases in Tibet as part of his subjugation of the local deities there).[7] Similarly, when discussing the World Peace stupas in Scotland, Akong Tulku equated their function to the 'nailing-down' temples built by Srongtsen Gampo (interview with author, 8 August 2003).

The degree to which such geomantic rites constitute important components of Tibetan tropes of state power can be seen in more contemporary examples. The geomantic use of vases in particular was one of the many ritual responsibilities of the pre-1959 Tibetan government at Lhasa: so-called *sa-chu* vases were placed in important sites around central Tibet in order to avert floods and earthquakes, and ensure the fertility of fields and herds (Atisa 1991); further vases were carried out to the outlying districts of Tibet by government 'postman' (*atrung*). The consecration and provision of such vases to Tibetan refugee households remains the responsibility of the Tibetan government-in-exile to this day.

An even more recent, but no less striking, example incorporates the use of both the Kalacakra and stupa symbolism for such apotropaic purposes: the construction of nine 'earthquake stupas' in and around the Dalai Lama's government in Dharamsala, north India. Built in the late 1990s in response to the seismic results produced by the Indian geological survey – which predicted imminent major earthquakes that threatened the very existence of the Tibetan government-in-exile's hill-station residence – the stupas were recommended by the Tibetan government's principal Nechung Oracle whilst in possession. The stupas were constructed primarily for the protection of the person of the Dalai Lama himself: the central stupa, dedicated to the deity Kalacakra, is placed immediately adjacent to His Holiness's residence; this was then surrounded by four directional stupas placed within the palace grounds. A further outer ring of four stupas was constructed on the outskirts of Dharamsala, designed to protect the population of the town.

7. Retrieved 26 November 2003 from http://www.siddharthasintent.org/peace/treasure_vases.html.

World Peace or Spiritual Colonialism?

The clear continuities between the various World Peace practices – carried out by high lamas closely associated with the Tibetan government-in-exile – and Tibetan modes of ritual statecraft should perhaps not surprise us when we recall that they emerged alongside the Dalai Lama's own Five Point Peace Plan, an explicit model for a future Tibetan state. Nonetheless, certain crucial caveats are required when applying a statist interpretation to this kind of material. Can we, for example, follow Lopez in his suggestion that such practices constituted a form of 'spiritual colonialism' (Lopez, 1996: 206–7)? Or, should such processes merely be included under the category of Tibetan 'soft power', as opposed to the coercive and co-optive 'hard power' of modern nation state action (Magnusson 2002; Nye 1990)?

Certainly, Lopez's perception of Tibetan Buddhist expansion in the wake of the events of 1959 as in some sense 'colonial' is far from counter-intuitive: when I first presented an early version of this paper to an interdisciplinary academic audience, some were struck by the sheer intellectual ambition of some of the World Peace projects, while many were shocked (even outraged) by what they saw as some kind of 'religious invasion' or a 'conversion by stealth'. The territorial aspect of the rites, in particular, caused consternation. Such responses are perhaps predictable, speaking as they do to the degree to which modern European cultures associate territorial sovereignty with encapsulating and unitary political identities. However, it also speaks to the profound clash of meanings between two understandings of the categories of religion and state, within European modernity, on the one hand, and Tibetan theocracy, on the other. To begin with, interpreting World Peace rites as 'conversion by stealth' makes sense only if Tibetan Buddhist practices are rendered as identical in form and purpose to modern Christian practices; in other words that their primary purpose is indeed conversion, and that any 'conversion to Buddhism' is logically assumed to be a conversion away from Christianity. In such a model the dynamics of ritual practices are reduced down to the politics of exclusivist identity. Self-evident though this portrait may be from the perspective of a Western history of religions, it stands at odds with both the ideological assertions of Tibetan Buddhist thinkers of the World Peace mould, and (more crucially) with the ethnography of their practice. The Dalai Lama in particular has strongly criticized those religions (such as Islam and certain forms of modern Hinduism) that assert conversion as a primary religious dynamic, and those Westerners who seek too swiftly to convert to Buddhism:

> I always tell my Western friends it's better to keep their own traditions. Changing religions is not easy and often is a cause of confusion …

> Because I'm teaching Buddhism does not mean I'm trying to promote or propagate Buddhism (Dalai Lama, cited in Samphel 1998).

On the assumption that such a distinction – between teaching Buddhism and propagating it – is genuinely meant, how are we to interpret it, particularly in the context of World Peace ceremonial? Much depends on how we understand the precise religious dynamic that occurs between Tibetan Buddhist ritual practices and the place in which it was performed. For example, when Srongtsen Gampo erected the temples that nailed down the she-demon of Tibet, or when Guru Rinpoche bound the local gods in magical battle, can we reasonably interpret these events in the manner in which they are usually glossed in English-language publications – as the moments when Tibet was 'converted to Buddhism'?

Akong Tulku, for one, has disagreed with such an interpretation. Discussing the similarity in principle between the purposes of the World Peace Stupa and Srongtsen Gampo's 'nailing-down' temples, he denied that the purpose of the latter was to convert Tibet to Buddhism, but asserted instead that they were to bring an end to quarrelling and conflict, and to generate peace (interview with author, 8 August 2003). From the perspective of post-Christian European modernity, such an interpretation looks frankly bizarre – perhaps even disingenuous – especially when we consider that the nailing-down temples were a functional prelude to the placing of Princess Kong-jo's newly-arrived statue of the Buddha at Lhasa, and that Guru Rinpoche's binding of the local gods was a prelude to his founding of the first Buddhist monastery in Tibet. However, seeing Akong Tulku's statement as disingenuous depends on interpreting the arrival of the Buddha figure and its attendant ritual practices as constituting the arrival of Buddhism as a unified and exclusive institutional presence – a system of belief focused on institutional membership of a group, manifest in the form of a Church (ecclesia). Arguably, this Durkheimian emphasis on group membership and institutional presence – the presence of a Church – depends on a fundamentally Christian picture of religion. As Spencer has noted in the Sri Lankan context (Spencer 1990), and Lopez in the Tibetan (Lopez 1997), the concept of Buddhism and Lamaism as functional equivalents of Christianity within our connotation of the term 'religion' is largely the product of a colonial rewriting which sought to mould indigenous Asian traditions within the conceptual framework of a specifically Christian understanding of religiosity.

We must be wary, therefore, of assuming that Buddhist religious practice and Christian religious practice must necessarily be designed to 'do the same thing'. In the Tibetan context, the nearest available rendition of 'Buddhism' is the phrase *nangpo chos*, a term that implies an adherence to ethical principles that pertain to the inner heart or mind, rather than the purity of the outer body (*chipa'i chos*, a term applied in particular to Indian Hindus, whom the Tibetans feel to be overly concerned with the purity of food and body as opposed to inner ethics). In this regard, I have heard several Tibetans refer to devout Christians as following *nangpo chos*, because of what was seen as their fundamentally inner morality.

Whilst it may perhaps be problematic to refer to devout Christians as 'good Buddhists' as a consequence, this nonetheless highlights much of the issue at hand: Tibetan renditions of religiosity – and most particularly those associated with the World Peace rhetoric – often cross-cut our understanding of religious group membership, identifying certain core moral properties as general to humanity, and therefore assert that certain general religious principles exist at the heart of all bona fide religious traditions. In particular, the Tibetan traditions to which the World Peace thinkers are primarily heirs – the so-called *ri-mé*, or 'non-sectarian', tradition of Tibetan religious thought that emerged as an institutional force in Tibet between the eighteenth and twentieth centuries, and that now dominates much of Tibetan religious politics – generally take an open position on the question of what counts as *dharma*, or Buddhist doctrine (Samuel 1993: ch. 27; Smith 2001).[8]

This open canonical position lent certain peculiar features to the World Peace movement: most obviously the Dalai Lama's use of it as a vehicle for the religious parity of all Tibetan Buddhist traditions, but also the endeavour to encompass other religious traditions within its ambit. This inclusivist stance characterizes many World Peace practices: recent Kalacakra initiations have incorporated teachings from all Tibetan Buddhist traditions, not simply those from the Dalai Lama's own Gelukpa school; Tarthang Tulku's World Peace Ceremonies, carried out initially by the Nyingmapa school at Bodhgaya, are now augmented by linked ceremonies performed at key Buddhist sites on the subcontinent by the other Tibetan orders.

More germane to this issue, however, there have also been moves to incorporate non-Buddhist traditions into their World Peace dynamic. Thus, while constructing the World Peace stupa at Samye Ling Tibetan monastery in Scotland – a monument normally 'consecrated' by including within its main body the accumulated texts of the Buddhist canon – Akong Tulku received

8. This position should not be seen as representative of a universal Tibetan view; indeed, the tendency to sectarianism is and always has been a particular feature of Tibetan institutional life. The *ri-mé* view has been opposed by a variety of Tibetan luminaries, in particular from the Gelukpa exclusivist stand of writers such as Sumpa Khenpo (Kapstein 2000a) and Pabonkha Rinpoche (Samuel 1993), who associated the 'true dharma' with a particular closed canon of Buddhist texts. Nor should it be assumed that the canonical openness of the *ri-mé* tradition universally equates with ecumenism: while it asserts the *recognition* of many other Buddhist traditions as the 'word of the Buddha' (*buddhavacana*), the Tibetan non-sectarian movement generally asserts the internal coherence of individual traditions rather than promoting an undifferentiated amalgamation of Buddhist schools.

several tape recordings of Christian teachings from Bishop Desmond Tutu. These were included within the stupa, alongside the Buddhist texts, on the grounds that they, like the Buddhist texts, were focused on the subjugation of 'afflictive emotions'.[9] Similarly, the second site for a World Peace stupa in Scotland – Samye Ling's retreat site on Holy Island of Arran – was deemed as particularly auspicious by its Tibetan retreat master Lama Yeshe Losal, because it was the retreat site of the ninth-century ascetic St Molaise, a solitary Christian ascetic who had lived for several years in one of the island's many caves. For Lama Yeshe, the meditative disciplines of his Christian predecessor had created on the island 'auspicious conditions' for ascetic practices during future Buddhist retreats. Christian teachings seem, therefore, to have been regarded in some sense as contributing to the 'pacification' process brought about by Buddhist ritual practices.

World Peace and the Modern Nation State

However, if – as is suggested above – we cannot easily understand the ritual propagation of Tibetan Buddhist practices through images of conversion and religious competition, then what are we to make of the regal (even statist) antecedents of the World Peace traditions? Here again we must be particularly careful about importing into Tibetan practices the implicit models of European statehood – specifically, the modern conception of secular, territorially bounded nation-states. In such a model, particular territories – like persons – are seen as ideally wholly enclosed by national identity: when I as a British citizen stand on British soil, I am the focus of all principal vectors of British state sovereignty – taxation, law, and identity. Within such a political ideology, all dimensions of state power and authority meet coterminously and uniformly on every square foot of a nation-state's territory; as a corollary, the 'infiltration' of any one dimension of a state's powers of sovereignty into the territory of another state is seen as synonymous with the whole of its presence. In the heartland of nationalist sentiment, any compromise of this principle of total sovereign enclosure of territory is a compromise that heralds 'invasion'. This theoretical sentiment exists regardless of the universal practice of such compromise in the daily running of states: extradition treaties, capitulatory rights, embassies and diplomatic immunities.

That such a theoretical vision of the ideal, hermetically sealed nation-state has never truly existed in practice should not surprise us. However it has also been the (largely vain) struggle of many historians to point out that neither has it always been the ideal vision of righteous sovereignty in the minds of kings and conquerors. Tambiah noted this when formulating his 'galactic polity' with

9. World Peace Stupa Office, Samye Ling Tibetan Centre, Scotland, August 2002.

reference to early Indian kingship (Tambiah 1976; see also Samuel 1993), and Southall saw the same thing when he proposed his model of the 'segmentary state' in order to explain the form of pre-colonial African states (Southall 1988). All of these were societies and states where the boundaries of rule were porous and labile: where villages would often pay their taxes to one state whilst owing their military service to another, and thinking of themselves as being members of neither. Perhaps the clearest example of this can be found in the old Gorkha regimes of the pre-British Indian subcontinent, political forebears of modern-day Nepal. As the late Richard Burghart noted (Burghart 1984), political identity in the region was modulated through a variety of differing relations with land, law, and tax affiliation: whilst people lived in one of a variety of 'countries' (*des*) to which they owed lifelong allegiance and rarely strayed out of, these had little or nothing to do with the sovereignty of the kingly state. The king's sovereignty, as we most commonly understand it, was mediated by legal authority, organized within a single, permanent territorial realm (*desa*) that overlapped across certain sections of these 'countries'. Centred on his ancestral temple and bounded by four directional shrines, within this realm the sovereign had to maintain the caste law of a Hindu king, and arrival here was strictly circumscribed by the rules of ritual purity. At the same time a further third set of territories (again only partially overlapping with the previous two) were the kings territorial 'possessions' (*muluk*), inhabitants of which owed the king tax obligations. These territorial possessions perpetually changed depending on the forcefulness and loyalty of the king's officers, and while often extending far beyond the boundaries of his realm (much to the annoyance of the British in India, who found this system perplexing and chaotic), also often failed to cover the territory of his legal realm (see Michael, this volume). Thus, there were large periods of time during which the Gorkha kings oversaw caste law and purity within a realm, much of the northern section of which owed their taxes to the Dalai Lamas to the north.

Emerging as they do from a political and historical milieu in which such 'loose' understandings of statehood and sovereignty prevailed, the imperial antecedents of the World Peace projects should be approached with a certain degree of caution. In particular, Srongtsen Gampo's 'nailing-down' of a wide swathe of the land of Tibet cannot easily be equated with the founding of the coterminous bounded polity, akin to the modern nation-state; nor (more pertinently) is it interpreted as being so by modern Tibetan religious writers. Thus, Dudjom Rinpoche (1904–87, late head of the Nyingmapa order of Tibetan Buddhism) notes that the three cycles of nailing-down temples constructed by Srongtsen Gampo were, respectively: the four District Controlling Temples (*ru-gnon gyi lhakhang*) in the centre, surrounded by the four Border Taming Temples (*tham-dul gi lhakhang*), with the final outer set of Further Taming Temples (*yang-dul gi lhakhang*) on the outside ring (Dudjom

Rinpoche 1991: vol. 2, p. 42, n. 543). Here, it is only the districts (*ru*) at the centre that constitute the actual domain of Srongtsen Gampo's rule: these are 'controlled' (*gnonpa*); whilst the regions beyond – the borders (*tha-*) and regions beyond (*yang-*) require 'subjugation' (*dulwa*). In other words, the conception of ritual sovereignty employed by Srongtsen Gampo was not simply one that 'nailed-down' his political territory, or merely asserted the boundaries of his state. Certainly his actions did those things. However, they also served to project ritual authority beyond the boundaries of direct political rule.

This was a feature of the organization of sovereignty common to Tambiah's galactic polity and Southall's segmentary state. It was, moreover, a characteristic feature of rule from Lhasa throughout the later history of the Dalai Lamas, the most powerful of whom sought to replicate the imperial stature of the reign of Srongtsen Gampo, to whom they saw themselves heirs (Kapstein 2000). The authority of the centre was projected far beyond the sovereign's actual coercive capacity to intervene in the lives of his subjects in either military or financial terms. Villages and provinces might look to Lhasa as a superordinate centre of political, legal, and religious authority, whilst at the same time never actually experiencing the direct effects of its rule. Lhasa and the Dalai Lamas sought to rule primarily through a system of religious authority and ritualized loyalty, rather than through the exercise of power, which – as with most pre-modern states – was generally beyond their capabilities.

In the modern context, this model of sovereignty is replicated within the more diffuse structures of the World Peace projects: centred on a vision of Tibet as a symbolic and imagined community that combines partially overlapping vectors of Tibetanness, it is felt to project its ritual authority outwards into the transnational community, far beyond its ill-defined borders. In the Dalai Lama's vision of the Five Point Peace Plan for Tibet, that authority is felt to bring peace to the surrounding Asian region; in the World Peace projects, to the world as a whole. In both cases the ritual authority of Tibet as a sacred centre cross-cuts the precisely clipped borders of the world's nation-states. It is, of course, an imagined picture; as are they all (Anderson 1989).

Conclusion

Modern anthropological discussions of identity and territory have, since the writings of Fredrik Barth and Anthony Cohen, strongly emphasized the importance of boundaries as core symbolic markers within the construction of social identities (Barth 1969; Cohen 1986). However, important though they often are, the overdetermination of boundaries as simple and global dividing lines within political and territorial landscapes has created within much postmodern social science writing an overemphasis on the notion of

'Otherness'. The postmodern oversensitivity to difference has tended to create a vision of the world in which those that see another as different must surely be treating them as opposite, as an opponent or competitor: we seem to live in a world in which dragons no longer live on the far edges of the world, but just outside our cultural front doors. Arguably, such a polarization of the world is a product of the preceding great project of modernity itself, which divided all the known world into nation-states, thus filling all territorial space with those who are either 'ourselves' or 'foreigners'.

Within the Tibetan evocation of 'World Peace', however, the dichotomies that have organized our understanding of political territory over the last three hundred years seem strangely absent. It is, nonetheless, a political vision in the way in which we would understand that term, one that clearly incorporates the exercise of sovereignty, building as it does on ancient Tibetan visions of righteous kingship. However, within such a model the symbolic authority of the righteous king is seen as territorially distinct from the space of his actual political power: rather than simply being 'inside' or 'outside' the boundaries of political and religious identity, differing structures of religious, political, and legal affiliation 'place' territories, communities, and persons more or less distant from sacred centres, which are themselves mirrored again and again across the globe. Such conceptions of sovereignty and influence exist outside, and indeed cross-cut, the set frameworks of European religious and political identities – frameworks historically and ideologically defined by the assertion of borders and the fear of conversion.

References

Aris, M. 1980. *Bhutan.* Warminster: Aris and Phillips.

Atisha, T. P. 1991. 'The Tibetan Approach to Ecology', *Tibetan Review* 26(2): 9–11, 14.

Barth, F. 1969. 'Introduction', in F. Barth (ed.), *Ethnic Groups and Boundaries: The Social Organisation of Culture Difference.* Oslo: Scandinavian University Press, pp. 9–38.

Burghart, R. 1984. 'The Formation of the Concept of Nation-State in Nepal', *The Journal of Asian Studies* 44(1): 101–25.

Cohen, A. (ed.). 1986. *Symbolising Boundaries: Identity and Diversity in British Cultures.* Manchester: Manchester University Press.

Dalai Lama, H. H. the XIVth. 1991. *My Tibet.* Berkeley: University of California Press.

Dalai Lama, H. H. the XIVth, and J. Hopkins, 1985. *The Kalacakra Tantra.* Boston: Wisdom.

Dudjom Rinpoche. 1991. *The Nyingmapa School of Tibetan Buddhism: Its Fundamentals and History.* Boston: Wisdom.

Gyaltsen, S. S. 1996. *The Clear Mirror: A Traditional Account of Tibet's Golden Age.* Ithaca, NY: Snow Lion.

Huber, T. 2001. 'Shangri-la in Exile: Representations of Tibetan Identity and Transnational Culture', in T. Dodin and H. Rather (eds), *Imagining Tibet: Perceptions, Projections and Fantasies.* Boston: Wisdom.

Kapstein, M. 2000a. 'The Purificatory Gem and Its Cleansing: A Late Polemical Discussion of Apocryphal Texts', in M. Kapstein, *The Tibetan Assimilation of Buddhism: Conversion, Contestation and Memory*. New York: Oxford University Press.

———. 2000b. 'The Imaginal Persistence of Empire', in M. Kapstein, *The Tibetan Assimilation of Buddhism: Conversion, Contestation and Memory*. New York: Oxford University Press.

Korom, F. 1997. 'Introduction', in F. Korom (ed.), *Constructing Tibetan Culture: Contemporary Perspectives*. Quebec: World Heritage Press.

Lopez, D. 1996. *Prisoners of Shangri-La: Tibetan Buddhism and the West*. Chicago, IL: University of Chicago Press.

———. 1997. '"Lamaism" and the Disappearance of Tibet', in F. Korom (ed.), *Constructing Tibetan Culture: Contemporary Perspectives*. Quebec: World Heritage Press.

McLagan, M. 1997. 'Mystical Visions in Manhattan: Deploying Culture in the Year of Tibet', in F. Korom (ed.), *Tibetan Culture in the Diaspora: Papers Presented at a Panel of the 7th Seminar of the International Association for Tibetan Studies, Graz 1995*. Wien: Verlag der Osterreichischen Akademie der Wissenschaften.

Magnusson, J. 2002. 'A Myth of Tibet: Reverse Orientalism and Soft Power', in P. C. Kleiger (ed.), *Tibet, Self and the Tibetan Diaspora: Proceedings of the Ninth Seminar of the IATS, 2000*. Leiden: Brill.

Mills, M. 2003a. *Identity, Ritual and State in Tibetan Buddhism: The Foundations of Authority in Gelukpa Monasticism*. London: Routledge Curzon.

———. 2003b. 'Lineages of World Peace', Tenth Conference of the International Association for Tibetan Studies, Oxford, September, 2003.

Mumford, S. R. 1989. *Himalayan Dialogue: Tibetan Lamas and Gurung Shamans in Nepal*. Madison: University of Wisconsin Press.

Nye, J. 1990. 'Soft Power', *Foreign Policy* 80: 153–71.

Samuel, G. 1993. *Civilized Shamans: Buddhism in Tibetan Societies*. Washington, DC: Smithsonian Institute Press.

Samphel, T. 1998. 'Review of Lopez' *Prisoners of Shangri-La*', *Tibet Journal* 23(4): 128–30.

Shiromany, A. A. (ed.). 1996a. *The Spirit of Tibet: Universal Heritage. Selected Speeches and Writings from H.H. the XIVth Dalai Lama*. Tibetan Parliamentary and Policy Research Centre. New Delhi: Vikas.

———. (ed.). 1996b. *The Spirit of Tibet – Visions of Human Liberation. Selected Speeches and Writings from H.H. the XIVth Dalai Lama*. Tibetan Parliamentary and Policy Research Centre. New Delhi: Vikas.

Smith, E. G. 2001. 'Jam Mgon Kong Sprul and the Non-Sectarian Movement', in *Among Tibetan Texts: History and Literature of the Himalayan Plateau*. Boston: Wisdom.

Southall, A. 1988. 'The Segmentary State in Africa and Asia', *Comparative Studies in History and Society* 30(1): 52–82.

Spencer, J. 1990. 'Tradition and Transformation: Recent Writings on the Anthropology of Buddhism in Sri Lanka', *Journal of the Anthropological Society of Oxford* 21(2): 129–40.

Stein, R. A. 1972. *Tibetan Civilisation*. London: Faber and Faber.

Stutchbury, E. 1994. 'Perceptions of Landscape in Karzha, *Tibet Journal* 14(4): 59–102.

Tambiah, S. J. 1976. *World Conqueror, World Renouncer*. Cambridge: Cambridge University Press.

Yeshe De Research Committee. 1994. *World Peace Ceremony, Bodhgaya*. Berkeley: Dharma Publishing.

Chapter 6
A Weft of Nexus: Changing Notions of Space and Geographical Identity in Vanuatu, Oceania

Carlos Mondragón

Earth is a womb; her sons are men. By contrast space is a sea, a 'floating' value that has no depth and no duration. What man considers valuable is the quality of his roots, in other words, his places of origin, like fixed points in a moving pattern of waves.

If this reticulated space is a structure knit in a fluid system, a 'weft of nexus', it cannot possess a centre. By contrast, it knows its 'foundations', which are the only places representing, perhaps, in this flowing universe, some truly stabilised realities. Melanesian routes converge toward junctions where they knit with others, but they also continue on those foundation-places which have been theirs from the beginning. The departure points hold, in themselves, the fundamental principles of origin.

Bonnemaison (1994: 234 and 1996: 37, respectively)

As the late Joël Bonnemaison sought to explain throughout his life, ideas about space in the maritime region of Melanesia are bound up within local understandings of geographical identity, ancestral origins, and socio-geographical networks that often challenge Western concepts of space, movement, and personhood (Bonnemaison 1991; 1997; and above).

The following pages offer a set of ethnographic data from Island Melanesia that invite us to transcend the reductionist dichotomy often inherent in the categories 'place' and 'space', and which, as Peter Wynn Kirby aptly points out in the introductory chapter to the present volume, arises from a 'lingering [Cartesian] bias that imagines places as simply fitting into a container-like volume of space'. More importantly, the following material compels us to reflect on the lived world as inseparable from the creation, reproduction, and flow of persons and things, while provoking us to eschew influential phenomenological propositions in which landscape is treated as a self-standing (i.e., external or self-contained) medium that is 'invested' with meaning through human acts of 'perception' (Feld and Basso 1997) or 'habitation' (Ingold 2000).

Rather than define the maritime and insular milieux of Melanesian life as a landscape (a category that, together with that of 'territorial identity', carries a problematic terrestrial bias), that is situated between place and space in the form of 'cultural process' (Hirsch and O'Hanlon 1995), I follow recent contributions from the Austronesian world that present the living milieu as a complex interweaving of land- and sea-scapes, personhood, and 'topogeny' (i.e., genealogical topographies, for which see Fox 1997: 91–102). Moreover, I seek to describe how this interweaving is continuously imagined and reiterated through flows of persons and things as a self-productive process that gives rise to a 'life-world of praxis and not just signification' (Biersack 1990: 67), thereby also stressing the importance of the 'human-scale experience' and the 'social dynamics' of movement (Kirby, Chapter One, this volume). In order to better reflect Torres people's own perceptions of these flows and transformations, I have chosen a narrative structure that moves from broad perspectives (key concepts of the lived world) to specific spheres of activity (villages, ritual grounds), and then back again to broader patterns of change in time and space. In this way I hope to mirror the inward–outward spiral processes of 'fluidity, improvisation, and change' (ibid.; see also Goldman and Ballard 1998; Hirsch and M. Strathern 2004) that are present in local metaphors of growth, exchange and transformation by which the inhabitants of the Torres Islands perceive and act upon the various contexts within which their lives unfold.

In respect of its debts to regional scholarship, this chapter follows from and speaks to many important anthropological writings regarding the nature and construction of Melanesian socio-scapes (e.g. Kahn 1990; Weiner 1988, 1991, 2001; Stürzenhofecker 1994; Crook 1999; Rumsey and Weiner 2001; Leach 2003). Moreover, it offers original ethnographic data and further theoretical elaboration for a growing volume of scholarly work regarding the social construction of the lived world in Vanuatu and Island Melanesia (Tryon 1996; Senft 1997; Bolton 1999b; Curtis 1999; Jolly 1999; Rio 2002; Mondragón 2004, 2006; Hess 2005; Scott 2007).[1]

1. Ten years ago, Margaret Jolly described the ethnography of North Vanuatu as 'an arcane dialect known only to a few' (1991: 49). Since then, important work has emerged regarding the main islands of North-Central Vanuatu. Yet Jolly's assertion continues to hold true for the northernmost province of the archipelago – the Banks and Torres Islands. Until now, the people of the Torres had never been the subject of ethnographic study. This article constitutes part of a series of texts in which I hope to provide an anthropological outline of the Torres islanders, whose existence, cosmology and contemporary concerns remain largely ignored, both inside Vanuatu and beyond (cf. Mondragón 2004).

An Oceanic Socio-scape

The Torres are a tightly knit group of small islands that straddle the edge of an invisible political divide that separates the modern nation-states of Vanuatu and the Solomon Islands. The Torres group is made up of six islands – Toga, Loh, Linua, Tegua, Metoma, and Hiw – which currently sustain a population of around 950 Island Melanesians who represent two distinct Austronesian languages (Hiw and Lo-Toga) and who are distributed across half a dozen coastal settlements.[2]

The immense oceanic region surrounding the Torres is dotted with a few scattered island groups that were the scene of an extensive complex of exchanges during the course of many centuries. In the past, the core of this complex encompassed the islands of Tikopia, Anuta, Vanikoro, Nendö (or Ndende), the Duff Islands, the Reef Islands and the greater Santa Cruz group in the Solomons, and the Banks Islands, Espiritu Santo, and Maewo in Vanuatu. Further abroad, the exchange cycles extended north into the main Solomons chain and south through central Vanuatu, perhaps reaching as far as the Loyalty group and Kanaky/New Caledonia (Huffman 1996; Dubois 1996). Moreover, the waters around the modern political frontiers that divide the South East Solomons from North Vanuatu constituted an extended cultural borderland of Remote Oceania where the influences of Maritime Melanesia and Eastern Polynesia met and overlapped (Green and Cressell 1978). But in the hundred years following first contact with non-Oceanic peoples, a rapid succession of displacements gave rise to the forcible clustering of previously separate inland hamlets into coastal mission settlements, outbound migratory movements, and long-term engagements with extra-local actors – namely, missionaries (Codrington 1885; Durrad 1940a, 1940b, 1940c; Hilliard 1978; Lange 2005: 247–81), plantation labour recruiters (Allen 1968; Corris 1970; Shineberg 1967), and colonial administrators (MacClancy 2002; M. Rodman 1978). All of these factors compelled the Torres people to dramatically reimagine their senses of place and belonging and to invent new forms of contact with the broader world.

In approaching Torres people's understandings and representations of these connections and transformations I have taken the following questions as my point of departure. How do contemporary Torres islanders imagine themselves and their islands? How does this image provide alternative approaches to anthropological discussions about space, landscape and movement? The outline of an answer was first offered to me by the inhabitants of Loh, one of the smallest islands in the Torres group.

2. According to the Vanuatu National Population Census 1999 and personal field census taken in 1999–2000 and again in 2004.

Vave and *Gwë* (Growth and Layering), and the Absence of Insularity[3]

Loh is a green island, with a surface area that encompasses less than twelve square kilometres shrouded by a dense covering rainforest and circumscribed by irregular, jagged coastlines of uplifted coral (Galipaud 1996: 1). Approximately one hundred and fifty people currently reside on Loh, sharing a distinct language and representing half a dozen *metaviv* – exogamous nucleated kin groups or extended families – that represent the basic household and landholding units of the Torres; in turn, each *metaviv* claims attachment to one of the three basic ancestral lineages (L: *tutumwe*) of the islands (Mondragón 2003: ch. 2).

Contemporary Torres people do not know the origin or significance of the name 'Loh'; indeed, it is unlikely that the island as a whole was ever given a particular name (see Van Trease 1987 regarding other islands in Vanuatu that did not traditionally have names as a whole). I once asked chief (B: *jif*) Peter Wotekwo of Loh what they called their island. It took some explaining before *jif* Peter understood that I was asking him for the name of the whole piece of land that is Loh, rather than a specific site or area within it, but even then he could not seem to evoke a term for island in Loh language. I then asked him whether he would use the Bislama word *ples* (place) instead of island. 'No', he replied, 'that type of word does not fit, it is not straight'. Then he made a sweeping up-and-down motion with his arms that indicated *stamba* (B: root, foundation) and said: 'It is this, it is here'. In the local vernacular, he explained, *lo* means a brief rainshower. 'Perhaps people called it Loh because of the frequent rainclouds that sweep overhead, or because our ancestors' weather magic was strong'. But this was only a guess. 'The island', he said finally, 'does not have a name. But in the past, some of the people of Ureparapara and the Banks called our islands *vave*'.

In the language of Lo-Toga, *vave* (also *wawë*) seems to be an archaic word that, while not unfamiliar, is no longer in everyday use. Various discussions with Loh islanders revealed, first, that in the past *vave* appeared to relate to a specific reef passage on the coast of Loh or Toga that became synonymous for neighbouring island groups, with the whole of the Torres, and, second, that *vave* translates as 'living growth' and may have functioned (as it appears to do in some Central and South East Solomons societies) as a metonym for the act

3. All indigenous language terms in this article are taken from two languages – Bislama (the neo-Melanesian pidgin of Vanuatu), and the autochthonous language of Lo-Toga, which is spoken mainly in the Torres islands of Toga, Loh and Tegua. Terms in Lo-Toga are indicated in brackets and preceded by an L, while all terms in Bislama are indicated in brackets, preceded by a B. Conversely, sometimes the term in Bislama or Loh appears in the body of text, while its meaning in English is provided in brackets and enclosed by inverted commas. All non-English language terms are italicized throughout.

of weeding and clearing ground in preparation for planting new gardens (Ross, Pawely and Osmond 1998: 122). More importantly, according to all of the informants who provided interpretations for this term, *vave* appears to relate to *vanuë*, more commonly pronounced *vanua* across north and central Vanuatu, where it functions as a term for what Euro-Americans identify as 'land' or 'island' (cf. M. Rodman and M. Allen, cited in Bolton 1999b: 45–46).

In the Torres Islands, *vanuë* represents land that is made meaningful through productive human effort, and stands as a metonym for the ancestral soil that provides territorial roots, nourishment and spatio-temporal continuity for the kin group (L: *metaviv*). In this context, *vanuë* encompasses and is coterminous with *tetot* (L: ancestral gardens), which are the origin-places of every *metaviv*, where the founding ancestors of every Torres lineage each cultivated their first plantings. Both *vanuë* and *vave* evoke generational continuity and the consubstantiality that links specific places with groups of kinspeople who are nourished ('grown', in Torres terms) in time and space (see Crook 1999, for a discussion of very similar concepts in the Mountain Ok region of Papua New Guinea). These meanings are neatly borne out in the commonplace Lo-Toga expression *vave lete*, which means 'to make a garden; to make it grow and/or bloom'. In any case, for the people of Loh *vave* seems to present itself as an active form of the category *vanuë* and translates literally as 'living growth'.

In relation to gardens and nourishment, living growth is one of the organizing principles of Torres effort, sociality, and reproduction. However, it is worthwhile stressing that growth, understood more broadly as nurturing, life-producing growth, is also evocative of ritualized transformations during initiation ceremonies, marriages, and mortuary feasting, which constitute the basic reproductive scenarios that enable the continuing flow of persons and things across the local socio-scape (e.g. Foster 1995). Importantly, in everyday contexts *vave lete* can only be successfully coaxed from the earth as a function of a person's *menä*, which is to say their capacity to evoke life-giving growth or potentiality from specific milieux (in this case, garden soils) within the circumambient world. In theoretical terms, the Torres islands' notion of *menä* is reminiscent of what Aletta Biersack (1990; after Touraine 1977), defines as the 'autopoietic' (self-productive) work of horticultural practice in Melanesia.[4] In sum, *vave* seems to be anchored within a set of practices and territorial concepts that refer to those processes whereby persons act on themselves and others in ways that give rise to nurturance and powerful forms of (re)productive capacity. Given that *vave* is evocative of a broad spectrum of

4. While there is no space here for a detailed discussion about *menä*, it is important to mention the pan-Austronesian reach of this term, which is more commonly known as *mana* in other parts of Oceania; cf. Keesing 1984; Shore 1989; Kirch and Green 2001: 239–47; see also Mondragón 2004, for a discussion about *menä* within the context of calendrical rituals and temporality.

'processes of becoming' it is not surprising that it presents itself as a multisemic concept, a symbol for the multifarious self-transformations of Torres persons and their (is)lands.

'The Torres', *jif* Peter concluded during the conversation cited previously, 'are *vave* because they are bright green. They bloom. Do you see?', and he pointed to the thick forest that was shining under the glare of the sun on the shores of the nearby islet of Linua. 'The vegetative growth is only stopped by the surrounding water'.

By contrast with the non-indigenous term 'island', which invokes essentialist notions of insularity, the notion of living growth does not operate in isolation from concepts of personhood, 'power' (which, as should be clear by now, is to be understood as productive capacity, potency or efficacy) and the interwoven nature of the land and the sea. In this sense, it is a concept that is best understood when placed alongside another term and artefact that is fundamental to Torres ideas about 'foundation-places' (following Bonnemaison) and the movement of persons and things in space and time. I am referring to the Torres Islands stone oven, or *gwë*, whose form and function during ritualized exchange neatly encapsulate the processes upon which the local matrilineal dynamics of social reproduction hinge.

In everyday usage, the term *gwë* (also pronounced '*gwa*' on the islands of Toga and Tegua) describes a stove or ground oven, but its full range of meanings conveys processes of containment, revelation, and distribution (of food and persons) that are generally incumbent on the ritual persona of the *wuluk* (L: maternal uncle). Importantly, these meanings are also present in other islands within the region, especially Tikopia (for which see Sir Raymond Firth's classic and highly engrossing but frequently overlooked description of ovens, food production and the role of the maternal uncle (*tuatina maori*) during ritualized exchange (Firth 1957: 394–427)). In what follows I forego discussion of kin relations and exchange in order to focus on the form of the ground oven in relation to genealogical layering in time and space.

In its most basic form a Torres Islands stone oven is a pile of heated stones, ashes, and vegetative substance that serves to cover and cook a tight bundle of leaf-wrapped food. The leaf-wrapped food that constitutes the core of the oven is not considered a separate part, but is intrinsic to the body of the oven. Hence, a stone oven only begins to acquire the status of a meaningful artefact, in the sense that it contains and transforms edible matter, at the moment when leaf-wrapped food is placed within – i.e., when it 'becomes' an oven. This becoming is indicative of the fact that a stone oven is viewed simultaneously as a *medium* through which the transformation of edible matter into cooked food is carried out and a *manifestation* of that transformative process.

Significantly, *gwë* also appears in the context of local toponymy, insofar as certain islands appear to stand as concrete manifestations of the 'topogeny' that operates between persons and places within the neighbouring region of the Torres group. Thus, from the perspective of Loh the neighbouring island of Ureparapara, which is visible as a small pile of land on the southeastern horizon, is known as Gwë. When asked to elaborate upon the meaning of this name, the men with whom I was speaking explained that Ureparapara was 'like a pile of stones, *like a stone oven*, because the sides of the island rise up and cover the hole [i.e., the bay] that is inside' (from fieldnotes during conversation on Tegua, September 1999, emphasis added). The toponym *gwë* is apparently not exclusive to one island, but appears across the Banks and Torres as the name for the island of Gaua (pronounced 'gwa' in Lo-Toga), as well as for the island of Tegua, which is part of the Torres group and is pronounced locally as 'degwe', with one of the possible meanings of this term having been confirmed, after cross-referenced inquiries, as representing 'a pile or covering of something'.

The meanings discussed above do not appear to be fortuitous, and cannot be reduced to the simple category of 'metaphors'; if generations of ancestors can be described as constituting parts of a layered body of persons (*metaviv*), and the same imagery is borne out in descriptions of yam-piles, which are products of the living earth, then perhaps it is not impossible to conceptualize whole islands as icons for the socio-territorial layering of persons and genealogical depth (note, however, that I approach these semantic relationships with caution, given that they may not constitute more than a series of casual associations arising from seemingly similar contexts and processes). In effect, it seems that the notion of an island standing as a 'pile' or 'layered' construct relates to the imagery of 'foundation-places' (*tetot*), which represent the basic 'layers' of soil and generations who share a continuity of substance, and to the temporal (transgenerational) movement of persons through ritualized exchange between nucleated kin groups (*metaviv*).

Having thus observed some of the ways in which land and sea are conceptualized I turn now to how the people of Loh imagine the ground on which they reside and the everyday milieux where the flow of persons and things inform the living world.

Pathways of Knowledge and Being

In their daily transit along the many paths that criss-cross their islands, Torres people traverse through different gardens and areas, each of which has a name and is associated with particular *metaviv*, or with spiritual and historical forces from the recent or remote past. Consequently, any given bush path is bursting with place names inscribed on stones, trees, dips in the road, and all manner of other objects, both stable and ephemeral. Toponyms provide constant points of reference for ongoing events and interpretations of the surrounding world. As Biersack rightly contends, the milieux within which toponyms are grounded cannot simply be called 'natural', because they are dependent on the transformative labour of humans, as well as non-human things and events (1990: 67).

Ni-Vanuatu villages and gardens constitute the grounding poles of human life and the everyday contexts for the circulation of people – circulation itself being an act of self-production, insofar as pathways represent an arena for partial disclosure and unfolding social relations. Specialized knowledge of plants and animals is transmitted, and transformed orally and visually, over the course of many years through such everyday acts as 'walking about' on a bush path (cf. Gell 1999: ch. 8). It follows that the physical surroundings within which people move are not 'inhabited' (pace Ingold 2000), so much as *produced*, day after day. In many cases place names and the understandings that are attached to them remain stable over long periods, due to the fact that they stand as topographical reference points for ancestral origins, group identity and descent.

The topogeny of the Torres Islands possesses an underlying instability that is not immediately apparent, but which arises from the strict limits on movement imposed as a result of ancestral, territorial, and maritime markers. While the 'land' (L: *vanua*) and 'water' (L: *pe* or *li*) are not necessarily viewed as separate realms, they are divided into scores of areas that are exclusive to specific *metaviv*, and into which non-*metaviv* members abstain from trespassing. Importantly, these patterns of territorial identity and controlled flow are never stable, given that *metaviv* are the outcome of ongoing social relations. As *metaviv* come and go (live and die, as one man from Ureparapara expressed it), or gardens are given and taken during cycles of marriage exchange, landholding patterns become entangled and members of different *metaviv* are involved in constant and complicated negotiations over specific areas (for descriptions of similar processes in other parts of Melanesia, see Ballard 1998; Carrier 1983; Foale and McIntyre 2001; Jolly 1999; and Weiner 1991). Generally it makes no sense to move within an unfamiliar area, particularly a garden which does not belong to one's own kin group, when there is nothing specific to be done there, but especially because violating someone else's horticultural ground is often associated with attempted theft, or even, in extreme cases, with sorcery (B: *nagaemas*).

One significant consequence, in terms of the imagination of landscape, that follows from these restrictions is that no single person ever comes to possess first-hand knowledge of every inch of their home island, no matter how small its surface area may be.[5] The fragmented view of the lived world that arises

5. The nature of Torres people's fragmented experience and knowledge of their lived world was made strikingly evident on a day when I was given the privilege of viewing a *tambu* (B: sacred; forbidden) site on the island of Loh. I was taken to this place in the company of two of the island's chiefs, Peter Wotekwo and Joseph Merelëte. Upon arrival, *jif* Peter, a septuagenarian who had come at the invitation of Joseph (the current custodian of this particular *tambu* site) was visibly moved by the sacred objects contained therein. I was then told that, despite seven decades of living on Loh, *jif* Peter had never before been to this site. When I inquired how this could be possible on such a small island, Peter simply stated: 'It is not my place'.

from these contexts further explains the absence of a term for 'insula' in Lo-Toga; rather, (is)lands and their maritime milieux are visualized as interconnected media through which a tracery of aquatic roads and bush paths are constantly being renewed or made redundant by the ongoing circulation, the ebb and flow, of persons and things.

Having discussed the ways in which the land, the sea, and the social world are laid out, it is towards the historical transformations of this living, networked context that I now turn.

A Weft of Nexus: Torres Past and Present

Today, as in the past, the people of this micro-archipelago are connected through a shifting matrix of relations that is configured by gender, kin ties, territorial affiliation, and particular types of everyday and ritualized flow. This relational matrix is sustained through various forms of exchange that overlap and complement each other at various junctures, thereby generating a range of iterations which preclude any single, stable image of the Torres Islands.

Thus far, I have argued that Torres people's self-perceptions are strongly influenced by the particular origin place that a person occupies within the 'reticulated space' of local relations and by particular patterns of displacement. Movement and action constitute the bases upon which self-perception, as well as intersubjective knowledge, are generated and expressed, but stress is often placed on the *stamba* (B: foundation, root) of home territory and on the strength that is drawn from being in one's proper 'place'. Across Vanuatu the most common way of verbally referring to the geographical identity of a person is through the conjoined and ubiquitous Bislama term *manples* ('person-place'), which indicates island and community of origin, as well as local *kastom* (customary knowledge practices) and purport; accordingly, specific forms of localization derive from the term *manples*, as in *man* Toga, *man* Hiu, *man* Metoma. 'We are Torres islanders, but the *metaviv* of my father and mother are both from Loh, and I am a man from the village of Lunharigi; I am a *man* Loh'. These words, spoken by Bretin Wokmagene Mweiu of Loh, convey the multiple emplacements by which Torres islanders localize and express their *stamba* within the overlapping network of 'person-places' that constitutes their lived milieu.

The local inter-island milieu is a living, shifting, relational thing composed of multiple agents and spatio-temporal horizons – of moments that can only ever be partially experienced, rather than abstracted as a whole (once again, it follows from this that no single 'island' is ever conceptualized as a self-contained entity). In order to grasp the basic pattern of foundation-places and general patterns of movement that have informed the Torres 'worldview' over several generations, it is worthwhile to consider a snapshot in time and space

– a single, if abstract, picture of the 'weft of nexus' that defines this social cosmos (as I confirmed in the field, this exercise is confusing to Torres people, given that it excludes movement and flow by attempting to 'freeze', on paper, the overlapping relationships that define the regional cultural socio-scape). I begin this exercise in frozen space-time with a picture of past flows as they are said to have taken place in the past, and subsequently link them to the transformations of the present.

The first of these two snapshots would place the two islands that lie at the extremes of the group, Toga in the south and Hiw in the north, as the principle hubs of Torres displacement throughout the past five hundred years. The most important patterns of migration and settlement within the Torres, and beyond, appear to have had their directing loci in these two islands. The boundary at which the social influence of Hiw and Toga met and clashed at various junctures in the past is the region encompassing the islands of Metoma, Tegua, and Nmwel. For their part, the people of Loh, while always retaining a certain measure of self-sufficiency and autonomy, were often under the powerful influence of Toga, to whose population they have been intricately linked for hundreds of years by virtue of marriage exchange, regional alliances, and linguistic proximity.

The patterns of settlement of the precolonial past were characterized by a large number of hamlets that lay dispersed across the upland plateaux of the main islands. Coastal settlements did not exist because they made no sense, given the constant threat posed by frequent hurricanes and cataclysmic oceanic swells. In the past, as in the present, these hamlets were connected to other hamlets by a tracery of bush paths and to other islands by maritime routes.

In the century prior to the arrival of Europeans, the inhabitants of Toga appear to have engaged in exchange cycles with Ureparapara and Mota Lava, which were prime donors and receivers of women and ritual artefacts.[6] For its part, Loh became the site of important in- and out-migrations to and from northern Vanua Lava and Rewa, in the Banks Islands. By contrast, Hiu held close ties with Vanikoro, and perhaps other of the South East Solomons, to the north. Following the arrival of Euro-American merchant vessels, labour recruiters, and missionaries throughout the nineteenth century, and of the iron, evangelical message and deadly diseases that they brought with them, these ties disintegrated and by the second decade of the twentieth century the population of the Torres Islands was almost completely wiped out (cf. Durrad 1922).

Throughout the twentieth century two processes dominated the interface between micro (by which read, Torres-based) and macro (regional and global)

6. Storied narratives from Loh and Toga tell of how the island of Ureparapara used to lie much closer to the Torres in the past, but after a series of kidnappings of Toga women by Ureparapara men, a group of powerful sorcerers from Loh and Toga gathered at the top of Mt. Luwovinie and conjured a cataclysmic spell that 'moved' Ureparapara far away, to the place in the ocean where it lies today.

interactions. The first of these was driven by the circular migration of Torres men and women to various islands within central Vanuatu (particularly Espiritu Santo) and the sugarcane plantations of Queensland in far away Australia. But circular migration has, on the whole, been limited, and most Torres migrants never went beyond Santo, where they sought temporary employment in copra plantations and in modern service sectors (Bedford 1973; Bonnemaison 1977). Contemporary Torres people's understandings of the outside world are, therefore, considerable but indirect; in contrast with the extended connections and maritime mobility that characterized their past, the sights and sounds of the world beyond their horizon remains distant and their situation is peripheral with respect to the modern nation's centres of government, finance, and education.

The second process of influence that changed local perceptions of lived space is more stable, continuous, and significant. It has been the process of Christianization and missionary work undertaken by various generations of foreign and Melanesian members of the Anglican Church. This process began in the 1870s and has gradually but radically changed traditional patterns of leadership and settlement, permanently transforming domestic and spiritual senses of place. The broad implications of the impact of Christianity on Island Melanesia is a subject that merits close analysis and has hitherto been absent from much of the ethnographic record of that region. In the following paragraphs I will focus on only one of the various ways in which Christianity and post-independence transformations affected the everyday spaces of Torres life (see Hilliard 1978; Hume 1986; Kolshus (in press); Lange 2005; and Rio (in press), for detailed accounts about the progress and effects of Christianity in other regions of Oceania).

In the present, Toga continues to host the bulk of the population of the Torres, and its greater surface area provides its inhabitants with opportunities to produce copra and sustain small-scale cattle farming. However, as a result of a series of transformations brought about by the establishment of postcolonial administrative relocations and aerial transport routes, the previously dominant contexts enjoyed by Hiw and Toga have been overshadowed by the sudden rise to regional influence of Loh – the third and traditionally less significant locus of Torres people's activities. In 1983, the Vanuatu Office of Civil Aviation built an airstrip on Linua, the flat islet next to Loh, and the single domestic national airline that services all of Vanuatu (originally named Melanesian Connections, which has now become the ailing company known as Vanair) began to operate an air transport service to the Torres. Hence, Loh unexpectedly became the main port of entry for people and goods arriving at or departing from the Torres. In recent years, the arrival of Twin Otters and Islanders from the Vanair fleet has become an almost weekly occurrence. 'Plane days', as Torres islanders informally refer to these visits, are now the single most important event that brings large numbers of people from across the islands together on a regular basis.

In a world where social relations and exchange are paramount, and the intricate movement of people and goods are markers of a group's prestige and influence, it is no small matter that Torres islanders wanting to gain access to the only regular and direct means of communication with the outside world now have no choice but to displace themselves to one specific island community.

Thus far, I have described the imagination of landscape in the Torres Islands from a general perspective that presents an image of the networks that characterize this micro-archipelago. In the next section I concentrate on the two most significant 'horizons of agency' (Biersack 1990) in the lives of Torres islanders, namely, the hamlet and the *hara* (L: ancestral and ritual ground, B: *nasara*).

Hamlet and *Hara*: The Dissolution of Customary Space

In Vanuatu, Bonnemaison once wrote, 'there is no descent group without a place or network of places and stones within its territory to which it can trace its attachment directly or indirectly' (1991: 73). Such associations are in evidence across Island Melanesia but, given the predominantly maritime nature of this world, Bonnemaison posited that territorial belonging was best conceptualized as a kind of 'geographical identity' (1997: 11–12). For his part, Lamont Lindstrom has described senses of place and identity on the Vanuatu island of Tanna as constituting a 'geographical subjectivity' (1990: 77–81). What is important here is that in many parts of North Central Vanuatu, the Bislama term *ples* (place) acts as a polysemic intercept for the complicated topogenic linkages that operate between gardens, hamlets, kin groups (*metaviv*), ritual grounds (*hara*), and traditional men's houses (L: *g'mel* or *gemel*). The elicitation of 'living growth' of a hamlet's inhabitants is primarily directed towards two of these *ples* contexts: one is the cultivable garden whose life-giving foodstuff is obtained through horticultural effort, and the other is the house, which stands as an icon of social relationships and reproduction that represent the nexus of local 'genealogical intercepts' (after Wagner 1987: 74).

According to contemporary descriptions, the 'traditional' form of hamlets on the island of Loh consisted of an area shaped roughly like an equilateral triangle several hundred metres across and was located on higher ground, within the forested hills. The number of residents tended to number no more than two dozen people who were closely related affines grouped around a paternal authority figure, usually the eldest first-born son from amongst the families. The ritual men's house (*g'mel*) was located opposite the row of family houses, in a privileged position within the clearing. At the front of the *g'mel* lay a line of sacred stone cylinders that represented the most powerful ancestors of the local kin group (*metaviv*). In the central part of the clearing, between the stones and the row of residential houses, were the ritual dancing grounds (*hara*) and burial stone piles reserved for very powerful persons. As a rule, women and children would always sleep in, and keep exclusively to, the surroundings of the house. The men, however, are reported to have frequently slept within the *g'mel*, where they would hold kava-drinking rituals almost on a daily basis. In the pre-European past, over a dozen of these triangular clearings appear to have been distributed across the hilltop areas of Loh, each one representing the dwelling area and ritual ground of every *metaviv* on the island. Conversely, the coastal areas, beaches, and reef passages, were used exclusively for going and coming to other islands within the group and beyond.

The above model of a traditional Torres hamlet is derived from contemporary oral accounts and is no more. It represents an ideal and frozen image that does not properly account for the mobility, variations, and interactions that took place within and between hamlets. But the icon of the triangular *hara* as an ideal manifestation of a *metaviv* remains a powerful, if abstract, socio-geographical marker of topogeny in the minds of Torres islanders. However, these markers are now being challenged by the transformations that followed contact, colonization, and independence.

In contemporary villages there are invisible spatial demarcations that determine people's everyday movement and attitudes; in essence, following unspoken codes of deportment, a person is not supposed to intrude into the area of a hamlet to which he or she is not directly related through *metaviv* ties. Similar codes of conduct are consistently observed across Island Melanesia.[7] However, in recent years there has been an increasing awareness among Torres islanders that the rules regarding the sanctity of the house have begun to break down as a result of recent social transformations.

The collapse of the Torres population in the early twentieth century forced radical changes on marriage practices, changes that were instigated in part by European missionaries who despaired of seeing their entire Torres congregation become extinct. Consequently – according to present day elders – they turned a blind eye to (some even say encouraged) the abandonment of certain taboos regarding marriage and reproduction, thereby condoning a process of unregulated incest the effects of which are still being felt today. This dramatic demographic transformation, in conjunction with the establishment of coastal villages, forced radical dislocation on traditional patterns of settlement and social relations, thereby collapsing the physical distance and socio-geographic differentiation that had previously operated between dwelling areas in the forest. A recent product of early missionary activity and

7. Wagner describes respectful attitudes towards the house among the Barok of New Ireland as follows: 'Person, family and clan are surrounded by an invisible wall of reserve and sanction, [which is] objectified in the dwelling house and its immediate surroundings. ... The dwelling house ... is a very visible sanctum of personal inviolability, to be approached by a nondweller with caution and formality'; he then explains these as prescribed, publicly exhibited forms of behaviour that is part of 'the differentiating elicitation of kin relationship' (1987: 50).

colonial administrative policies is Lunharigi village, which is the main settlement of Loh.

Many of the inhabitants of Lunharigi claim that current manifestations of communal disrespect began with the generation of men that are now approaching middle age (35–40 years old), largely because Lunharigi was founded around 1963, at the time when they were children. Lunharigi represented the first successful attempt at concentrating the entire population of the island into one single dwelling area (previously, around 1905, the Rev. W.J. Durrad had created a small coastal settlement named Vipaka on the south-west coast of Loh, but it was abandoned soon after he departed). The constricted spatial disposition of the mission station in Lunharigi imposed new patterns of cohabitation on a people whose codes of conduct had, for many centuries, been based on a sociality dependent on the strict separation of hamlets. Significantly, the name 'Lunharigi' summarizes the phrase 'many *haras* where kava is consumed' (L: *lun*, things of the same type clustered in a group, often said of a group of trees or bushes, + *hara*, ritual clearing + *gí*, kava), and is reflective of the coming together of different *metaviv* and their associated kava-drinking houses and ancestral grounds within one expanded context.

Both Jadran Mimica (1988) and Roy Wagner (1991) have suggested that the cosmogony, or cosmic beginning, as well as the apocalyptic demise, of Melanesian social life can be represented by the collapse into a unitary whole of all of the different parts and agents within the existing world of human relations. As recounted in the Torres creation myth (as well as those of many other Melanesian peoples, e.g., Biersack 1992; Gell 1999), the wholeness or 'oneness' prior to creation represents the absence of movement, the absence of opposites, the absence of distinct agents and parts. What has occurred on Loh, with the 'bringing together of many *haras*', is suggestive of this kind of social breakdown in previous inter-hamlet and *metaviv* relations, and provides one possible (although incomplete) explanation of the perceived erosion of respectful deportment between those persons who now inhabit a single, congregated arena.

This possibility is borne out by what the eldest man on Loh, Ben Ara'ana, once told me: 'This way of life', Ben said, referring to the creation of Lunharigi forty years ago, 'this living like ants, it confused everyone. Nobody knew where their *hara* began or ended, and the children have grown up without knowing how to follow the paths of their fathers and mothers'. Around ten years ago, following the unease that he felt about living in such close quarters, Ben decided to move his home to a new place and established a clearing, a *hara*, on ground belonging to his *metaviv* in an area that is distant from the island's two villages. From his *hara*, Ben has, in the words of other Loh islanders, been able to freely practice and transmit the specialized knowledge and respect that he learned when he was young and used to live in a single hamlet with his parents and grandparents.

> Torres. You are isolated from other islands of Vanuatu. Communication is poor. Transport is [un]satisfactory.
> What can I do? Depending largely on my sea resources and land resources. When is the improvement come about? Nobody knows. People of Vanuatu forget you, but you are the most beautiful place in the world with white fine sand like sugar, coconut crabs, lobsters, fish, birds, reefs and beautiful palm trees which sing in the wind ('My Remote Island', written by Sixth-grade Torres students at Robin Primary School on Loh).

Conclusion

Since their arrival in the Torres over 2,000 years ago, the Austronesian peoples of this island group held intense connections with the world around them. During prehistoric times the extent and intensity of their linkages underwent periodic contractions and expansions; one century ago, they suffered a catastrophic population collapse that nearly brought about their complete demise. Today, the Torres are connected to the rest of the archipelago mainly by a tiny airstrip and by the infrequent visits of copra-carrying vessels. Ironically, while modern forms of telecommunication have also dramatically increased the nature of (indirect) engagement with extra-local actors, the prohibitive cost of air travel and the paucity of shipping services pose insurmountable limitations to the actual mobility of ordinary Torres people.

In response to these situations, Torres islanders have developed a narrative in which they present themselves as a small, vulnerable community at the periphery of Vanuatu and the world. This vision of insularity and abandonment contrasts sharply with local expressions of geographical identity and customary practice; indeed, it is clear that current notions of remoteness are often adopted from extra-local discourses that posit the Torres group as marginal, primitive, and powerless. But current ideas about insularity are also serious and local, insofar as they are informed by a deep sense of anxiety over the perceived dwindling of social values, traditional skills, and wisdom, and the disappearance of respectful behaviour that is believed to have been paramount in an idealized past. As I have demonstrated, part of this angst can be traced to changing patterns of settlement and socio-geographical interaction.

In the present, Torres islanders are creating new ways of relating; they are also rethinking ancestral ideas about geographical identity. In some cases these reconceptualizations are resolved by turning to neo-traditional living arrangements (such is the case of Ben Ara'ana). But deeply-rooted perceptions about the interlinked nature of the land, the sea, and the capacity of efficacious persons continue to play a key role in the perspectives and relations of Torres people with their circumambient spaces (cf. Mondragón 2004, 2006), even as the transformations of an increasingly interconnected but paradoxically marginalizing modernity dislocate their ancestral senses of place and space.

As I stated at the beginning of this text, by rendering explicit some of the concepts and processes by which the Torres people construct the contexts in which they live, I hope to contribute to emerging understandings of place and space in Island Melanesia. At a broader anthropological level I seek to advance alternative forms of analysing and theorizing space and movement that are informed by Austronesian principles and that suggest, for example, that some of the more attractive phenomenological approaches to landscape can easily take for granted such ubiquitous concepts as that of insularity. Such a naturalized notion of maritime environments may, indeed, be absent from the perceptions of those people who inhabit a 'sea of islands' such as Island Melanesia. On the whole, the dislocation of commonplace ideas about space and movement requires us to reconceptualize lived contexts as arising from the interconnections of the social with the geographical. Importantly, it compels us to pay greater attention to movement in the broadest sense of the term – be it as in the ethnographic data presented here, in the long-term form of genealogical layering, the periodical re-placement of houses and the consequent mobility of villages, or the daily displacement of persons within changing networks of paths and maritime routes. Movement, in this sense, functions as the necessary processual component in the constant renewal, abandonment, and re-creation that accompany the act of localizing oneself in 'place' and 'space'.

References

Allen, M. 1968. 'The Establishment of Christianity and Cash-Cropping in a New Hebridean Community', *Journal of Pacific History* 3: 25–46.

Ballard, C. 1998. 'The Sun by Night: Huli Moral Topography and Myths of the Time of Darkness', in L. R. Goldman and C. Ballard (eds), *Fluid Ontologies: Myth, Ritual and Philosophy in the Highlands of Papua New Guinea*. London: Bergin and Garvey, pp. 67–85.

Bedford, R. D. 1973. *New Hebridean Mobility: A Study of Circular Migration.* Canberra: Australian National University.

Biersack, A. 1982. 'Ginger Gardens for the Ginger Woman: Rites and Passages in a Melanesian Society', *Man* (n.s.) 17: 239–58.

———. 1990. 'Histories in the Making: Paiela and Historical Anthropology', *History and Anthropology* 5: 63–85.

Bolton, L. 1999a. 'Introduction', in L. Bolton (ed.), *Fieldwork and Fieldworkers in Vanuatu. Oceania* Special Issue 70: 1–8.

———. 1999b. 'Women, Place and Practice in Vanuatu: A View from Ambae', *Oceania* 70: 43–55.

Bonnemaison, J. 1977. *Système de Migration et Croissance Urbaine a Port-Vila et Luganville (Nouvelles-Hébrides).* Collection Travaux et Documents No. 60. Paris: Éditions de l'ORSTOM.

———. 1991. 'Magic Gardens in Tanna', *Pacific Studies* 14: 71–89.
———. 1994. *The Tree and the Canoe*. Honolulu: University of Hawai'i Press.
———. 1996. 'The Metaphor of the Tree and the Canoe', in J. Bonnemaison et al. (eds), *Arts of Vanuatu*. Bathurst, NSW: Crawford House Publishing, pp. 34–38.
———. 1997. *Les Gens des Lieux: Histoire et Géosymboles d'une Société Enrancinée: Tanna. Vol II: Les Fondements Géographiques d'une Idéntité: Essai de Géographie Culturelle*. Paris: Éditions de l'ORSTOM.
Carrier, J. 1983. 'Profitless Property: Marine Ownership and Access to Wealth on Ponam Island, Manus Province', *Ethnology* 22: 133–51.
Codrington, Rev. R. H. 1885. *The Melanesian Languages*. Oxford: The Clarendon Press.
Corris, P. 1970. 'Pacific Island Labour Migrants in Queensland', *Journal of Pacific History* 5: 43–64.
Crook, T. 1999, 'Growing Knowledge in Bolivia, Papua New Guinea', *Oceania* 69: 225–42.
Curtis, T. 1999. 'Tom's Tambu House: Spacing, Status and Sacredness in South Malakula', *Oceania* 70: 56–71.
Dubois, M.-J. 1996. 'Vanuatu Seen from Maré', in J. Bonnemaison et al. (eds), *Arts of Vanuatu*, Bathurst, NSW: Crawford House Publishing.
Durrad, Rev. W. J. 1922. 'Chapter 1', in W. H. R. Rivers (ed.), *Essays on the Depopulation of Melanesia*. Cambridge: Cambridge University Press, pp. 79–82.
———. 1940a. 'Notes on the Torres Islands', *Oceania* 10: 389–403.
———. 1940b. 'Notes on the Torres Islands', *Oceania* 11: 75–109.
———. 1940c. 'Notes on the Torres Islands', *Oceania* 11: 186–201.
Feld, S. and K. Basso (eds). 1997. *Senses of Place*. Santa Fe, NM: School of American Research Press.
Foale, S. and M. Macintyre. 2001. 'Dynamic and Flexible Aspects of Land and Marine Tenure at West Nggela: Implications for a Marine Resource Management', *Oceania* 52: 30–43.
Foster, R. 1995. *Social Reproduction and History in Melanesia: Mortuary Ritual, Gift Exchange and Custom in the Tanga Islands*. Cambridge: Cambridge University Press.
Fox, J. 1997. *The Poetic Power of Place: Comparative Perspectives on Austronesian Ideas of Locality*. Canberra: Australian National University.
Galipaud, J.-C. 1996. *Recherches Archéologiques aux Iles Torres: Premiers Resultants de la Mission Realise du 9 au 23 Novembre 1990 dans les Iles de Metoma, Tegua et Toga*. Rapport de Terrain No. 5. Port Vila: ORSTOM.
Gell, A. 1998. *Art and Agency: An Anthropological Theory*. Oxford: Clarendon.
———. 1999. *The Art of Anthropology: Essays and Diagrams*. E. Hirsch (ed.). London: Athlone Press.
Gillespie, S. 2000. 'Beyond Kinship: An Introduction', in R. Joyce and S. Gillespie (eds), *Beyond Kinship: Social and Material Reproduction in House Societies*. Philadelphia: University of Pennsylvania Press, pp. 1–21.
Goldmand, L. R. and C. Ballard (eds), *Fluid Ontologies: Myth, Ritual and Philosophy in the Highlands of Papua New Guinea*. London: Bergin and Garvey.
Green, R. C. and M. M. Cressell (eds). 1978. *South-East Solomon Islands Cultural History: A Preliminary Survey*. Bulletin 11. Wellington: The Royal Society of New Zealand.
Hess, S. 2005. 'Person and Place on Vanua Lava, Vanuatu', Ph.D. dissertation. Canberra: Australian National University.
Hilliard, D. 1978. *God's Gentlemen: A History of the Melanesian Mission, 1849–1942*. St. Lucia: University of Queensland Press.
Hirsch, E. and M. O'Hanlon (eds). 1995. *The Anthropology of Landscape: Perspectives on Place and Space*. Oxford: Oxford University Press.
Hirsch, E. and M. Strathern (eds). 2004. *Transactions and Creations: Property Debates and the Stimulus of Melanesia*. Oxford: Berghahn.

Huffman, K. 1996. 'Trading, Cultural Exchange and Copyright: Important Aspects of Vanuatu Arts', in J. Bonnemaison et al. (eds), *Arts of Vanuatu*. Bathurst, NSW: Crawford House Publishing.

Hume, L. 1986. 'Church and Kastom on Maewo, Vanuatu', *Oceania* 56: 304–12.

Ingold, T. 2000. *The Perception of the Environment: Essays in Livelihood, Dwelling and Skill.* London: Routledge.

Jolly, M. 1982. 'Birds and Banyans of South Pentecost: Kastom in the Anti-Colonial Struggle', *Mankind* 13: 338–73.

———. 1991. 'Soaring Hawks and Grounded Persons: The Politics of Rank and Gender in North Vanuatu', in M. Godelier and M. Strathern (eds), *Big Men and Great Men: Personifications of Power in Melanesia*. Cambridge: Cambridge University Press, pp. 48–80.

———. 1999. 'Another Time, Another Place', *Oceania* 69: 282–99.

Keesing, R. 1984. 'Rethinking Mana', *Journal of Anthropological Research* 40: 137–56.

Kolshus, T. (in press), 'Anticuados y Novedosos: Los Usos de la Cronometría en una Historia de Conversión en la Melanesia', in C. Mondragón (ed.), *Más Allá de la Religiosidad: Historia y Antropología del Cristianismo en México, la Melanesia y el Sur de Asia*. México: El Colegio de México.

Lange, R. 2005. *Island Ministers: Indigenous Leadership in Nineteenth Century Pacific Islands Christianity*. Canberra: Pandanus Books.

Leach, J. 2003. *Creative Land: Place and Procreation on the Rai Coast of Papua New Guinea*. New York: Berghahn Books.

Lindstrom, L. 1990. *Knoweldge and Power in a South Pacific Society*. Washington: Smithsonian Institution Press.

Lynch, J. 1994. *An Annotated Bibliography of Vanuatu Languages*. Suva: University of the South Pacific.

MacClancy, J. 2002. *To Kill a Bird With Two Stones: A Short History of Vanuatu*. Port Vila: Vanuatu Kaljoral Senta.

Mimica, J. 1988. *Intimations of Infinity: The Mythopoeia of the Iqwaye Counting System and Number.* Oxford: Berg.

Mondragón, C. 2003. '*Las Ples, Las Aelan, Las Tingting*: Living Respect and Knowledge in the Torres Islands, Vanuatu', Ph.D. dissertation. Cambridge: University of Cambridge.

———. 2004. 'Of Winds, Worms and *Mana*: The Traditional Calendar of the Torres Islands, Vanuatu', *Oceania* 74: 289–308.

———. 2006. 'El Temps i l'Expressió de la Temporalitat a les Illes Torres, Vanuatu', *Revista d'Etnología de Catalunya* 28: 8–19.

———. forthcoming. 'Yam Gardening, Substance and "Respect" in the Torres Islands, Vanuatu'.

Mondragón, C. (ed.). In press. *Más Allá de la Religiosidad: Historia y Antropología del Cristianismo en México, la Melanesia y el Sur de Asia*. México: El Colegio de México.

Neyret, J. 1959. *Pirogues Océannienes, Tome I: Première Partie: Mélanésie*. Paris: Association des Amis des Musées de la Marine.

Rio, K. 2002. 'The Third Man: Manifestations of Agency on Ambrym Island, Vanuatu', Ph.D. dissertation. Bergen: The University of Bergen.

———. In press. 'El Ascenso y la Caída de un Misionero y la Inesperada Aparición de un Movimiento Cristiano en la Isla de Ambrym (Vanuatu)', in C. Mondragón (ed.), *Más Allá de la Religiosidad: Historia y Antropología del Cristianismo en México, la Melanesia y el Sur de Asia*. México: El Colegio de México.

Rodman, M. 1987. 'Moving Houses: Residential Mobility and the Mobility of Residences in Longana, Vanuatu', *American Anthropologist* 87: 56–72.

Ross, M., A. Pawley, and M. Osmond. 1998. *The Lexicon of Proto-Oceanic: The Culture and Environment of Ancestral Oceanic Society, Vol. 1: Material Culture*. Canberra: Research School of Pacific and Asian Studies, Australian National University.

Rumsey, A. and J. Weiner (eds). 2001. *Space, Narrative and Knowledge in Aboriginal Australia and Papua New Guinea*. Honolulu: Hawai'i University Press.

Scott, M. 2007. *The Severed Snake: Matrilineages, Making Place, and a Melanesian Christianity in Southeast Solomon Islands*. Durham: Carolina Academic Press.

Senft, G. (ed.). 1997. *Referring to Space: Studies in Austronesian and Papuan Languages*. Oxford: Oxford University Press.

Shineberg, D. 1967. *They Came for Sandalwood: A Study of the Sandalwood Trade in the South-West Pacific 1830-1865*. Melbourne: Melbourne University Press.

Shore, B. 1989. 'Mana and Tapu', in A. Howard and R. Borofsky (eds), *Developments in Polynesian Ethnology*. Honolulu: University of Hawai'i Press, pp. 137–73.

Touraine, A. 1977. *The Self-Production of Society*. Chicago: University of Chicago Press.

Tryon, D. 1976. *New Hebrides Languages: An Internal Classification*. Pacific Linguistics, Series C 50. Canberra: Australian National University.

———. 1996. 'Dialect Chaining and the Use of Geographical Space', in J. Bonnemaison et al. (eds), *Arts of Vanuatu*. Bathurst, NSW: Crawford House Publishing.

Van Trease, H. 1987. *The Politics of Land in Vanuatu: From Colony to Independence*. Suva: University of the South Pacific.

Wagner, R. 1986. *Asiwinarong: Ethos, Image and Social Power among the Usen Barok of New Ireland*. Princeton: Princeton University Press.

———. 1991. 'The fractal person', in M. Godelier and M. Strathern (eds), *Big Men and Great Men: Personifications of Power in Melanesia*. Cambridge: Cambridge University Press, pp. 159–73.

Weiner, J. 1988. *The Heart of the Pearl Shell: The Mythological Dimension of Foi Sociality*. Berkeley: University of California Press.

———. 1991. *The Empty Place*. Bloomington, IN: Indiana University Press.

———. 2001. *Tree Leaf Talk: A Heideggerian Anthropology*. Oxford: Berg.

Chapter 7
At Home Away from Homes: Navigating the *Taiga* in Northern Mongolia

Morten Axel Pedersen

Introduction

Deleuze and Guattari, in their essay 'On Nomadology', suggest that 'even though the nomadic trajectory may follow trails or customary routes, it does not fulfil the function of the sedentary road, which is to parcel out a closed space to people'. Rather, they argue, 'the nomadic trajectory does the opposite: it distributes people (or animals) in an open space, one that is indefinite' (1999: 380, emphases omitted). While it should be remembered that Deleuze and Guattari's work represents an attempt to develop new philosophical concepts rather than anthropological ones – indeed, their reading of the ethnographic literature on nomads is rather dubious (Pedersen 2007a) – it is striking how well their concepts of nomadic space resonate with how some nomads in present-day Mongolia perceive and navigate within their environment. Based on fieldwork among the reindeer-breeding Duxa of northern Mongolia, this paper[1] contends that the Duxa landscape can be described as 'nomadic', as opposed to the 'sedentary' landscape of, say, contemporary Euro-Western agriculturists. People whose landscape is nomadic, I propose, tend to highlight places at the expense of spaces, whereas people whose landscape is sedentary tend to highlight spaces at the expense of places, for, whereas sedentary landscapes are perceived as largely homogeneous and bounded, nomadic landscapes are perceived as largely heterogeneous and infinite.

1. The present chapter is a shortened and substantially rewritten version of Pedersen (2003). I thank Peter Kirby for his encouragement as well as his insightful comments. My 1995–96 fieldwork among the Duxa was supported by HM Queen Margrethe and Prince Henrik's Foundation, by King Christian X's Foundation, by Mindefondet, and by the University of Aarhus. Subsequent fieldwork among the neighbouring Darxads was carried out between June 1998 and October 1999 as well as during the summer of 2000, and was funded by the Danish Research Academy, by the William Wyse Foundation, and by King's College, Cambridge.

This is not to say that Duxa nomads and Euro-Western agriculturists live in radically different cultural worlds. Nomadic and sedentary landscapes are not the result of two different cultures constructing their own natures (cf. Ingold 1993). Rather, I argue, the marked differences between the two landscapes are the outcome of particular geographical and politico-economic trajectories, which, in the course of history, seem to have brought about a figure–ground reversal within the perceptual hierarchy of place and space within the two contexts in question. Following an introduction to the Duxa people and their landscape, I open by using actor-network theory to show how the Duxa conceive of their landscape as a heterogeneous network of prominent places. I then turn, more specifically, to the phenomenology of nomadic movement. It is suggested that, immersed in the boundlessness of their nomadic landscape, the Duxa perform a range of ritual actions that mould their spatial sensibilities in significant ways. Indeed, inasmuch as these practices clearly serve to anchor people's perceptions within an otherwise infinite vortex of relations, these ritual movements seem to be aimed towards an intimation of spatial finitude. The Duxa, it would appear, have truly learned the art of making a home away from homes.

The Duxa People

The Duxa (also known among Mongolians as the Tsaatang, or 'the reindeer people') are a group of approximately 500 ethnic Tuvinians inhabiting the Tsagaan Nuur district situated in the far north-western corner of Mongolia's Xövsgöl province. The Duxa's first language is Tuvinian, but they all speak fluent Mongolian.[2] Half of the Duxa live in or around the district centre of Tsagaan Nuur alongside Mongolian Darxad and Xalx semi-pastoralists, whereas the other half is dispersed over two large territories of coniferous forests and high alpine lands (*taiga*) where, since the collapse of Mongolian state-socialism in 1990, they have practiced a combined economy of reindeer-breeding, hunting, and trading. The adult members of this *taiga* community – the primary focus of this chapter – are fully nomadic. These nomadic Duxa move camp some ten to fifteen times each year, using their reindeer as pack and riding animals. They are divided into two semi-corporate groups – an 'Eastern' camp and a 'Western' camp – each tracing themselves back to a specific area of the (now) Tuvinian Autonomous Region of Russia, from where they migrated 200 years and 50 years ago respectively. The inhabitants of each camp live in tepee-shaped dwellings (*orts*) during the entire year, although, as elsewhere in rural Mongolia, the composition and size of each household (*ail*)

2. In this chapter all indigenous terms are presented in Mongolian as my data on the Duxa are the result of conversations and interviews carried out in this language.

varies according to the season. Unusually for Mongolia, the traditional clan system is still intact among the Duxa, the descendants of the original immigrant groups being divided into five exogamous clans. Descent is patrilineal, and each semi-corporate group is headed by an elderly male (informal) leader, who, among other things, has the final say in determining when and where the encampment will move. (For more on the Duxa, see Badamxatan 1987 and Wheeler 1999, 2000, and forthcoming. Cf. also Vainsthein 1980).

The Duxa inhabit the northernmost part of the Republic of Mongolia. This area – known as the Darxad Depression after its main indigenous group – is characterized by its many forests, rivers, and lakes, by its abundant wildlife, and by its extreme remoteness. High mountains – up to 3,500 meters – tower around a large, flat depression, and in between this upper alpine land and the lower steppe zone (which is inhabited by Darxad pastoralists), vast forests make possible the Duxa's reindeer-based nomadic livelihood. Among the (predominantly Buddhist) Xalx Mongolians, this area is renowned for its wild and beautiful nature, but also for its fierce and impoverished population of indigenous Duxa and Darxad nomads. Tellingly, one young city-dweller of the Mongolian capital Ulaanbaatar called the area the 'Dark Valley', a name referring not only to its rugged mountains and deep forests, but also to its feared shaman population of the 'black faith' (*xar mörgöl*) (see also Pedersen 2007b).

Indeed, the Duxa have a flourishing shamanist religion, and practicing shamans (*böö*) live in both *taiga* encampments and in the Tsagaan Nuur village, although, especially among those Duxa living in close proximity to Darxad and Xalx Mongolians, Lamaist Buddhism is having a significant religious impact as well. Being shamanist, or we could say animist (Pedersen 2001, 2007a), the nomadic Duxa regard their landscape as animated by both human and non-human agents. In particular, a multitude of spirits are understood to dwell within different phenomena of the *taiga*, such as prominent mountains, trees, rivers or wild animals. This sacred geography plays a significant role in Duxa everyday life. A successful hunt, for example, cannot be carried out without proper knowledge of the landscape, and, as we shall see below, such knowledge includes being aware of how to deal with its different spiritual entities.

Theorizing the Duxa Landscape

The Duxa landscape, then, is not simply comprised by the physical contours of the environment surrounding the nomadic camp. For one thing, a given camp does not define an enclosure of cultural space on the other side of which its inhabitants encounter a natural wilderness. 'Wild' spaces can be found inside each Duxa camp, just as 'tame' places can be found outside it. For another thing, the Duxa landscape is a combination of a spiritual background reality and a physical foreground reality (cf. Hirsch 1995). It is important, however, to keep in mind that this distinction is largely analytical. For the Duxa, it seems, the invisible background and the visible foreground of their landscape are collapsed into a simultaneously spiritual and physical presence of spirit 'owners' (*ezed*).[3] Each of these spirits is believed to control something within the environment, be that the fireplace inside a tepee, the wild animals roaming around in the *taiga*, or the barren peaks of the highest mountains.

Let us consider a concrete example. Among the Duxa, most prominent mountains are believed to have 'owners', that is, intentional non-human agents with whom humans have to engage in a friendly and submissive manner so as to avoid trouble. One such mountain is called Agaya ('White Cliff') and many stories are told about this place. A special kind of spirit, the so-called *avlin*, 'own' this mountain. Normally, *avlin* are invisible but a few experienced hunters claim to have encountered them whilst travelling alone in the *taiga*. When the *avlin* show themselves to man, they always do so in the half shape of something. One hunter reports that he once saw the *avlin* in the form of 'half-people' (humans with only half of the face, their body being vertically sliced); another reports having encountered them in the shape of deer with only half the antlers.

As a rule, *avlin* are benevolent: they harm neither man nor beast. Once, a story goes, a group of children got lost in the vicinity of Agaya Mountain and had to spend the night alone in the *taiga*. But, mysteriously, the following morning they were found near to the camp, without a scratch. Though not able to provide any details of what had happened, the children did remember being fed with candy and kept warm by 'someone' during the night. However, the event later turned out to have harmful effects, for it was followed by a number of unusual deaths among the households involved in the incident. Another popular story involves a domestic reindeer disappearing near Agaya Mountain, only to return several days later. By then it had grown oddly twisted and beautifully coloured antlers, and, when eventually milked, was found to have wild flowers in its milk (for an account and analysis of a similar tale among the neighbouring Darxad people, see Pedersen 2007a).

As the following story shows, the wild animals belonging to Agaya Mountain 'owner' are also being watched over by the *avlin*. Once, a hunter had been tracking a wild reindeer for several days. He finally managed to shoot it,

3. Mongolian concepts of property are too complex to discuss in any detail here, but it should be emphasized that the terminology and practices pertaining to the proprietorial authority over land are essentially similar in the case of humans and non-human *ezed*. Indeed, the term *ezen* (pl. *ezed*) is used for any entity recognized to be the 'master' or 'owner' of a given constellation of subjects (e.g., *geriin ezen*, 'master of the yurt', a status which designates also 'ownership' of the household's domestic animals; or *uulyn ezen*, 'master of the mountain', a status involving proprietorship over all life forms associated with the mountain, including the wild animals living in its vicinity). See also Humphrey (1996) and Sneath (2000).

only then to realize that he was uncomfortably near Agaya Mountain. Angered, the mountain spirit said to him: 'Why did you kill my animal?' The hunter was very scared, but, as it was getting dark, he had to spend the night on the spot. Upon awaking at dawn, he caught a glimpse of several half-people climbing the mountain. Turning around, he saw the wild reindeer rising from the spot where he had killed it the previous evening. The *avlin* had revitalized it. The hunter now looked at the mountain again, and at the very moment the half-people reached the top, a terrible blizzard broke out. Following this event, no one has hunted near Agaya Mountain. Instead, hunters occasionally go there to present offerings to its spirit owner.

This is not the place to make a comprehensive exegesis of the cultural context behind the above stories. Instead, I want to pursue a more specific point, namely that these stories seem to illustrate a general conception of the landscape as a fragmented totality of prominent places each surrounded by local fields of power. Indeed, the 'field' concept is particularly apt for describing the unfamiliar ontology described above, for this term conveys a recurring theme in Duxa animist thought, namely the idea of a focal point out of which beams of spiritual ownership somehow 'radiate' so as to produce a gradient halo-effect of non-human agency.

More stories could be retold to further substantiate that, while the Duxa landscape is imbued with many different kinds powerful places, they all seem to share the field morphology outlined above. As mentioned earlier, these places are not necessarily mountains, but also include freak trees (the so-called *böö mod*, or 'shaman trees') and other outstanding locations in the *taiga* or on the steppe. Often, the prominence of such places is explained as the result of shamans' actions in the past, as in the case of the burial places of deceased shamans (*ongod asar*), who, apparently, decided on these locations before passing away (see also Vainsthein 1996; Dioszegi 1963). Other places are considered prominent due to their connection to evil or unusual events which once occurred within particular households which used to live there. And, as we have seen, also the deeds (and misdeeds) of hunters continuously serve to instantiate particular qualities in the Duxa landscape. Finally, a significant number of places seem to be imbued with power simply because they are considered intrinsically beautiful, frightening or odd, such as in the case of the highest mountain, the fastest river, or the lone tree on the steppe (cf. Humphrey 1996).

The Duxa landscape, then, is heterogeneous. This should be understood both in the 'physical' sense, as a landscape consisting of different prominent places, and in the 'metaphysical' sense, as a landscape whose invisible qualities originate from the actions of different social agencies, be they human or non-human ones. In the Duxa landscape, then, it is not only that the multiplicity of prominent places adds up to a heterogeneous topography, it is also that their spiritual fields together constitute an ontology of heterogeneous powers.

If newer anthropological writings on landscape constitute the overarching theoretical framework behind this chapter, Bruno Latour's 'actor-network theory' (ANT) provides much of its theoretical vocabulary. Three ANT lessons are worthwhile to emphasize in light of the present analysis.

First, according to the ANT perspective, an actor is defined semiotically, that is, an actor is anyone or anything – be that a human or a non-human – 'granted to be the source of an action'. (Latour 1996: 374; see also Latour 1993: 62–65). Second, a network is neither just a social structure, nor is it simply a technological thing. A network is rather a sort of fragmented totality cross-cutting the domains of society (humans) and environment (non-humans), for it is comprised of all the connections that can be traced between a given constellation of human and non-human actors (cf. Latour 1996). Third, an actor-network is never homogeneous, it is always heterogeneous. A given actor-network is not confined to a finite, homogeneous territory demarcated by clear-cut boundaries; rather, it carries the potential of infinite expansion due to the unproblematic incorporation of all the kinds of actors, however different, the network may mobilize (cf. Latour 1993).

Now, if we paraphrase one of Latour's definitions of the actor-network by substituting the word 'networks' with 'Duxa landscapes', the following proposition appears: '[Duxa landscapes] are simultaneously real, like nature, narrated, like discourse, and collective, like society' (Latour 1993: 6). This theoretical rendition of the Duxa landscape is highly satisfactory. As we have seen, the Duxa clearly conceive their landscape as an arena of intentional actors, that is, as a quasi-social collective. The Agaya Mountain example showed that, while the Duxa evidently do not conflate humans with non-humans, they seem to incorporate a number of non-humans – such as the mountain 'owners' – into their concept of sociality. Also, the Duxa landscape is subject to an ever accumulating number of stories; that is, the landscape also takes the form of a narrative. Indeed, the ongoing narration of hunting stories is not only inseparable from what makes a Duxa hunter a good hunter, it is also constitutive for the perception of the environment as such, since, for a significant number of Duxa (notably the women), listening to hunting stories is all they will ever experience about certain places in the landscape, such as Agaya Mountain. Finally, the Duxa landscape is obviously also very real. The magnitude of its mountains, the strong currents of its many rivers, the bitter cold of the winter gales from the North – these all give rise to powerful bodily and aesthetic experiences (e.g., that the highest mountains are bound to have spirit masters) that are hard to overestimate.

Place and Space in the Duxa Landscape

Perhaps the most striking characteristic of the Duxa perception of the environment is their focus on places at the expense of spaces. As already hinted at, the fields radiating from non-human entities in the landscape have well-defined centres, but their external boundaries seem correspondingly ill-defined. Certainly, the case of the sacred mountains fits this characterization. As we saw in the above Agaya Mountain examples, the peak of this mountain unquestionably is the genius loci of the *avlin* spirits. Little attention, however, is paid to spatial boundaries in these and other stories. It is true that the hunter of wild reindeer 'suddenly realized' that he was near this mountain, but it is still impossible to establish any demarcation of the 'owner's' domain of influence from this story. The same goes for other Duxa narratives about this mountain. What really seems to matter is that something unusual took place in the *taiga*, and that this event was linked to the agency of the Agaya spirit, not so much where it happened.

I once asked a young Darxad herdsman to draw a map of the immediate landscape surrounding us. We were standing on top of a hilltop near the border zone between the *taiga* and the steppe, and the herdsman was very careful in his depiction of the various mountain peaks on the horizon. Many of these had 'owners' and each of these mountains/spirits had a particular nickname. Asked about the existence of boundaries (*xil*) in the landscape, my friend insisted that there were no boundaries at all. Perplexed by this answer, I asked him whether a highly sacred mountain pass in the far distance did not represent a boundary of sorts. After all, I added, people on the two sides of the mountain pass call themselves by different names, just as the two areas belong to different sub-districts (*bag*). But the herdsman persisted: his homeland was boundless (*xilgüi*), and the political distinctions were merely names of the land (*gazaryn ner*), not boundaries in the land.[4] Finally, I pointed towards a river at our feet, cross-cutting the entire view towards the west, and asked him whether this river did not define a boundary. But again he stressed the lack of spatial boundaries; in fact, judging from his laughter, my question about rivers as boundaries did not seem to make much sense to him.[5]

4. Not surprisingly, Mongolia's national borders present a quite different story. Indeed, given that the Duxa live at Mongolia's remote northern border, and may occasionally cross (illegally) into Russia to hunt, it seems that this national border has become embedded within their place-oriented nomadic landscape. Based on recent fieldwork among the Duxa, Wheeler thus argues that, for the Duxa nomads, 'the state as a [homeland], which is left behind and never occupied, becomes visible precisely at the point of movement from it' (Wheeler, forthcoming).
5. Of course, rivers do constitute natural barriers in the Darxad Depression, something that is clearly recognized by people at the level of everyday practice. Still, it is rather telling that the Mongolian word for river, *gol*, also denotes the idea of a centre. *Gol* is thus used for a range of 'intrinsically centred' phenomena, such as an 'aorta' (*gol sudas*), the 'heartwood of a tree' (*modyn gol*), the 'axle of a wagon' (*tergenii gol*); as well as, more metaphorically, a 'moral imperative' (*gol yos*) and what is 'most important' (*xamgiin gol*) (Hangin et al. 1986). This would seem to imply that, at least at the ideological level, rivers are conceived of as much as life-giving *cores* of the land as spatial boundaries constituting its outer fringes. Certain practices in Inner Mongolia seem to convey an analogous idea. There, local pastoralists treat the Great Wall not so much as an impassable obstacle for nomadic movement but, rather, as a particularly attractive route to follow in their annual migrations (Caroline Humphrey, personal communication).

In sum, it is my impression that, whereas few residents of the Darxad Depression will doubt that the genius loci of mountain 'owners' is the very heart of the mountains (the peaks), people will either disagree or not even know where the possible boundary between two mountain owners' realms goes. And, as the above example illustrates, this lack of spatial boundaries not only refers to the metaphysical qualities of the landscape, it refers to physical, ethnic, and political aspects as well (to the extent that this atomization into aspects of the landscape makes sense in the present case at all). Put differently, many domains of the Duxa landscape do not seem to be 'owned' by anyone in particular, be that humans or non-humans. At the same time, however, many specific locations in the landscape have 'owners', be they particular trees, lakes or – as we have seen – mountains.

So, whereas a number of places are imbued with particular qualities (spirit-powers), most of the spaces in between these places are ontologically neutral, that is, they are devoid of any invisible spiritual substance. This, of course, does not imply that such spaces are not perceived at all, it only means that they do not qualify as (permanent) loci of powerful non-human entities. This difference is also expressed in the different toponymical regimes employed for places and spaces respectively. Sacred places such as mountains are usually known by their nicknames, since enunciation and indeed knowledge of their real names is conceived of as dangerous, which is why this domain is left to the shamans to deal with. Names of spaces, on the other hand, such as administrative districts, are unproblematic to utter and are regarded as common knowledge.[6]

Nomadic and Sedentary Landscapes

Why, then, do the Duxa seem to highlight places at the expense of spaces? One good answer is that a topology of spaces and boundaries is not really workable when people constantly move from one place to another. The effect of a spatial boundary, one may argue, is to separate one finite domain from another, and one wider implication of such a demarcation seems to be the denial of frequent movement between such enclosed spaces. So what, one may ask, is the use of spatial boundaries when the nomadic lifestyle evidently implies their continuous crossing?

6. Arguably, many of Mongolia's *official* place names originate from now forgotten cases of such toponymical substitution. It certainly is striking that every fifty to a hundred kilometres place names such as 'White Lake' (Tsagaan Nuur) or 'Red Hill' (Ulaan Tolgoi) reappear across Mongolia's territory (Humphrey 1995). Given that the ruthless Communist persecution of Mongolia's shamans is recognized to have left a large gap in people's esoteric knowledge, it is entirely conceivable that the topogenic systems once used to link different patriclans to their respective shamanic burial grounds have now been forgotten, with the secondary effect that the former *nicknames* of these places have today acquired the role of official names.

Think about the herdsman who was asked to make a depiction of his landscape with respect to the different 'spirit-owners' inhabiting it. Evidently, the result was quite unlike a conventional political map using different colours to depict distinct, bounded territories. Instead, his representation was one depicting a multitude of dots in between which there were large gaps of unqualified space. Now think of the stereotypical Balinese landscape consisting of neat terraces of rice paddies, or, even better, the characteristic Northern European countryside with its well-demarcated agricultural fields, each consisting of a single and pure crop. Imagine an aerial photograph of such a landscape. Clearly, the result will be a pattern of different, finite spaces that, just like the political map, are internally homogenous and externally heterogeneous. Then imagine moving around within this configuration. This would seem to give rise to a feeling of spatial discontinuity; of having to jump from one pure domain to another.

Sedentary landscapes, I suggest, are precisely characterized by such finite, homogeneous spaces with clear-cut boundaries between them. For the Duxa and possibly also for other nomadic people as well, however, a dominant topology of places and boundlessness seems much more meaningful given their life on the move. Unlike the 'economy of spaces' characteristic of sedentary landscapes, the 'economy of places' characteristic of nomadic landscapes engenders neither boundaries nor finite spaces. Certainly, the Duxa economy of places has been shown to lead to something quite different, namely a multitude of spatial centres – or focal points – from each of which a (potentially) infinite spatial realm takes its beginning.

A given Duxa camp can thus be said to constitute a distinct place from which vectors point towards the different sacred mountains located at varying distances from it. From one camp, the main vectors will point towards, say, mountains A and B, and, from another, they will point towards, say, mountains C and D. However, neither encampment is for this reason enclosed within a finite space, nor can one talk of any clear-cut spatial boundary marking the transition from the one campsite to the other. Rather, the two camps differ with respect to the two unique configurations of powerful places that arise from their respective locations. What distinguishes a given point in this nomadic landscape, then, is the impure mixture of distinct places, not a purist demarcation into distinct spaces.

This brings us back to Latour. A given actor-network, we may recall, consists of different nodes – actors – from which threads towards disparate directions take their beginning. In principle, such a network knows no ending, it has no boundaries. Each node is the starting point of its own unique network, but any one such network is not qualitatively different from the network defined by another position, it is always a potential part of it. Movement within a network thus implies continuity; or what Latour calls 'translation', from one network to another, neither of which was ever pure. As Latour puts it, 'a network has no outside' (1996: 373).

In that sense, the distinct place defined by a Duxa encampment is the starting point of a temporary actor-network, i.e., a unique blend of human and non-human agents, and this actor-network will not differ in kind from the one instantiated by a neighbouring (past or future) encampment; it will only differ in degree. For a given Duxa camp is just one place among a number of places (e.g., camps) from where the human actors, who temporally reside there, are compelled to engage with the non-human actors, who (may) permanently reside there. A Duxa camp can therefore be said to constitute a distinct configuration of human agents temporarily embedded within a unique animist configuration of non-human agents; they must therefore seek to act within this actor-network to facilitate their desired effects, however mundane or esoteric these might be.

Landscape Inside-Out

It must be emphasized that the proposed difference between nomadic and sedentary landscapes does not assume the problematic existence of two monolithic cultures radically different in kind (cf. Gupta and Ferguson 1997). What in my view can be said to differ in kind is rather the two modes of spatial perception – the economy of place and the economy of space – which seem to be dominant in the two landscape-ontologies respectively. Neither spatial economy, I would argue, is restricted to particular socio-cultural settings. Instead, the two modes should be conceived of as universal spatial dispositions, which may or may not be foregrounded in a given form of social life. This, however, should not be understood in the hardcore mentalist sense that the materiality of the lived environment does not play a significant role in the cognitive construction of the two landscape-ontologies in question. Following Hutchins (1995: xiv), I rather take the softer position according to which cognition always occurs in the wild, in the form of an 'ecology of thinking in which human cognition interacts with an environment rich in organizational resources'. What have here been dubbed nomadic and sedentary landscapes, therefore, might alternatively be described as two complex socio-material nexi (viz. horizons of situated cognition) through which Mongolia's nomads navigate in a certain – but only to a very limited degree predisposed – way (see also Pedersen 2007 c).

So exactly what lies behind the apparent figure–ground reversal in the perceptual hierarchy between place and space outlined in this chapter? This brings me to another reservation that might be raised against my argument so far, namely that it appears to downplay the impact of politico-economic upheavals in the constitution of the two landscapes in question. Clearly, the dominance of the space-economy of northern Europe's sedentary landscapes is inseparable from particular Euro-Western histories of governmentality, rationalization, and secularization (see Berglund, this volume), just as the dominant place-economy of the Duxa nomadic landscape is intimately linked to the complex history of overlapping polities and empires within the Inner Asian region generally, and in north-western Mongolia specifically.

Elsewhere (Pedersen 2002 and 2007b), I have described the historical trajectories by which the current inhabitants of the Darxad Depression have come to be positioned at the extreme margin of the modern Mongolian nation-state. Without going into detail, it should be emphasized that we are not talking about one singular colonial narrative of Euro-Western hegemony here. The processes which have led to the current livelihood of the Duxa nomads date back at least 300 years, to the time when the (then) powerful Mongolian Buddhist church gained de facto sovereignty over most of the Darxad Depression within the overarching colonial framework of the Manchu empire. Confined to the outer periphery of this ecclesiastical estate, and being classified as 'external subjects' (*xariyat*) of the so-called Xövsgöl Urianxai Borderland (Wheeler, forthcoming), the predominantly Tuvinian inhabitants of the *taiga* gained a reputation as a bunch of wild shamanists, who, unlike their Darxad neighbours, had yet to taste the fruits of (Gelugpa) Buddhist civilization. Ironically, this process of stigmatization only gained momentum during Mongolia's seven decades of state-socialist rule, when the Duxa became the unwilling subjects of the often paradoxical discourses and interventions of Marxist cultural politics (cf. Grant 1995). Although the majority of the Duxa population was enrolled in Mongolia's collectivization programme from the mid-1950s, their proper integration into the planned economy was always subject to a good deal of official doubt. Indeed, a small group of mainly elderly Duxa were apparently deemed to be beyond the reach of historical-materialist progress, and were effectively left to 'nomadize' in the *taiga* in accordance with their 'backwards' pre-revolutionary way of life. It was against this historical background that, in the early 1990s, some descendants of the aforementioned group decided to settle in the *taiga* following the sudden collapse of the state-run hunting and fishing collective, which had hitherto constituted the social and economic basis of their lives (see also Wheeler 2000).

Like many other nomadic peoples, then, the story of the Duxa is one of extreme political, economic, and cultural marginalization. What makes the Duxa case quite unique, however, is not only the fact that most of them have only become (full-time) nomads quite recently, but also the fact that, in contemporary Mongolia, more than one third of the population is registered as nomads – a fact which, it should perhaps be noted, is highly appreciated by most Mongolians. So, where my previous analyses at first glance might appear to suffer from a traditionalist anthropological bias towards the study of small-scale societies mysteriously sheltered from wider political and economical processes, the truth is that the Duxa case seems to represent a particularly revealing illustration of the more general process in which, to turn Bloch's argument (1986) on its head, ideology is turned into cognition. For it is clear that, inasmuch as the unfamiliar landscape described above could be interpreted as a subaltern perspective construed in accordance with the counter-hegemonic agendas of a certain marginalized group (see, e.g., Day et al. 1999), this nomadic ideology nonetheless has significant ontological implications for those people whose life is on the move. After all, if the horizon within which one's navigation occurs is dominated by the sort of heterogeneous socio-geographical networks elucidated above, then it seems to matter precious little whether or not this nomadic landscape is, in fact, the indirect outcome of certain critical events that took place in late twentieth-century Moscow.

To conclude this section let me briefly consider a very different nomadic landscape, namely that of central London. For this cityscape can be conceived of as an environment that entails a reactivation of the place-economy – and consequently a deactivation of the space-economy – at the very heart of Euro-Western society. When travelling around London, and particularly with the London Underground, one's perception of the environment is clearly very place-oriented. Imagine taking the Tube from, say, Piccadilly Circus to Holborn. Even for long-time residents, the perception of these two domains of the central London landscape must be significantly moulded by the recurring experience of suddenly emerging above ground from the two underground stations respectively. Following an initial lack of orientation, one will focus on a significant place near or at the station – such as a tall building – and literally move on from there.

Central London, then, should perhaps not so much be described as a typical sedentary landscape characterized by bounded spaces and fixed boundaries (its many parks being a notable exception), but rather as a sort of urban nomadic landscape defined by prominent places, such as Underground stations, from which particular networks of both human and non-human actors take their beginning.

A Home Away from Homes

I now turn my attention to the Duxa perception of the landscape while they are on the move. In order to engage with this question, I will concentrate solely on Duxa migration. (Obviously, the Duxa interact with their environment in many other ways, such as when hunting, herding reindeer, or collecting firewood or pine nuts in the *taiga*.)

Migration among the Duxa is highly ritualized. When the Duxa move camp, they begin by packing up their belongings in a very specific order, and when they arrive at the new campsite, they end the journey by unpacking these things in exactly the reverse order. On either occasion each household also makes a sacrifice to the mountain 'owners' believed to preside over the given campsite. It is also significant that the Duxa do not tear down their tepees completely. Rather, just before departure, the men carefully take down the wooden poles of the tepee one by one and put these on the ground, only to leave a skeleton of naked poles. After that, the women carefully clean the inside ground of each dismantled tepee. When one travels through the Duxa landscape one occasionally notices these abandoned camp sites which, were it not for their characteristic wooden structures, would be indistinguishable from the surrounding environment (see also Wheeler, forthcoming).

Why are the Duxa so keen on carrying out these highly formalized practices; why do they not just move? To move camp is, although it happens frequently, a highly significant event. The day of migration is a special day, and potentially a dangerous day. Things may go wrong; the 'owners', for example, of either campsite might become offended by people's wrongdoings (such as forgetting to present them with a sacrifice). On a more implicit level, the ritual practices occurring at the new as well as in the old camp also seem to represent a celebration of place, or rather a facilitation of the transfer of spatial sensibility from one place to another. For when the Duxa carry out the same formalized practices, but in reversed order, at the new and old camp respectively, they seem to effect the lifting of the 'home-ish' qualities of their previous campsite to the new one. The Duxa's careful cleaning of the campsite to be abandoned also supports this point. Given the existence of the tepee skeletons at former campsites, it would however be wrong to say that the Duxa, when moving, reduce their former places of dwelling into unqualified, neutral space. Rather, the abandoned campsites continue their existence as distinct places; it is only that their home-ish qualities, by virtue of the aforementioned ritual practices, seem to be reduced to potentials now latent in these places. Indeed, like many nomads, the Duxa usually return to a former campsite the following year, thus rendering possible a reverse transformation of this place from a potential home into an actual one.

The Duxa, then, are not just packing up their various physical belongings to later unpack these at the new camp site. They also seem momentarily to wrap their metaphysical 'sense of place', to borrow a term from Feld and Basso (1996), only to start unwrapping this sensibility at the moment they reach their new home.

Turning now to the phenomenology of nomadic movement itself, the Duxa, whilst on the move, will ride in a certain order, just as they will follow particular tracks in the land and make great efforts not to stop, except at those places where, as I was told, 'people usually make a halt'. Amongst these, the so-called *ovoo* are particularly interesting. The typical Mongolian *ovoo* consists of a cairn of stones, although in forested regions some are made of tree branches (the form and function of these *ovoo* are identical to the stone type). Generally, *ovoo* are found at those places – in particular, mountain peaks and passes – known to be genii loci of land 'masters'. For the same reason, *ovoo* traditionally were bound up with the social reproduction of patrilocal clans, whose male members performed annual sacrificial rites (*ovoony taxilga*) at the *ovoo* site corresponding to the land appropriated by them (e.g., Heissig 1985). During communism, the *ovoo* institution lost most of its politico-religious salience. Today, the *ovoo* institution is being re-invigorated across Mongolia. On the one hand, this is happening in the form of elaborate sacrificial rituals involving politico-religious communities corresponding to local districts or sub-districts. On the other hand, the *ovoo* are also subject to more everyday ritual practices. When people, including the Duxa, travel in rural Mongolia many will stop at any given *ovoo* encountered on their way. Ideally, one must then pick up three stones and circumambulate the *ovoo* three times in a clockwise direction, each time throwing a stone at the *ovoo* and perhaps also making a silent prayer to the spirit it incarnates.

My concern here is not to analyse the systems of belief (whether shamanist or Buddhist) connected with *ovoo*. My more limited aim is to discuss what effects the aforementioned ritual actions have on the Duxa perception of their environment. Essentially, I want to argue that the highly formalized bodily practices performed at the Mongolian *ovoo* sites bring about a continuous re-evocation of the nomadic landscape. The fact that people circumambulate the *ovoo*, I believe, only further underscores my previous assertion that, in the nomadic landscape, places are highlighted at the expense of spaces. For, when the Duxa stop at an *ovoo*, they seem to instantiate a fixed point of reference resembling that of a given campsite. The *ovoo* circumambulation, in short, serves to (re)establish yet another node in the network of prominent places earlier described.

Keeping in mind the Duxa's nomadic livelihood, any given *ovoo* might therefore be described as 'a home away from homes'. Of course, like all homes that are not real homes, the *ovoo* site is not a site of permanent dwelling, but a temporary place of rest. But my point is that the Duxa, in order to activate this spatial refuge, must act in certain ways so as to intimate a perception of spatial finitude. As I shall show in the final section of this chapter, the practice of *ovoo* circumambulation, itself occurring within the wider framework of ritualized nomadic movement, serves momentarily to untangle the Duxa from the infinite nomadic landscape in which they are otherwise entangled whilst on the move.

Intimations of Finitude

We have seen that the animist geography of the Duxa landscape, taken together with the downplaying of bounded spaces seemingly inherent to nomadic livelihood, allow us to characterize the Duxa landscape as an actor-network.

Strictly speaking, however, the infinity of an actor-network is measured in relational, not spatial, terms. For Latour (1996), networks do not exist in a conventional space, where distances are expressed for example by 'near' and 'far'. Rather, an actor-network has a distinct topology in which a given extent is measured, vector-like, as either 'long' or 'short'. Consequently, a given actor-network is not suspended in a container of empty space, it rather contains itself by instantiating boundaries that paradoxically do not demarcate any limits (which is also why networks exist independently of concepts of inside and the outside). Strictly speaking, then, an actor-network cannot be described with reference to the category of space at all, for what really counts is the number of actors, or places, standing in a certain relationship to each other.

Yet the infinity of the Duxa landscape clearly is measured in terms of spatial limitlessness. In fact, and very much like the Euro-Western case (see Kirby, Chapter One, this volume), the Duxa (and more generally the Mongolian) perception of the environment is highly ocularcentric. To shamanists and Buddhists alike, the greatest power imaginable is the Sky (*Tenger*), which, being represented as simultaneously omnipresent and transcendental, is praised in countless prayers, songs, and tales. Immersed in an environment of often limitless views, and living under an 'eternal blue sky' (as they like to put it themselves), Mongolia's nomads have – at least in their own understanding – come to despise spatial confinement. However, this Mongolian 'space' is not quite the same as (modernist) Euro-Western space. At a less ideological level, the Mongolian steppe environment is thus perceived in a manner that brings to mind the 'non-insular' perspective from Island Melanesia, as described by Mondragón (this volume). As pointed out by several anthropologists, Mongolia's pastoralists conceive of the vast steppe expanses not as unified blocks of unqualified space severely restricting one's actions (as deserts or oceans are often represented in Western traditions), but rather as a limitless haecceity of potential action comprised by sociologically as well as spiritually distributed tracks and routes (i.e., vectors) cross-cutting domains that a Euro-Westerner would regard as ontologically distinct (Humphrey 1995; Pedersen 2001, 2007c; cf. Deleuze and Guattari 1999: 380 ff.).

My point, however, is that exactly this positivization of the limitless expanse renders necessary a converse fetishization of particular places. Following Strathern (1996), I would thus insist that man cannot tolerate being continuously part of an infinite actor-network: at some point he will need to 'cut it', somehow or another. So, if the Mongolian nomadic landscape can be described as an actor-network, then the Duxa must have developed particular ways of curtailing this infinite horizon of action.

This is exactly what the *ovoo* rituals, amongst other things, accomplish. Indeed the *ovoo* circumambulations seem to have a double impact with respect to Duxa manipulations of spatial perception. On the one hand, as we have seen, people's clockwise movements around the *ovoo* instantiate an anchored point from which the entirety of the environment can be apprehended – a spatial vantage from which people can loop into the infinity of the nomadic landscape, as it were. But, on the other hand, people's circumambulation of the *ovoo* also seems to make possible a simultaneous looping out of this landscape by enacting a sort of 'magic circle', within the nebulous perimeter of which a finite space is intimated. Try, thus, to imagine moving 360 degrees around an object, clockwise, as the Duxa do in the everyday *ovoo* ritual. If you look straight ahead, you are part of the motion. If you turn your head to the left, you fall out of the motion, towards an infinite expanse. If you look right, however, as people do when carefully throwing the stones at the *ovoo*, you fall into the axis of your motion towards an impermanently self-contained micro-cosmos. This is what I mean by 'looping out' of the nomadic landscape.

By way of conclusion, allow me to note the potentially significant fact that Duxa and Mongolian nomads alike prefer to live in round dwellings, or, we could say, permanently self-contained micro-cosmoses. The forest Duxa live, as already mentioned, in tepees (*orts*), whereas most pastoralist Mongols live in felt yurts (*ger*). The different architecture and symbolism of the two dwellings aside, their general design is similar in form as well as function, as are the highly formalized rules governing the manner in which both groups are supposed to navigate within these miniature landscapes. In fact, one might speculate whether a detailed analysis of the distinct modes of spatial perception within these dwellings would reveal a tension between the bounded and the limitless, between the finite and the infinite, very similar to the one that I have sought to expose in this chapter.

References

Badamxatan, S. 1987. 'Le Mode de Vie des Caatan Eleveurs de Rennes du Xövsgol', *Études mongoles et sibériennes* 18.

Bloch, M. 1986. 'From Cognition to Ideology', in R. Fardon (ed.), *Knowledge and Power: Anthropological and Sociological Approaches*. Edinburgh: Scottish University Press.

Day, S., E. Papataxiarchis, and M. Stewart. 1999. *Lilies of the Field: Marginal People who Live for the Moment*. Oxford: Westview Press.

Deleuze, G. and F. Guattari. 1999. *A Thousand Plateaus: Capitalism and Schizophrenia*. London: The Athlone Press.

Dioszegi, V. 1963. 'Ethnogenic Aspects of Darkhat Shamanism', *Acta Orientalia Hungaria* 16: 55–81.

Feld, S. and K. Basso. 1996. 'Introduction', in S. Feld and K. Basso (eds), *Senses of Place*. Santa Fe, NM: School of American Research Press.

Grant, B. 1995. *In the Soviet House of Culture: A Century of Perestroikas*. Princeton: Princeton University Press.

Gupta, A. and J. Ferguson (eds). 1997. *Culture, Power, Place: Explorations in Critical Anthropology*. Durham, NC: Duke University Press.

Hangin, G. et al. 1986. *A Modern Mongolian-English Dictionary*. Bloomington, IN: Research Institute for Inner Asian Studies.

Heissig, W. 1980. *The Religions of Mongolia*. London: Routledge and Kegan Paul.

Hirsch, E. 1995. 'Introduction', in E. Hirsch and M. O'Hanlon (eds), *The Anthropology of Landscape: Perspectives on Place and Space*. Oxford: Oxford University Press.

Humphrey, C. 1995. 'Chiefly and Shamanist Landscapes in Mongolia', in E. Hirsch and M. O'Hanlon (eds), *The Anthropology of Landscape: Perspectives on Space and Place*. Oxford: Oxford University Press.

———. 1996. *Shamans and Elders: Experience, Knowledge, and Power among the Daur Mongols*. Oxford: Clarendon Press.

Hutchins, E. 1995. *Cognition in the Wild*. Cambridge, MA: MIT Press.

Ingold, T. 1993. 'Hunting and Gathering as Ways of Perceiving the Environment', in K. Fukui and R. Ellen (eds), *Beyond Nature and Culture*. Oxford: Berg.

Latour, B. 1993. *We Have Never Been Modern*, trans. C. Porter. London: Harvester Wheatsheaf.

———. 1996. 'On Actor Network Theory: A few clarifications', *Soziale Welt* 47(4): 369–81.

Pedersen, M. A. 2001. 'Totemism, Animism and North Asian Indigenous Ontologies', *Journal of the Royal Anthropological Institute* 7(3): 411–27

———. 2002. 'In the Hollow of the Taiga. Landscape, Prominence and Humour among the Shishged Darxads of Northern Mongolia', Ph.D. dissertation. Cambridge: University of Cambridge.

———. 2003. 'Networking the Landscape: Space, Power and Decision-Making among the Tsaatang of Northern Mongolia', in A. Roebstorff, N. Bubandt and K. Kull (eds), *Imagining Nature: Practices of Cosmology and Identity*. Aarhus: Aarhus University Press.

———. 2007a. "Multiplicity Minus Myth. Theorizing Darhad Perspectivism". Special issue of *Inner Asia* 10(1), M. A. Pedersen, R. Empson and C. Humphrey (eds.).

———. 2007b. 'Tame from Within. Terrains of the Religious Imagination among the Darxads of Northern Mongolia', in U. Bulag and H. Dienberger (eds), *The Tibetan Mongolian Interface: Opening New Research Terrains in Inner Asia*. Proceedings from the 10th Seminar of the International Association of Tibetan Studies. Leiden: Brill.

———. 2007c. 'Talismans of Thought. Shamanist Ontology and Extended Cognition in Northern Mongolia'. In A. Henare, M. Holbraad and S. Wastell (eds.), *Thinking Through Things. Theorizing Artefacts Ethnographically*. London: Routledge.

Sneath, D. 2000. *Changing Inner Mongolia: Pastoral Mongolian Society and the Chinese State*. Oxford: Oxford University Press.

Strathern, M. 1996. 'Cutting the Network', *Journal of the Royal Anthropological Institute* (n.s.) 2: 517–35.

Vainsthein, S. 1980. *Nomads of South Siberia: The Pastoral Economies of Tuva*. Cambridge: Cambridge University Press.

———. 1996. 'The *Erens* in Tuva Shamanism', in V. Dioszegi and M. Hoppal (eds), *Shamanism in Siberia*. Budapest: Akademiai Kiado.

Wheeler, W. A. 1999. 'The Dukha: Mongolia's Reindeer Herders', *Mongolia Survey* 6: 58–66.

———. 2000. 'Lords of the Mongolian Taiga: An Ethnohistory of the Dukha Reindeer Herders', M.A. thesis. Bloomington, IN: Department of Central Eurasian Studies.

———. Forthcoming. 'Where is "Home" in a Nomadic "Homeland"? State Territoriality and Mobility among the Dukha Reindeer Herders of Mongolia', *Nomadic Peoples*.

Chapter 8
Toxins Without Borders: Interpreting Spaces of Contamination and Suffering

Peter Wynn Kirby

If the poisons are everywhere, you can move all you want but there's nowhere to go.
Awaki-san, Izawa resident

Introduction

The world's largest cities offer many attractions but are frequently most intriguing for the spaces in between: the nooks, alleyways, ghettoes, dumps, warrens, and local establishments hidden away there. In Tokyo – a megalopolis both fastidious and prone to neglect, depending on what's at stake – rather unremarked pockets of the capital can stir with life. Ramshackle structures or overgrown thickets of wan greenery in 'no-man's lands' tucked between buildings or elsewhere may seem uninhabited, even uninhabitable, but can be populated. Small cities of tarpaulin, twine, and cardboard – dwelled in by 'homeless' denizens at the fringes of some Tokyo parks – provide ready glimpses of an underclass living on the margins, albeit in the centre. Other 'pariahs' (including descendants of Japan's traditionally excluded out-caste of untouchables (*burakumin*)) live in fringe communities elsewhere in the city. But there also exist other groups of contemporary Japanese 'untouchables' – recent former members of mainstream Japan who fell ill or suffered other misfortune – who remain less well known. Ostracized by their neighbors, and sometimes driven away, they give testament to rips and unravellings in the social quilting of Japanese communities. Such de facto 'untouchables' frequently keep to themselves, more or less sequestered in the bleak spaces they find, and yet – as I show in this chapter – their understanding is crucial in interpreting a group-oriented, vertically configured society like Japan where social exclusion can be used to police group membership and reinforce solidarity. Movement for 'pariahs' like those I studied may be difficult, and yet sometimes, unbeknownst to observers, these social spaces in between allow the forging of new networks of relation and support that create new places to go and new worlds to inhabit.

Of course, 'space' in Japan has seduced outsiders for quite some time (e.g., Morse 1960 [1866]; Alcock 1863; for 'Japonisme', see for example Meech and Weisberg 1990), and the 'hyperspace' (Jameson 1999: 43) of certain architectural complexes or teeming districts of major Japanese cities has drawn considerable attention to visually seductive footage representing the sometimes intense, and often highly mediated, experience of life in urban Japan.[1] For social scientists, urban planners, architects, designers, and artists, not to mention journalists, the complexity, density, cultural otherness, and traditional legacy of Japan make mega-cities such as Tokyo seem like ideal social laboratories for (or vivid tableaux of) the developments and pressures of a globalizing, postmodern world (e.g., Rheingold 2003; Clammer 1997; Sassen 2001; Sorkin 1994). Furthermore, traces of Japanese traditional architecture and material culture that linger on in cities like Tokyo inspire imaginings of ways of life that bespeak poetry and elegance in striking contrast to the expanses of concrete development and the 'sea of signs' (Yatsuka 1990) that engulf present-day urbanites there.

Yet a real city exists there beneath the layers of rhetoric, ideology, nostalgia, and hype; daily life in urban Japanese communities offers urbanists and others an important, less-hyped alternative. Take communities facing vexing waste issues and miasmic conditions, for example. At a remove from the bright lights and flashy shopping districts, we can see the flipside of technology obsession, hyper-consumption, and large-scale disposal for which urban Japan is emblematic but certainly not unique: flows of (frequently at some stage toxic) waste and pollutants in cities that make waves, triggering a ripple-effect of community-wide responses as denizens struggle to protect themselves and their families from deleterious living conditions. Indeed, as I demonstrate here, sometimes movement in cities involves movement away.

This chapter takes contaminated community 'space' as its point of departure in probing the fraught political terrain of the contemporary Japanese wastescape and social exclusion there. The following pages scrutinize the dislocation that victims of extreme toxic illness can experience in contaminated communities and address the ways in which this dislocation can alter forms of 'Japanese' engagement with surroundings. In so doing, the chapter explores the implications of how concerns over threats to health altered established patterns of movement, leading to self-sequesterment in the home, the use of the automobile-as-refuge, elaborate evasive manoeuvres when out and about on foot, and even eventual exodus in order to reduce toxic exposure for some of the afflicted and their families. Other contributions to the present volume

1. While mass media coverage of mobile phone use in Japan, for instance, frequently involves sending a camera crew to one crowd-swarmed Tokyo street corner or another, a good and reasonably well-contextualized airing of these sorts of images of Tokyo would be the film *Lost in Translation*.

furnish theorizations of movement in different social contexts and bring a sense of ethnographic emplacement through their writing; this chapter, to balance out the volume, puts relatively more emphasis on how socio-cultural reckonings of relation, proximity, and exclusion can be undermined and demonstrates the impact this collapsing of boundaries can have on movement, identity, and community. First, I examine the initial social and political fallout surrounding toxic emissions from a contested waste facility located in the centre of Izawa, a Tokyo community where I conducted research. I then delve more deeply into how the scourge of toxic damage altered afflicted residents' 'top(ont)ological' conceptions and embodied experience of their community – and describe subsequent political agitation and ostracism that further intensified victims' sense of alienation in a zone that became utterly transformed. Throughout, I make reference to the tension between Japanese society's complex logic of relationality – embedded in both traditional and contemporary ideas of hygiene, purity, and exclusion – and the movement of people, pollutants, and political alliances in a dense, non-'Western' city that belies static conceptions of space.

Living with Toxic Waste: 'Location, Location, Location'

Due to the exigencies of waste policy, one of my field-sites – a quiet community called Izawa,[2] located in western Tokyo – became a key flow-channel in the macro-functioning of Tokyo. Without becoming too swept up in recent globalist rhetoric, Tokyo is, like all cities, in essence an aggregation of flows. The introductory chapter to this volume adds a voice to a growing chorus of critics (Tsing 2000; Jameson and Miyoshi 1998) who see globalist ideas such as 'flow' as concepts invoked far too frequently as some sort of *ne plus ultra* metonym of transnational processes, often to the diminution or exclusion of other important elements of socio-cultural inquiry, such as human-scale action. Scepticism of scholarly focus on flow should not, however, lead to an underemphasis on flows encountered ethnographically, and along with those movements of capital, labour, and culture more commonly focused upon in analyses of 'global' cities (Sassen 2001; Kirby, Chapter One, this volume), extensive flows of waste and pollutants (and linked environmental illness) in Tokyo expose an oft-unspoken, miasmic underbelly of the global city

2. Such characterizations are based on informants' recollections. Throughout the chapter, I excerpt quotations from both field interviews (conducted intermittently between August 1998 and October 1999 and between September 2005 and April 2006, as well as during ten other shorter field trips to Tokyo) and responses to questionnaires handled by the Izawa-based protest group.

phenomenon. Some of these waves of waste and pollution are experienced in ambient forms throughout the megalopolis. But to the extent that toxic waste always has specific sources or sites of concentration, particularly at processing and disposal sites, certain hapless communities in Tokyo found themselves vulnerable to unexpectedly high levels of toxic pollutants; this exposure reflected state-level calculus selecting specific, often lower-income, areas as acceptable for greater proximity to risk (Beck 1992). Izawa, one of two communities I studied in western Tokyo, discovered itself an unwitting host to particularly noxious and profuse toxic residues, subjecting a considerable proportion of residents to symptoms that ranged from merely frustrating to debilitating and grave. Below, I describe some of the factors involved in Izawa's peculiar toxic waste predicament before delving into the ethnographic murk of residents' experiences of toxic anxieties and toxic damage in the contaminated precincts of the community.

In waste macro-management, as in other sectors, location counts. When Azuma Ward[3] agreed to allow a metropolitan waste facility built within its boundaries, ward authorities hit upon Izawa as a highly favourable location. Nestled alongside the ward border and intersected by a major thoroughfare heading out of the capital, Izawa was both convenient in terms of access and in terms of political and socio-economic concerns; being coterminous with another ward, the site reduced the potential level of exhaust exposure of Azuma residents and, furthermore, Izawa was less affluent than many communities in Azuma Ward and by extension in possession of less political capital. (These points raise, of course, the question of which bodies 'matter'. In bureaucrats' and politicians' calculus, poorer and extra-ward bodies apparently seemed less deserving of consideration – though officials declined to discuss these policy dimensions. Naturally, this logic of risk is hardly exclusive to Japan (e.g., Casper 2003).) But unlike waste incineration complexes and other 'trouble facilities' (*meiwaku shisetsu*) like nuclear plants, all of which inflamed opposition in Japanese communities after the more acquiescent and holistic early decades of the postwar period (Lesbirel 1998; Broadbent 1998), the proposed facility was assumed to be bereft of the kinds of toxic complaints that typically alienate local residents and doom present-day waste planning. For the complex was to be only a waste transfer facility (*gomi chūkeisho*), a way station that would allow waste to be moved (from smaller trucks able to navigate the narrow byways of the capital), then compressed with extreme force by huge compactors, and finally placed in containers loaded onto larger trucks that could deliver the waste more economically to landfill sites sometimes far from the capital. Since none of this

3. Based on the terms of my interviews with Tokyo informants (some of whom were willing to go on the record, many of whom were not), 'Azuma' Ward and Izawa are pseudonyms, as are most of the names given in this chapter. I have made some adjustments to other distinctive details elsewhere while attempting to preserve as much ethnographic detail as possible.

waste was to be incinerated, the *chūkeisho* was billed as a benign facility that, far from harming the community, would bring state-funded amenities to Izawa without the usual risks of proximity to waste and its processing. (I describe some of these deal sweeteners, and disputes surrounding them, in a later section.)

Given the pressures of waste collection throughout the megalopolis, the financial and logistical efficiencies Izawa's facility offered (convenient access and the means to compress waste bound for disposal sites – some charging by the container-load, rather than by weight) made the Izawa facility an important node in the capital's waste network, with millions of tons of waste flowing through Izawa annually. Designers opted not to follow the example of another waste complex in western Tokyo, the 'cleansing facility' (*seisōkōjō*, a common euphemism for incinerator) at Takaido, which had a half-kilometre subterranean passage connecting the facility to a nearby highway to reduce unpleasant toxic, olfactory, and noise emissions into the residential community there. The Tokyo Public Cleansing Bureau chose to make the facility relatively unobtrusive otherwise, however – in ways that suited its ends. For example, instead of providing an elaborate ventilation apparatus, like the chimney some 480 feet tall at Takaido, the bureau decided on a far more modest exhaust tower that attempted to disguise its purpose.[4] Incessant truck movement through the community, however, did not go unnoticed. Izawa residents complained of putrid odours emanating from both the trucks and, reportedly, from the facility – this despite the fact that the *chūkeisho*'s design as an underground complex four floors deep was supposed to help control the emission of waste fumes and reduce noise pollution.

While the subterranean design and other features of the *chūkeisho* helped 'sanitize', to a certain extent, the presence of waste in close proximity, numerous residents responded that, even before the advent of toxic consciousness there, they were uncomfortable with the idea of waste from literally millions of Tokyo households moving through the precincts of the community. A young female office-worker summed up this attitude by saying, 'It feels a little weird (*chotto kimochi warui ne*)'. (Below, I explain Japanese distancing protocols designed to segregate 'social pollution' that, through their collapsing, made this discomfort with proximity to pollutants more acute.) Some of those who rejected environmental protests in Izawa admitted that, incentives aside, they would have preferred the facility elsewhere (though most who did were quick to add that this preference had nothing to do with any

4. From most of the park, a ventilation tower some nine metres tall standing at the top of a small rise is the only visible sign of the subterranean waste facility buried under Izawa's 'Forest Park'. The tower's rendering, somewhat reminiscent of the architecture of I. M. Pei and matching two pyramidal skylights embedded nearby in the grass and hedges of the hillock, uses transparent plastic panels and an angular crown design to give these elements the veneer of high-tech. These protrusions also appear autonomous, as if they were not appendages of the facility at all but, rather, mere sculptural features of the park.

perceived toxic threat, which they challenged).[5] Intentionally generous incentives that the Metropolitan Government dangled in front of community leaders for siting the facility in Izawa eventually closed the deal and went a long way towards alleviating unease with any waste-related associations of (social) pollution for many in the community.

The *chūkeisho* was, strategically, built beneath parkland. The state began negotiating for access to a plot of wooded, relatively 'wild' land in the centre of the community (a small part of which was once the site of a state institute for machine technology) that had become a rare trove of verdure in an otherwise highly constructed area of the megalopolis. Government authorities proposed to re-landscape the wooded land (making it conform more closely with notions of tidiness and control that epitomize contemporary Japanese ideals of 'nature' (Berque 1997b; Asquith and Kalland 1997; Kerr 2001; Kirby 2004)), creating a far more tailored public resource than the 'neglected' wooded expanse had been. In addition to more extensive grassy open spaces and severe extirpation of undergrowth, the plan for the 'Forest Park', as it came to be called, was to add a sports field, a rock garden, a playground, flowers, a recreation centre, and the familiar augmentation of cherry trees ringing the park confines (the last dendrological feature being virtually *de rigueur* in contemporary Japanese public landscaping (cf. Moeran and Skov 1997)). Furthermore, the ramped truck entrance to the waste transfer facility was placed behind a man-made hillock and screened behind trees and shrubbery, creating what was effectively a 'natural' veil to obscure facility operations as park-goers consumed the recreational resources available on the other side.

While most of the community was, in the end, won over by these incentives and lifestyle concessions, a minority of residents was opposed to transforming the sylvan tract. For example, many owners of houses along the street facing the proposed 'Forest Park' were wary of the plan to transform the land, which had been a verdant backdrop beyond their stoops and windows for many years in some cases. And when, in the end, the city stripped the 'Forest Park' of considerably more trees than originally indicated, some residents in the area believed this was an intentional deception and expressed irritation at the sudden change from woods to (rather denuded) 'forest'.[6] The combined effect of the noise of trucks, the stench of waste, displeasure with the capital's intervention into the community's most prized amenity, and discomfort with

5. More than a few also pointed out that *some* community had to take the facility. This stereotypically group-focused Japanese response has become less common in recent decades (cf. Broadbent 1998; Lesbirel 1998), and has to be understood in the context of a divisive protest in progress – those who did not sympathize with protesters sometimes characterized them not only as hypochondriacs but as selfish as well.
6. Contemporary Japanese development projects, whether public or private initiatives, are full of such Orwellian euphemisms as 'Forest Park', indexing greenery or wildlife or breathtaking vistas in the relative (or, frequently, total) absence of the 'real' thing (e.g., Kerr 2001).

massive amounts of Tokyo's waste streaming through the area, meant that the imposition of the *chūkeisho* did not go uncontested or uncriticized. It also constituted one visible level of transformation in the community that would help contribute to the sense of dislocation that residents experienced.

But it was upon growing recognition of an invisible toxic threat in the community that the social mapping of the Izawa community became destabilized, distorting existing patterns of relation and transforming the Izawa facility from a sought-after boon to a divisive flashpoint. Below, I describe the discovery of a toxic scourge in the community and its socio-political repercussions before moving on to discuss the ways in which this environmental health problem split the community and led to distressing shifts and adjustments in engagement and movement in the area.

Perils of Proximity

> *When I went for a stroll through the Forest Park the day it opened, I could feel something was wrong. My eyes got really irritated and they started watering. The next morning, there were these thin rashes on my cheeks where the tears had streamed down my face. Talk about a bad omen! I was really shocked, but those tears were the least of my worries, and they certainly weren't my last.*
>
> Tsubō-san

The toxic fallout from the operations of the waste transfer facility in Izawa was nearly immediate, though political fallout was delayed by the indeterminate nature of toxic pollution and features of Japanese social topography in the community. *Chūkeisho* operations commenced in April 1996. Though protesters insist that they did not at first make a connection between the facility's waste processing and their own worsening health, soon after the waste began flowing through the facility members of the community began to contract mysterious combinations of symptoms (including headaches, shortness of breath, burning eyes, hacking coughs, insomnia, acute skin rashes, swollen glands). Because many of these complaints occur in all sorts of living environments in a wide range of circumstances and can accompany common sicknesses such as bronchitis, colds, and influenza (or even simply stress, overwork, and sleep deficit – not at all uncommon in urban Japan), at first many of these cases were seen to be difficult, even troubling, but not necessarily alarming. Indeed, in this light it is important to recall that toxic pollution is nearly impossible to discern and isolate without recourse to scientific measurement (Beck 1992; Berglund 1998); toxic substances such as dioxins[7] are tasteless, odourless,

7. Dioxins (deadly carcinogens that rank as the most lethal of all man-made substances) were only the most dreaded item on a long list of toxins that protesters argued contaminated the air in and around the waste transfer facility, claims supported by technoscientific studies they commissioned.

and invisible, and the health problems that they cause are all too easily explained away as the result of any number of lifestyle choices or seasonal and meteorological vicissitudes. (Burning eyes and feeling under the weather during pollen season are far from unusual complaints in Japan, as elsewhere, for instance.) But for the most severe cases, and even less serious cases over time, the destabilizing effects of toxic pollution and declining health led to shifts in how residents experienced their surroundings and engaged with their community on a variety of levels.

One day in early April 1996, Tsubō-san, a diminutive woman then in her sixties, was assaulted by noxious fumes. 'It was like a bomb exploded in the middle of my life. Until you've felt [such a thing], you can't imagine what it's like'. In its aftermath, nothing in her life felt the same. Her skin and breathing were the first casualties – after a difficult exploratory stroll through the new 'Forest Park', described above, she later began coughing violently with intense pain in her throat. Her saliva developed a bitter taste and, with swelling in her oesophagus, she frequently found she could no longer swallow it down. Yet this, unfortunately for Tsubō-san, was only the beginning. Her leg muscles cramped severely and, when she went to a medical clinic to investigate, her blood pressure had surged to 195 systolic, far above her normal readings. Her thinking became languid and hazy, as if she were floating her way through the days. She felt that, if anything, symptoms like laboured breathing and extraordinary chest pressure helped keep her from drifting away entirely.

The first indication that Tsubō-san's afflictions might be the result of a scourge within her community came when she travelled to a clinic outside the area and her cough and sore throat disappeared. (Upon returning, symptoms rematerialized.) Stress and nerve-related irregularities became so acute that she found her limbs beginning to shake. 'My hands trembled like leaves on a tree', she confessed. 'It got to where I couldn't even keep a simple diary [for recording symptoms] anymore'. Her condition reached its apogee from the life she only now dimly remembered when she could no longer breathe and an ambulance came to take her away. Even in the hospital, mere contact with clothes or utensils from her Izawa home caused severe reactions, so that through friends and family she was forced to buy daily necessities anew.

Tsubō-san was the first resident afflicted with what came to be called Azuma Disease. And while friends and neighbours were aware that she had been evacuated from the area, only over time and through informal networks of communication such as local gossip did they come to associate her predicament with their own health complaints. Indeed, there was an almost epidemiological character to the spread of information regarding the mysterious blight plaguing the community. Early concern with ill-health, or with ill friends or neighbours, created pockets of anxiety that seeded discontent and grew to plague the community. Residents began to discern commonalities;

close neighbours exchanged stories and made contact with family, friends, or acquaintances in more distant neighbourhoods in overlapping circuits of discourse. One of these, Awaki-san, a middle-aged woman who lived near Tsubō-san, had a difficult cough, pain in her eyes, skin problems, and trouble breathing. Her finger joints began to swell up abnormally. Having learned of her neighbour's condition, she began taking her own deteriorating health more seriously until she became convinced that this was no passing illness. Eager to give me visual proof of her plight during an interview, Awaki-san held out her hands: the sections of finger between joints were, to be sure, reddened and puffed up. Perhaps underwhelmed by my laconic reaction, however, she then produced more dramatic photographic evidence: on sheets of colour-copied paper, she had assembled pictures of violent skin rashes, strange protuberances, and other irregularities that had appeared on her parents' and children's bodies since the waste facility had commenced operations. She then went on: 'It's too embarrassing to show you, but I have swelling all over as well. Lymph nodes. … You wouldn't believe what it's like'. Hesitating, and apparently reconsidering, Awaki-san then produced another colour-copied page with a photograph of blue-veined breasts (hers) with lumps and discolourations. Though the political stakes involved in showing an ethnographic researcher striking images (that could lead to wider coverage of Izawa's plight) cannot be ignored, the gesture made it seem as if, in the wake of this toxic scourge, all shame had been lost (cf. Edelstein 1988).

Like Tsubō-san, Awaki-san, too, noticed that many of these symptoms would subside when she left the community. But it was only over time, and upon finding out more about other neighbours' own localized reactions, that afflicted members of the community determined that the waste transfer facility in the area was the source of their troubles. A number of them organized themselves into the Group to End Azuma Disease (*Azuma-Byō wo Nakusu-Kai*, hereafter referred to as the GEAD); after commissioning scientific evidence demonstrating that the facility was emitting dangerous toxins, these protesters began to counter (in their mind, politically tainted) state evidence to the contrary and to pressure the ward and metropolitan governments to shut the facility down. The machinations of the state (eager to keep this facility operational by misrepresenting and even suppressing negative scientific and other evidence, actions that came to light most dramatically during ward and metropolitan hearings) and the activities of the GEAD (equally eager to call attention to the toxic dangers of the facility and the mendacity of the state) created a 'toxic' political atmosphere that influenced greatly the experience of living in Izawa at this time (analysed in more detail in Kirby 2003 and Kirby 2004). Below, I focus on the extent to which the toxic contamination of this community led to different ways of conceiving of, experiencing, and moving through the precincts of Izawa that both aid and benefit from a nuanced reading of contemporary Japanese socio-cultural practices.

Spaces of Contamination

The mysterious toxicity of the pollution circulating through Izawa made those afflicted with Azuma Disease feel violated – sufferers began to conceive of their environs as contaminated, even hostile – and interpretation of this alienation begs a deeper analysis of prevalent Japanese ideas of relation and exclusion. Japanese social history, like that of many other parts of the world (e.g., Deliége 1999; Douglas 1966, 1992; Parker 1983), bears witness to ingrained notions of social pollution that can help interpret the political terrain of toxic pollution in contemporary Japan. Largely after Tokugawa-era Japan was organized into a strict hierarchy of different social strata, with an 'untouchable' out-caste at the bottom whose role it was to carry out polluting tasks deemed unsuitable for higher ranks – such as slaughter and the handling of animal carcasses (expressly condemned in Buddhist scripture (Davis 2000)) – Japanese communities developed a finely calibrated system of spatial practices that acted to keep undesirable external influences from contaminating the home and to segregate pollution within the home (Ohnuki-Tierney 1984; Pezeu-Massabuau 1981). And while the thresholds of these different domains might remain unrecognized by an outsider, movement within Japanese communities entailed the penetration and/or avoidance of zones that made navigating within Japanese communities a far more nuanced and complicated enterprise than simply drifting through empty 'space'.

While much in contemporary Japan has changed in recent decades, one key element of Japanese life that has not changed markedly is the constellation of spatial logics bound up in hygienic practices there. Traditionally, Japanese society depended on an elaborate set of protocols designed to cleanse people when they encountered spaces (and/or periods) of contamination. Largely informed by a Shinto, or animist, reckoning of sites of good or bad energy that dotted the landscape, sometimes spawned by auspicious or accursed events, an elaborate set of rites allowed Japanese to manage the pollution that came from moving through hazardous spaces, from travelling (i.e., vulnerability to communicable disease), from contact with dead bodies, from proximity to outcasts, and so on (e.g., Namihira 1977, 1984, 1985; Miyake 1996, 1977; Sakurai 1970, 1988). Most of these practices have atrophied considerably, but the social logic of contamination and purification lingers on in Japanese society, with inevitable permutations.[8] Awaki-san's husband, who was an executive in a small high-tech company, described the reaction of the community in terms of Japan's history of avoidance and ostracism (*mura hachibu*):

8. I explore this question in greater detail in an unpublished manuscript entitled *Troubled Natures: The Politics of Waste in Japan* (Kirby [under review])

> Back when people lived in villages, say, in the mountains … there were contagious disease epidemics (*densenbyō*) … like tuberculosis, for instance. … If someone got sick, the family wouldn't say. If at all possible, they wouldn't [tell anyone]. Because if they did, not just that one person, but everyone in that family would be driven out of the area completely. What's called *mura hachibu*, getting driven from the village. … Well, just like that, here with Azuma Disease I don't know if they'd call it a contagious disease (*hayari-yamai*) per se here, but there's a mysterious (*etai wo irenai*) illness.

In numerous informants' households all over Tokyo, when family members returned home they would disinfect their hands and gargle with mouthwash, particularly in winter when contagious illnesses were deemed to be rampant. These efforts were used to limit exposure of the interior of the home to *baikin*, or germs, a concept closely related to the perceived danger and filth of the outside sphere (explored comprehensively in Ohnuki-Tierney 1984). Koda-san, an informant in her forties who lived in another Tokyo community, explained it like this: 'My father and uncle are doctors, so when we were kids we all washed our hands and gargled right after we came back [home]. That way, we knew that it would be safe (*anshin*)'. Squeamishness with the outside and the unknown shaped domestic choreography fundamentally. To put it bluntly, 'inside' in Japan is typically associated with cleanliness and social warmth, while 'outside' implies social distance and has associations with impurity and possible disease.[9] This distinction is reflected for example in Japanese domestic spatial practice, where people remove their footwear before entering the home, leaving the dirt of the outside sphere behind on the soles of their shoes. Yet even within contemporary homes, and even within 'Western-style' homes, there exist zones of relative purity and impurity well segregated from each other. For example, almost all Japanese toilet rooms offer a dedicated pair of slippers to wear upon entering. This allows undesirable germs on the floor to remain within the toilet area rather than spreading to the rest of the home. Furthermore, nearly all my informants' homes, even tiny studios, had separate outdoor sandals or slippers on open-air balconies that they would wear when hanging wet laundry, for example. Since many Japanese like to wear yet another pair of ordinary indoor slippers in the home (particularly in colder months) and usually remove these before stepping into rooms floored with tatami mats, moving about a Japanese home could become

9. *Uchi*, a term for 'inside' or '[my] home', also enjoys a wider social usage, invoked metaphorically to index 'my' group or 'my' corporation in contrast to someone else's. This usage is highly relational, as well as plastic, so that while the cadastral and structural boundaries of the home are relatively fixed, ideas of social inclusion and exclusion can be adapted to one's emergent networks (cf. Kondo 1990).

a laborious balancing act of footwear changes, though one to which Japanese residents were fully accustomed.[10]

If the interior of the home can symbolize a (relatively) unpolluted realm for many Japanese, where what impure elements exist are rarely 'out of place' (Douglas 1966), then the prospect of airborne toxic pollution in the community becomes deeply unnerving. Even the purest part of the home, which might be the formal *tatami* room often reserved for guests or the baby's crib or futon, were likely to be just as tainted as anywhere else.

The impact of this reconceptualization of surroundings in Izawa was concussive. What once seemed familiar and reassuring became hooded, oppressive, a source of unease. No one seemed to know the extent of the danger or how to avoid it. Residents suffering from toxic exposure in Izawa complained that they had to keep their windows tightly shut at all times, this in a society where open windows traditionally provide a cherished alternative to air-conditioning – particularly at night in summer months, when the air cools down. (Depending on the household and the condition of its occupants, this domestic lock-down sometimes did little, if anything, to alleviate symptoms on the one hand or toxic anxieties on the other.) Residents were also quick to point out that they even felt unable to hang their laundry or bedding out in the air to dry, as was their custom. This latter point is extremely resonant for most Japanese. On sunny days in Japan, even in winter, Japanese buildings are festooned with laundry and futon mattresses hanging over railings in an effort to take advantage of the perceived healthfulness of the sun's rays – a few of my informants, lacking available space, would even drape their futon mattresses over a newly washed automobile outside. Yet with toxins apparently swirling around in the air and omnipresent in the community, many residents were unwilling to expose their homes and their bodies, through contaminated laundry and bedding, to the toxins around them. This feeling deepened when residents noticed traces of 'dirty' air left on their laundry frames. (Of course, those most sensitive, like Tsubō-san, mentioned above, had to discard their old clothes and bedding entirely to avoid toxic reactions.) But despite these extreme measures, few of those afflicted with Azuma Disease felt free of contamination in their homes. While attempting to seal off the domestic interior appeared to help periodically, more often sufferers reported how the space of the home became so foul that they despaired of ever succeeding in

10. While there is a great deal of interpretation of and improvisation within these codes of hygienic practice – like, for example, whether or not one steps onto the 'polluted' floor when putting on footwear – for the most part it is striking how enduring and pervasive these conceptions of hygiene have remained since the (albeit mythologized) days of raised wooden *geta* clogs and houses on stilts. For a detailed analysis of hygienic dimensions of Japanese traditional and contemporary architecture, as well as polysemic notions of 'pollution', refer to Ohnuki-Tierney 1984.

returning to the 'normal', healthy life they remembered having before the waste transfer facility commenced operations. Some complained of smelly, filthy water pouring from the tap and sharp reactions while bathing. Others found their 'allergies' were far worse, even while sequestered indoors, and found that they were falling ill with far greater frequency.[11]

The enveloping, all but inescapable, toxicity of the air that sufferers experienced led to a sharp transformation in the social topography of the community and, by extension, movement there. Like some celestial black hole of immense force come to earth, the buried waste facility loomed large in the minds of those afflicted with Azuma Disease, pulling at their thoughts even at a distance. There were those residents who could no longer move save shuffling around in their homes, better off than the bedridden but only just – they continued to feel human (somewhat) only through visits from friends and family, visits that sufferers, indeed, tried to discourage lest loved ones fall ill as well. But ambulant residents faced difficulties of their own. If afflicted residents took a walk, they might now choose a far-flung route to avoid any proximity to the waste facility and might even plan their itinerary literally with regard to which way the wind was blowing that day. Early on, those with acute cases (like Kōga-san, a male retiree in the area) might wait to go outside until they thought the wind had changed direction so as to decrease their exposure to what they termed the 'smoke' (*kemuri*) coming from the facility. Some sufferers discerned seasonal variations in patterns of exposure, one meteorological contribution to the upsurge in local brainstorming, even conspiracy-theorizing, as residents struggled to interpret the problem. For example, a man in his twenties who had lived in Izawa for three years tried to make sense of his newfound condition, explaining, 'My [skin problems] have gotten dramatically worse (*atopī no akka ha ichijirushiku*) … especially in winter [with] the north wind … I'm going to the hospital all the time like when I was a kid … my symptoms [change] a lot with regard to the direction of the wind'. Given these hostile environs, those with cars might drive short distances within the community rather than walk in the open air or choose to patronize shops and businesses far from the immediate community. One couple I

11. In time, these domestic concerns – sometimes invoked by opponents as partial proof that ambient toxic pollution did not exist in the community – were vindicated. Five years after the facility opened, Tokyo's government continued to deny that facility operations routinely created toxic emissions but admitted that rotting waste and other unanticipated toxic irregularities in a catchment tank beneath the facility had allowed chemical gases to spread through Izawa's sewage system, entering residents' homes through drains such as in their bathrooms and spreading throughout their homes. Protesters, while welcoming this rare acknowledgement of local illness and admission of culpability, argued that this did not nearly go far enough; for instance, it did not explain the many cases of toxic illness on the far side of Azuma Ward's border, just a stone's throw away from the facility but under a different administration and therefore with a separate sewage network.

interviewed closed down the small business they ran near the waste facility, partly because running it entailed spending long hours, daily, within the perceived toxic zone. If, as Lynch suggests, the spatial experience of living in a community can be understood through the landmarks by which people choose to orient their (practical and mnemonic) navigations (Lynch 1960), then the waste facility itself became a negative landmark, a site to be avoided, and yet which loomed in the mind as an undesirable spectre of insalubrity. And as residents' iterative ambits throughout the community shifted with regard to the field of 'reverse-gravity' their aversion to the facility created, it became increasingly difficult for the afflicted to recognize the intimate contours of their community through the toxic anxiety.

The social repercussions were severe and created complex knock-on effects that hit different community factions in divergent ways in what became a politically fragmented social terrain. On the part of those battling Azuma Disease, once the affliction began to take its toll, sufferers in the community found it very difficult to separate their feelings of ill-health from their attitudes towards Izawa itself. Echoing in a sense Watsuji's nativist conceit of *aidagara* ('betweenness') (Watsuji 1975), which he believed distinguished social engagement in the Japanese milieu, Japanese informants described Tokyo as comprised of sites of intensive relationality. Between the familiarity of a person's home and community and the familiarity of their place of work, for example, can be an indeterminate, acontextualized liminal zone of 'colourless indifference' (Berque 1997a: 90–95) where a lack of relations led to a lack of emotional engagement (compare with place-focused nomadic and animist 'landscape-ontologies' described by Pedersen with reference to Mongolia, or the 'meshwork' of Ingold (both this volume)). Along this theme, Lock (1980: 255) writes, 'The average Japanese is interested in the problem of pollution, for example, not in its global aspects, but only insofar as it affects one of the groups to which he or she belongs'. The flipside of this coin is that, when one's community is afflicted by this pollution, the relational mapping, and affective ties, of the area can be utterly changed.

In Izawa this result was magnified by the contested nature of the pollution. To be sure, in notorious cases of extreme toxic contamination such as in Bhopal or in Chernobyl, relatively straightforward evidence of considerable human suffering is complicated enormously by factors such as difficulties in definition and quantification of illness, political jockeying by interested parties, and inequities in access to information and resources for those most debilitated by the environmental disaster in question (Fortun 2001; Petryna 2002). Whereas in Izawa, where toxic defilement was not – objectively speaking – nearly so catastrophic as in these aforementioned environmental debacles, heated infighting ensued as to whether any toxic pollution existed at all. According to systematic GEAD studies (corroborated by my own investigations), approximately 10 per cent of the population living within 500 metres of the facility reported toxic symptoms that, in aggregate, came to be called Azuma Disease. While numerous residents suffered disastrous symptoms due to the presence of toxins in their midst – measured by a Tokyo-based academic toxicologist originally commissioned by the Tokyo government who saw his findings twisted by the state and who then conducted subsequent measurements under GEAD auspices – other members of the community relatively unaffected by the pollution found it very difficult to accept protesters' claims. Some unaffected parents, furthermore, had children manifesting symptoms. Afflicted members of the community, presented with this puzzling inconsistency of illness, chalked it up to the vagaries of chemical sensitivity (*kagaku busshitsu kabinshō*). According to this explanation (which has a provenance in Japanese and international pathological research (cf. Ishikawa et al. 2003)), some individuals – like Tsubō-san, mentioned above – with a low tolerance for toxins fell prey to the toxins almost immediately. Others carried on with their lives as though nothing had changed in their environment (though their health still suffered, according to the claims of GEAD protesters and environmental scientists, as a result of daily exposure). Most of the rest of the population, including the approximately 400 residents afflicted with varying levels of Azuma Disease, fell somewhere between these two extremes. Due to the vicissitudes of chemical sensitivity, then, a facility might have a grave effect on a fraction of the population while seeming relatively innocuous to the majority. Such was the case, protesters reasoned, in Izawa.

Theirs was a controversial claim, and resulting divisions in the community created social obstacles to movement that roughly mirrored toxic impediments there. A comment from Fujimura-san, a woman in her late fifties who was not a member of the GEAD protest group and who did not 'feel' Azuma Disease, was representative of many who were touched by the political controversy around them: 'I've lived here for twenty-one years. Some things have changed a lot since [my family] moved here, but the area always seemed the same. Now things are different'. Not least was the stigma of illness for the victims: once some residents began to feel the symptoms, they enjoyed sympathy from some but surprising coldness from others. Such hostility made journeying through the community something of a minefield for sufferers who were already hard-put physically to make it through the days. As Kamida-san, a woman in her seventies, explained: 'At first, I was really uncomfortable bumping into my neighbours. I'd do almost anything to avoid it. ... Getting [the cold shoulder] from people who'd been close to me, that was really hurtful. After a while, though, I relished it – I began fighting for all of us'. (Members of the GEAD, for their part, argued convincingly that the opposition of at least some other members of the community was driven by baser concerns – such as protecting the value of their real estate holdings and local businesses, or perhaps simply reacting against the tarnishing of the good name of their community – to play down their own ill health.) But whatever one's opinion of the purity or defilement of Izawa's precincts, in social terms the community was riven with suspicion and discrimination. Such Japanese social exclusion resembles that reported to novelist Haruki Murakami in his chilling non-fictional oral history of the victims of the Sarin nerve gas attack on the Tokyo subway in 1995. He found that those who survived the attack found it extremely hard to assimilate back into their groups at work and in communities, partly due to the ostracism of unsympathetic former friends and peers (Murakami 2000: 3, 61–64).

In many ways, the controversy surrounding Azuma Disease in Izawa comprised an example of larger-scale cases of environmental and health calamities writ small. For example, Azuma Ward is hardly the only political entity to locate a noxious facility near a border (e.g., the German toxic waste dump described in Berglund 1998, among many examples). And with toxic emissions (notoriously those of the Chernobyl disaster) and disease pandemics, such as HIV or SARS, dangerous and undesirable agents that pass across boundaries lead to conditions that are, nevertheless, acutely 'bounded' by national and regional political concerns. Social boundaries on a smaller scale, however, show themselves to be acutely sensitive to environmental health crises, as the present account explores. Conditions suffered by residents in Izawa demonstrate both how easily such boundaries can be undermined by pollutants and illness and also how resolution of such problems can be influenced by political action there and lead to unexpected remappings. Indeed, polluted zones become bizarrely liminal, an unsettling mix of features that can leave those afflicted feeling as if the groundedness and intimacy their communities once offered are forever beyond their grasp, bringing unanticipated consequences.

Members of the community like Tsubō-san, presented with contaminated surroundings, polluted homes and belongings, poisoned social relations, and a government more concerned about protecting the integrity of macro-scale metropolitan sanitation strategy than the micro-scale of community environmental health, took the only decision they felt was left to them: they moved. Of the core members of the GEAD, after a few years, only one remained in the community. Several others stayed relatively nearby (a quick bike ride, bus ride, or train trip away), sometimes making daily trips to Izawa. The rest, and other non-members, chose to relocate to new and sometimes remote communities with clean air and other treasured amenities, like easy access to forest or mountains. This led, thus, to a strangely disembodied, often virtual protest. Tsubō-san lived in the suburbs in a nearby prefecture with clean air and open terrain but commuted regularly, bundles of files in hand, to ward and Tokyo Metropolitan meetings and environmental symposia. Others, like Kimura-san, continued to work in the community – in his case as a playground monitor and self-styled ecology instructor at a local primary school – and constituted part of the small but influential 'live' daily presence in Izawa. The self-exiles, both relieved at their improved health and embittered by political wrangling with recalcitrant local leaders and mendacious bureaucrats,[12] frequently looked back at their aborted life in Izawa with some nostalgia. But with the upheaval they experienced, these were only qualified regrets. For the most part, from a safe remove, they reflected on the distressing memory of wrestling with a toxic blight that penetrated their bodies, subverted domestic and relational boundaries, and spawned dislocation in their engagement with environs and community and which they are determined never to encounter again. And this is no abstract, decontextualized, Cartesian notion, but a memory that is held bodily. Tsubō-san's frail voice lowers when she states: 'I have no interest in going back. … Sometimes my body feels [like spasming] even to think of it'.

12. Several official meetings, such as one ward hearing in October 1999, have been punctuated by commission members berating officials of the Tokyo Public Cleansing Bureau for clear and egregious manipulations of statistical data related to toxic levels in Izawa and for other transparent, failed attempts to undermine GEAD's assertions.

References

Alcock, Sir R. 1863. *The Capital of the Tycoon: A Narrative of Three Years' Residence in Japan.* London: Longman, Green, Longman, Roberts and Green.

Asquith, P. and A. Kalland (eds). 1997. *Japanese Images of Nature: Cultural Perspectives.* Nordic Institute of Asian Studies, Man and Nature in Asia, No. 1. Richmond, Surrey: Curzon Press.

Beck, U. 1992. *Risk Society: Towards a New Modernity.* London: Sage Books.

Berglund, E. 1998. *Knowing Nature, Knowing Science: An Ethnography of Local Environmental Activism.* Cambridge: White Horse Press.

Berque, A. 1997a [1986]. *Japan: Nature, Artifice and Japanese Culture*, trans. R. Schwarz. Yelvertoft Manor, Northamptonshire: Pilkington Press.

———. 1997b [1993]. *Japan: Cities and Social Bonds*, trans. C. Turner. Yelvertoft Manor, Northamptonshire: Pilkington Press.

Bourdieu, P. 1977. *Outline of a Theory of Practice.* Cambridge: Cambridge University Press.

Broadbent, J. 1998. *Environmental Politics in Japan: Networks of Power and Protest.* Cambridge: Cambridge University Press.

Casper, M. (ed.). 2003. *Synthetic Planet: Chemical Politics and the Hazards of Modern Life.* New York: Routledge.

Clammer, J. 1997. *Contemporary Urban Japan: A Sociology of Consumption.* Oxford: Blackwell.

Csordas, T. J. 1993. 'Somatic Modes of Attention', *Cultural Anthropology* 8(2):135–56.

———. 1994. *Embodiment and Experience: The Existential Ground of Culture and Self.* Cambridge: Cambridge University Press.

Davis, J. H., Jr. 2000. 'Blurring the Boundaries of the Buraku(min)', in J. Eades, T. Gill, and H. Befu (eds), *Globalization and Social Change in Contemporary Japan.* Melbourne: Trans Pacific Press.

Deliége, R. 1999. *The Untouchables of India*, trans. N. Scott. Oxford and New York: Berg.

Douglas, M. 1966. *Purity and Danger: An Analysis of the Concepts of Pollution and Taboo*. London: Routledge and Kegan Paul.

———. 1992. *Risk and Blame: Essays in Cultural Theory*. London and New York: Routledge.

Edelstein, M. 1988. *Contaminated Communities: The Social and Psychological Impacts of Residential Toxic Exposure*. Boulder, CO, and London: Westview Press.

Fortun, K. 2001. *Advocacy after Bhopal: Environmentalism, Disaster, New Global Orders*. Chicago: University of Chicago Press.

Ishikawa S, et al (eds). 2003. *Watashi no Kagaku Busshitsu Kabinshō: Kanshatachi no Kiroku*. (*My Chemical Hypersensitivity: Patients' Journals*. Published in Japanese.) Publication of the Association of Patients of Chemical Hypersensitivity. Tokyo: Jissensha.

Jameson, F. 1999. *Postmodernism, or, the Cultural Logic of Late Capitalism*. Durham, NC: Duke University Press.

Jameson, F. and M. Miyoshi (eds). 1998. *The Cultures of Globalization*. Durham, NC: Duke University Press.

Kerr, A. 2001. *Dogs and Demons: Tales from the Dark Side of Japan*. New York: Hill and Wang.

Kirby, P. W. 2002. 'Environmental Consciousness and the Politics of Waste in Tokyo: "Nature", Health, Pollution, and the Predicament of Toxic Japan', Ph.D. dissertation. Cambridge: University of Cambridge.

———. 2003. 'Troubled Natures: Toxic Pollutants and Japanese Identity in Tokyo', in M. Casper (ed.), *Synthetic Planet: Chemical Politics and the Hazards of Modern Life*. New York: Routledge.

———. 2004. 'Getting Engaged: Pollution, Toxic Illness, and Discursive Shift in a Tokyo Community', in J. Carrier (ed.), *Contesting Environments: Power, Places, People*. Walnut Creek, CA: AltaMira.

———. (under review). *Troubled Natures: The Politics of Waste in Japan*. Unpublished monograph.

Kondo, D. 1990. *Crafting Selves: Power, Gender, and Discourses of Identity in a Japanese Workplace*. Chicago: University of Chicago Press.

Lesbirel, S. H. 1998. *NIMBY Politics in Japan: Energy Siting and the Management of Environmental Conflict*. Ithaca, NY: Cornell University Press.

Lock, M. 1980. *East Asian Medicine in Urban Japan*. Berkeley, Los Angeles, and London: University of California Press.

Lynch, K. 1960. *The Image of the City*. Cambridge, MA, and London: MIT Press.

Meech, J. and G. P. Weisberg. 1990. *Japonisme Comes to America: The Japanese Impact on the Graphic Arts, 1872-1925*. New York: Abrams.

Miyata N. 1977. *Minzoku Shūkyōron no Kadai*. (*On Folk Religious Discourse*. Published in Japanese.) Tokyo: Miraisha.

———. 1996. *Kegare no Minzokushi: Sabetsu no Bunkateki yōin*. (*An Ethnology of Pollution: Discrimination's Primary Cultural Factors*. Published in Japanese.) Kyoto: Jimbun Shoin.

Moeran, B. and L. Skov. 1997. 'Mount Fuji and the Cherry Blossoms: A View from Afar', in P. Asquith and A. Kalland (eds), *Japanese Images of Nature: Cultural Perspectives*. Nordic Institute of Asian Studies, Man and Nature in Asia, No. 1. Richmond, Surrey: Curzon Press.

Morse, E. 1961 [1886]. *Japanese Homes and their Surroundings*. New York: Dover.

Murakami H. 2000. *Underground: The Tokyo Gas Attack and the Japanese Psyche*, trans. A. Birnbaum and P. Gabriel. London: Harvill.

Namihira E. 1977. '*Hare, Ke* and *Kegare*: The Structure of Japanese Folk Belief', Ph.D. dissertation. Austin, TX: The University of Texas at Austin.

———. 1984. *Kegare no Kōzō*. (*The Structure of Ritual Pollution*. Published in Japanese.) Tokyo: Seidosha.

———. 1985. *Kegare*. (*Ritual Pollution*. Published in Japanese.) Tokyo: Tōkyōdō.

Ohnuki-Tierney, E. 1984. *Illness and Culture in Contemporary Japan: An Anthropological View*. Cambridge: Cambridge University Press.
Parker, R. 1983. *Miasma: Pollution and Purification in Early Greek Religion*. Oxford: Clarendon Press.
Petryna, A. 2002. *Life Exposed: Biological Citizens after Chernobyl*. Princeton, NJ: Princeton University Press.
Pezeu-Massabuau, J. 1981. *La Maison Japonaise*. (*The Japanese House*. Published in French.) Paris: Publications Orientalistes de France.
Rheingold, H. 2003. *Smart Mobs: The Next Social Revolution*. New York: Basic Books.
Sakurai T. 1970. *Nihon Minkan Shinkōron*. (*A Discussion of Japanese Folk Beliefs*. Published in Japanese.) Tokyo: Kōbundō.
Sakurai T. (ed.). 1988. *Nihon Minzoku no Dentō to Kōzō: Shin-Minzokugaku no Kōzō*. (*Japanese Folk Tradition and Creation: Concepts of the New Folklore*. Published in Japanese.) Tokyo: Kōbundō.
Sassen, S. 2001. *The Global City: New York, London, Tokyo*, 2nd ed. Princeton, NJ: Princeton University Press.
Sorkin, M. (ed.). 1994. *Variations on a Theme Park: The New American City and the End of Public Space*. New York: Hill and Wang.
Tsing, A. 2000. 'The Global Situation', *Cultural Anthropology* 15(3): 327–60.
Watsuji T. 1975 [1935]. *Fūdo*. (*Milieux*. Published in Japanese.) Tokyo: Iwanami Shoten.
Yatsuka H. 1990. 'An Architecture Floating on the Sea of Signs', in B. Bognar (ed.), *The New Japanese Architecture*. New York: Rizzoli.

Chapter 9

Movements in Corporate Space: Organizing a Japanese Multinational in France

Mitchell W. Sedgwick

Introduction

We understand interpersonal contact as the context in which human relations, work, and, indeed, life itself are acutely and actively negotiated. Physical spaces are ordinarily taken to be vessels that place, or formally structure, and, so, contain, more quintessential human interactions. However, the apparent solidity, or exaggerated durability, of such 'structures' is a projection of our desire to stabilize our environments. These perceptions are convenient, but fully artificial, artefacts of our work of sense making; they are means of orientation – *fixations* – if largely unconscious. The plasticity of spaces is more durable than, but it is not different in principle from, the plasticity of interpersonal interactions: they are, rather, the same processes moving in different relations to perceptions of time. By no means am I implying that movement in spaces is thereby false, ephemeral or unreal. On the contrary, like interpersonal interactions, I hope to describe spaces as fully effective, evolving productions – described elsewhere as 'social space' (Lefebvre 1991) – made meaningful as territory that is marked, *taking place* through social relations. Indeed, making visible such processual and contextually-oriented activities hones our appreciation of human volition and authority over space, and its co-production with perceptions of time.

In this chapter I examine social relations at YamaMax: pseudonym for a rural French subsidiary of a major Japanese consumer electronics multinational, the 'Yama' Corporation. A factory like YamaMax would traditionally be understood as fully contained: a discrete formal organization. However movement across the boundaries of formal organizations is, of course, required in their reproduction. This point is especially pronounced at factories, which take in raw materials, process and sell them, and where employees are both members of the firm and other communities that are often more meaningful to them. In addition, in the case of YamaMax, the organization is but a minor node within an enormous multinational corporation, but, nonetheless, a factory whose goods can literally be found in every corner of the globe. This grand, fully-networked image notwithstanding, in this chapter I contextualize one large office area at YamaMax, understanding it as an expression of YamaMax's forms of organizing social relations, both cross-cultural and otherwise. Significant for our purposes, my central 'data' in the chapter – a blueprint-like diagram of the office space, a time chart identifying seven stages, or 'steps', in the social life of the office, and the stories demarcating the 'steps' – were generated by a group of French engineers/informants. All of the events recorded, meanwhile, occurred before my 18-month period of ethnographic fieldwork at YamaMax. The production of the French engineers' 'data' – their diagrams, charts, and storytelling – was, however, prompted by our discussions. And it is analysis of our co-production of (retrospective) research, animating movement across time and space in the office, that is the core contribution of the chapter. I will cover this matter in detail after a presentation of the formal 'data'.

Briefly, however, it is worth noting how our research project began. My initial queries with the French engineers about social relations at YamaMax – in the 'ethnographic' present – concerned the most obvious, observable things: 'Who is it sitting over there, and what do they do?' While eliciting brief responses, my queries stimulated surprisingly urgent reflections – especially for engineers – concerning 'Who used to be there, and why?' These were sufficiently potent, and unusual in my long experience of research in modern organizational settings, that I was drawn to them. It was determined that our discussions on the past would be formed explicitly through what was placed before us: open-plan office space, private offices, and conference rooms, punctuated by identical desks that, due to their surplus, remained for the most part *in situ* down the years. This choice replaced a progressive consultation of that more self-evident codifier of factory social relations: the endemic organizational chart. I rather quickly discovered that organizational charts were but flimsy approximations of organizational dynamics and, indeed, power at YamaMax. (Indeed, over the 18 months that I followed and collected artefacts 'in use' at YamaMax, there were seven different organizational charts alone representing the engineering section where my French informants worked. Apparently, no one at YamaMax paid any attention to organizational charts because they were produced and replaced with such rapidity.) The apparently 'fixed' features of office walls and desks may suggest a contradiction of my initial point regarding the plasticity of 'physical' spaces. On the contrary, our project concerned the production of office space as social space and, as would be apparent to anyone who works in offices, 'artificial' walls and offices themselves are carefully graded, traded, and moved: they are, indeed, hotly contested, visible forms of social politics, the most stable of discourses reflecting social movement.

Along with presenting the French engineers' data and elaborating its work as a joint research project, I interpret their transformations of forms of commonplace, and highly 'sensitive', 'scientific' knowledge – of rational design and *x,y,z* calibrations in the production of consumer goods – into exceptionally rich data regarding the movement of boundedness in producing organization. Their new, and delicate, social codifications – motivated, it is argued, by a gradual decline in their relative hierarchical authority in the workplace – compels consideration of who is an ethnographer, who an informant, and what constitutes and validates data and interpretation. The joint analytic process to be described here, therefore, throws up questions regarding memory, participation, cultural and intellectual background, language, research design, and the uses of knowledge. Based in an appreciation of Sorokin and Merton's (1937) work in elaborating 'social-time', I am concerned here, then, with questioning analytic representations, e.g., social science stories (cf. Czarniawska 1997; Watson 2000) based in the ethnographer's sharing of 'coeval … intersubjective Time … [with the] Other' (Fabian 1983: 148), socio-spatial constructions in organizing (Yeung 1998) and, therefore, general problems of research strategy (Latour 1999; Lee and Hassard 1999) in accounting for social space in that core feature productive of the modernity in which we continue to live: organizations.

Taking Place

At YamaMax the decision to expand the factory for start-to-finish production of videotape had been taken in Japan in 1989. It was an investment of a very large scale; initially between £30 and £40 million. The design of the expanded factory – adding building TP3, to the already-present TP1 and TP2 – was undertaken in consultation with a major Japanese construction firm to which several French construction firms were subcontracted. Setting up the machinery for the technically demanding work of the early stages of magnetic tape production required new, and more highly qualified, engineers. Following up advertisements for employment in several French engineering publications, from early 1990 a specially selected and highly skilled group of French engineers (my informants) was hired by YamaMax from various engineering jobs throughout France. They had varied educational backgrounds – from, at the extremes, a postgraduate degree in aeronautics, to a vocational school graduate – but all were in their mid-to-late thirties and had substantial engineering experience. Although none of them had any previous experience of working at Japanese firms or in doing business at any level with the Japanese, they began working intensively, apparently pleasurably and for extremely long hours with a group of Japanese Yama Corporation engineers: a Japanese 'start-up' team assigned solely to the task of overseeing the installation of new machinery and getting production up and running. The shell and floor space of TP3 were completed by mid-1991, when staff and workers were able to move in and, so, start-to-finish production of magnetic tape could begin at YamaMax. From then, whereas the Japanese 'start-up' team dispersed back to various Yama jobs in Japan and elsewhere, the French 'start-up' team took up other engineering posts at YamaMax.

Because of the large scale of TP3's tape production machinery only one section of 'floor space' in TP3 is currently divided into three floors. The bottom floor has storage areas and a few machine maintenance shops. The top floor is a windowed, empty space; a repository for computer equipment boxes, old fluorescent light bulbs, files of production information at least two years out of date, slices of magnetic tape (now collecting dust while propped against a wall) that had been subject to 'visual' (microscopic) inspection (and thereby provided a physical record of the quality of tape produced), and the odd cigarette butt. Especially hot in summer, in my few visits I never saw anyone on this top floor. While its objects may represent an archaeology of YamaMax, it is a social void. Our interests focus, rather, on the middle floor where the engineers, managers, and staff overseeing the work of TP3 have their desks, computers, telephones, and fax machines: their office lives. I had a desk in the open-plan area of TP3 – nearby the French engineer informants (as well as two Japanese engineers) – from which I could follow all of the comings and goings of the office. While of course observing the French engineers at work at their desks, on the shopfloor and in YamaMax's various robotic control rooms, I also had many opportunities during breaks, over lunch, and, indeed, during working hours, to discuss YamaMax and its evolution with them. They assisted me with explanations of the factory's technical tasks, past and present, and were interested in my queries about their experiences of the firm's socio-technical and cross-cultural dynamics. It was eventually determined that headway into this topic could be gained by drawing a time map outlining various phases in the office evolution, to be used in combination with a blueprint of the TP3 office space. (As described above, in the final sections of the chapter I will account in detail for the process of coming up with this analytic tool.) This space was divided into fourteen 'areas'. (See Figure 9.1) Four of these are within a large, central open space with windows to the outside of TP3 along one entire side. This central space serves both as offices and hallways between each of the other ten areas of various sizes, each with floor-to-ceiling walls and a door opening onto the central space. Two of these ten areas (Area 6 and Area 10) have a windowed wall facing the outside.[1] A further chart made by my informants (also shown in Figure 9.1) outlines a longitudinal series of seven 'steps', within each of which but the last, when I was present, they described to me various aspects of the office's organizational

1. In addition there are four areas on the left side of the layout, also opening onto the central space. Two are large meeting rooms (named 'Arc de Triomphe' and 'Tour Eiffel'), one a room with a highly efficient copy machine and a fax machine divided off from a space holding supplies and files, and the last a small office where two technicians track production processes on computers. These areas are irrelevant to the current discussion.

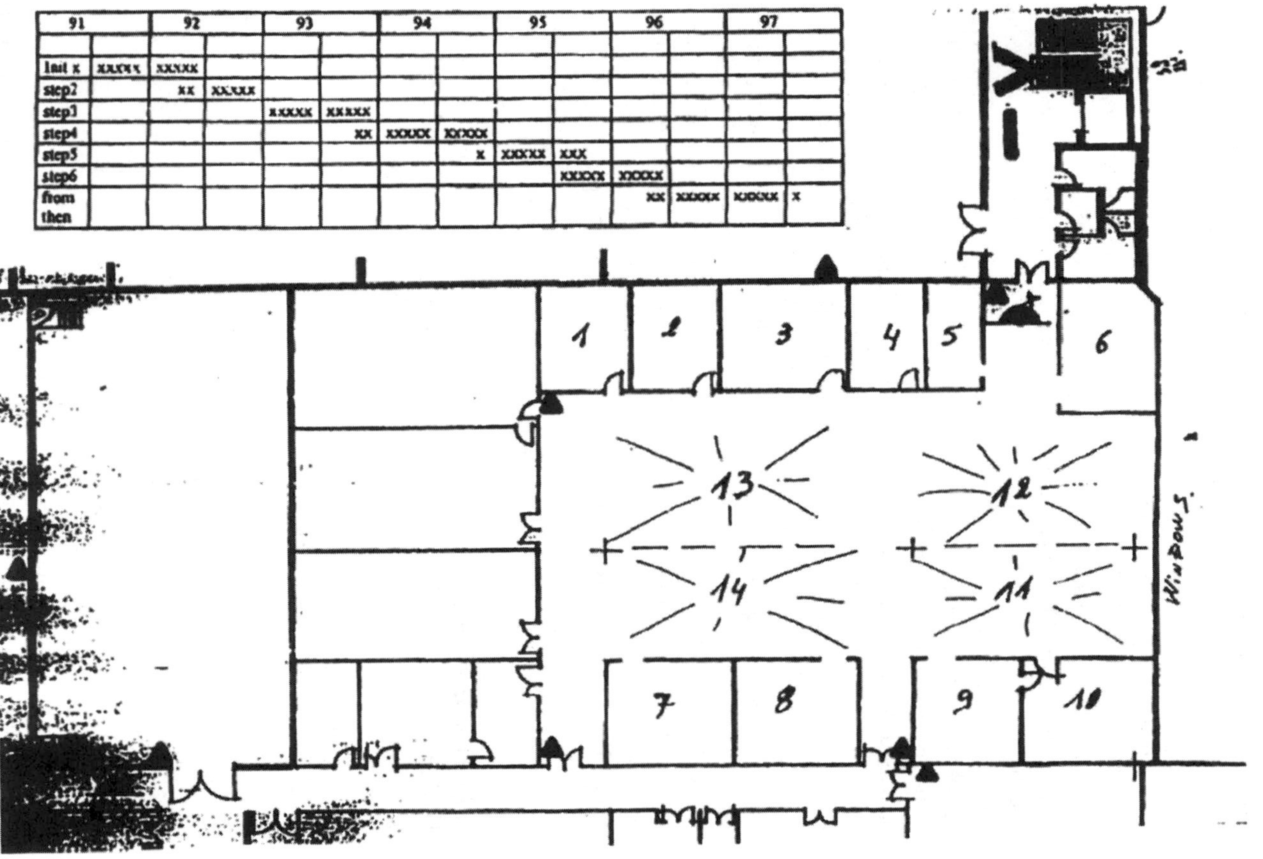

91		92		93		94		95		96		97	
Init x	xxxxx	xxxxx											
step2		xx	xxxxx										
step3				xxxxx	xxxxx								
step4					xx	xxxxx	xxxxx						
step5							x	xxxxx	xxx				
step6									xxxxx	xxxxx			
from then										xx	xxxxx	xxxxx	x

Figure 9.1 The office space divided into 14 areas

sociology and, so, personal (personnel) dramas. It should also be noted that for the most part the 'steps' overlap in chronological time – as represented by an overlapping of each 'step's' series of 'x's. This is a matter I take up with interest in my analysis following the presentation of the data.

I will not burden the reader with the complete record of office movement in TP3 as it was recalled to me for the entire 1991 through mid-1996 period. Rather, I briefly discuss particularly interesting situations that were highlighted by my French engineer informants, who were present throughout the period (as well as, obviously, throughout my fieldwork). In 'inverted commas', and *italics* on occasion, I add some of their specific comments, translated from the French. It should be recalled here that I was the *recipient* of this core data: the analytic decisions about when to make demarcations, and so bound the positions of persons working in particular places as a 'step', were made by the French engineers, based on their interpretation of organizational dynamics as reflected in the social space of the office. That said, as my central ethnographic work at YamaMax concerned 'cross-cultural relations' between the French and the Japanese, based on my expertise regarding the Japanese I do lightly embellish their observations with my own impressions. As suggested above, I discussed possible interpretations of the history of the office space with my French engineers/informants, who engaged naturally in discussion on the topic as they had worked with Japanese engineers and managers at YamaMax, a Japanese corporation, for seven years by that time.

Data

Initial Configuration

With the diagram to hand, then, the TP3 office space was initially occupied – as period 'Init' (May 1991 – June 1992) – in the following way:

Room:

1: French production manager
2: French engineering manager
3: French chemical laboratory manager
4: French utility manager
5: Meeting room
6: Meeting room
7: Quality assurance (QA) office: 1 French, 1 Japanese
8: Planning office: 1 French, 1 Japanese
9: Japanese plant manager (carpeted room)
10: Japanese plant manager's meeting room (carpeted and windowed)
11: Japanese (female) secretary
12: Utility group: 1 Japanese, 4 French

13: Engineering group: 2 Japanese, 5 French
14: Miscellaneous: office temps and French (female) secretary

The number of personnel at the end of period 'Init' was twenty-five, of which seven were Japanese and eighteen were French.

There are three matters of interest here. First, in Japan the Japanese are accustomed to working together at blocks of perhaps six or eight desks that face one another, where all phone conversations and interpersonal interactions of colleagues can be overheard and, indeed, commented upon. In effect, over time, through this arrangement, knowledge pertaining to 'work' (and a good deal of personal information) becomes communal knowledge. The two Japanese managers in Area 13 and the one in Area 12 re-enacted this familiar arrangement in the foreign environment of France. The Japanese are, thus, sharing space with the second hierarchical tier of, if highly skilled, French engineers – my informants for this chapter. (It might be noted that the formal hierarchy of the Japanese engineers in Areas 12 and 13 vis-à-vis their French colleagues is formally ambiguous as the Japanese engineers' titles are simply 'advisor'.)

Second, those single French managers in hierarchical positions higher than their French colleagues in Areas 13 and 12 have their own private offices (in Areas 2 and 4), thus reflecting their expectations about office space and, thereby, authority.

Third, the Japanese plant manager, who is the highest ranked Japanese at YamaMax, is the only Japanese with a private office (Area 9). He keeps the carpeted and windowed room next to him (Area 10) – the most pleasant room in the TP3 office – as his private meeting room. Most meetings here are with his Japanese staff. However, occasionally there are meetings in this room (Area 10) with Japanese guests, who are likely to be impressed by this space, in which formal Japanese seating arrangements would be recreated. These arrangements are such that the highest ranking person sits furthest from the door with his back to either art work and/or a flower arrangement, or an impressive exterior view, so that others, looking at him, will associate him with these grand, aesthetic splendours. Here the Japanese plant manager at YamaMax has literally re-enacted space arrangements, including the placement of his secretary (in Area 11), as they would be found in Japan only among the highest ranking private sector and public sector managers. Notably, this Japanese plant manager is unlikely ever to have the possibility of an office in Japan in which an arrangement of this sort could be organized. His overseas posting is an opportunity to – temporarily – expand the spatial horizons of his office and his commensurate sense of authority.[2]

2. While foreign postings are certainly challenging and strenuous for Japanese managers (and their families), it should also be recognized how the return to Japan into cramped offices (and homes), where superiors stand heavily and numerously on a manager's shoulders, is a cause for substantial reverse culture shock in terms of relative individual volition and decision-making opportunities enjoyed while abroad.

Step 2 (May 1992 - December 1992)

The number of personnel at the end of period 'Step 2' was twenty-five, of which seven were Japanese and eighteen were French.

Areas 13 and 2: The work of the French engineering manager in Area 2 is not up to the expectations of the Japanese, so one of the Japanese 'advisors' in Area 13 moves into the French engineering manager's office. This is obviously highly intrusive from the French perspective. My French informants (in Area 13), ranked lower than their French colleague in Area 2, indicate that while 'the Japanese managers say that, "He is joining the French manager for better support", in fact it is for close control'.

Areas 12 and 4: The French utility manager in Area 4 has a conflict with his Japanese counterpart (who sits in Area 12). The Frenchman is eventually sacked. According to my French informants, 'He is given a "window promotion" [stated in English], staying in room 4; thus, in the "environment", but has been stripped of authority until his departure five months later'. I have no details on the conflict between the Japanese and French utility managers. Interestingly the description by my informants (in 1997), seven years after they had begun work with the Japanese, of the French utility manager's 'window promotion' is a direct translation into English of a Japanese concept. A 'window promotion' is a typical Japanese managerial phrase used to describe someone who has been deemed useless to the organization but who, under the lifetime employment system, cannot be removed. He is now merely near the window (to look out of?); in any case he is irrelevant to organizational action. I expect that the French manager was not sacked outright because such a radical move would not be found in the workplace repertoire of Japanese managers at first-tier Japanese corporations like Yama.

Area 9: A new Japanese plant manager comes from Japan, replacing the previous Japanese plant manager who had overseen the set-up of TP3.

Step 3 (January 1993 – December 1993)

The number of personnel at the end of period 'Step 3' was twenty-two, of whom six were Japanese and sixteen were French.

Area 12: The Japanese utility manager returns to Japan, thus reducing their number by one.

Areas 2, 13, and 8: The beleaguered French engineering manager and his Japanese engineering manager – who share Area 2 – move to (larger) Area 8. The Japanese engineering manager in Area 13 joins them in Area 8. The consolidation of all engineering managers (two Japanese and one French) in Area 8, with the return to Japan of the Japanese utility manager, means that no Japanese is sitting in an open space office. The open blocked-desks arrangement, 'natural' to the Japanese at the outset of their work in France, has been transformed into a failed experiment in the cross-cultural negotiation in the spacing of social relations.

Step 4 (November 1993 – December 1994)

The number of personnel at the end of period 'Step 4' was twenty-one, of whom one was American, four were Japanese, and sixteen were French.

Areas 9 and 10: The Japanese plant manager is replaced by an American plant manager. The American comes from a 'sister' Yama plant in the US, which is already doing complete start-to-finish production of magnetic tape. The American plant manager makes Area 10, with a window, his office; Area 9 becomes his meeting room.

Areas 8 and 4: The French engineering manager in Area 8 is, according to my informants, 'kicked out' of engineering to a 'special project'. He joins the French utility manager who is on a 'window promotion' in his room (Area 4). The French engineering manager is fired three months later by the American plant manager and is given two weeks to depart.

Area 1: The French production manager is fired by the American plant manager. He is given three hours to depart.

Area 11: The Japanese (female) secretary returns to Japan and is replaced by a French (female) secretary.

This was a period of radical change in the TP3 office that was recalled during my fieldwork at YamaMax by all the French staff who were present during the period as dramatic and exhausting. Note that at this point the original work of setting-up the machinery has been long completed and the goal is to stabilize production. The posting of the second Japanese plant manager in France, who took over from the Japanese plant manager who had been overseeing set-up, is brief: less than two years. This suggests he has not been successful. Indeed, production has been well behind schedule and the company is generating significant operational losses. These losses are covered financially by 'Japan' – which understands them as part and parcel of YamaMax's 'learning period' – but they are apparently accompanied in Japan by considerable unease. Using an American Yama plant manager as a replacement suggests that the Japanese directors in Japan, frustrated with the progress of YamaMax, decide to let Yama foreigners (French and American) work with each other, i.e., they collapse the French and Americans into one category – 'foreign' – external to the Japanese. I would suggest that 'Japan' is feeling 'out of its depth' at handling YamaMax after having just invested tens of millions of pounds to build up a – technologically speaking – cutting-edge factory.

The American plant manager obviously has no qualms or restraint in shaking things up on the personnel level: he fires both a French engineering manager and a French production manager. Judging from conversations with French members of YamaMax during my fieldwork the American had a reputation for constantly coming up with interesting ideas but not stabilizing them in practice by providing the guidance to see them through. The French found this management style very disconcerting. Whereas, vis-à-vis the French, the Japanese are often indirect, or obtuse, about what should be done, the American provides constantly shifting directions. Stylistically he expects (perhaps as among many American managers?) his subordinates to debate his ideas with him, while the French, very reticent about openly challenging hierarchical authority and, perhaps also, concerned about language barriers, are made uncomfortable and are unable to engage him in this manner. In addition, note that the American's spatial aesthetic of authority is more privately driven – he takes the 'best' office (Area 10) as his own – than that of his Japanese predecessors who prioritized the visual and physical 'impression-management' of relatively infrequent Japanese guests.

Step 5 (December 1994 – September 1995)

The number of personnel at the end of period 'Step 5' was seventeen, of whom three were Japanese and fourteen were French.

Area 10: The American plant manager is replaced by a Japanese plant manager, Otake-san, who had visited the plant in April 1994, and again in May 1994 with a three-man Japanese 'recovery' team sent from Japan as YamaMax is running a huge loss.

Area 3: The production planning function leaves TP3 when the French planning manager quits and the Japanese planning manager returns to Japan (and is not replaced). Area 3 is left vacant.

Area 8: One of two Japanese engineering managers in Area 8 returns to Japan and is not replaced. He is said to have been 'broken' by Otake-san. Now Area 8 is the office of a single Japanese manager who oversees 'quality assessment' (QA).

In an interview with Otake-san (in 1997), he relates that the American plant manager felt threatened by him and his Japanese recovery team's visits, feeling that Otake-san was after his job. Indeed, while the American was put in 'to turn the factory around', the experimental nature of the move is evident: he was in France for just over one year when most overseas postings are for at least three years. According to my French informants, Otake-san's impact on the TP3 office and general activities throughout the factory are increasingly sensed. Overall, in anticipation of Step 6, we can note a general thinning down in terms of personnel and general responsibilities of the TP3 office. Otake-san keeps Area 10 as his office.

Step 6 (July 1995 – June 1996)

The number of personnel at the end of period 'Step 6' was nineteen, of whom seven were Japanese and twelve were French.

Areas 9 and 10: M. Marchalot, a production manager, is made plant manager, formally replacing Otake-san in this role. Otake-san formally becomes an 'advisor'. M. Marchalot's office is Area 9, right next to Otake-san in Area 10, and in fact there is a door directly between Areas 9 and 10.

Areas 13 to 12: A new French engineering manager arrives from another Yama factory in France – which does not produce magnetic tape – and is joined in open Area 12 by four French engineering staff members (my informants), who have moved from Area 13.

Areas 11 to 8 to 11 (and 7): A new Japanese team, of Otake-san's choice, of three young Japanese engineers arrives from Japan in February 1996. While Otake-san stays in Area 10, he places all four (three new and one remaining) TP3 Japanese engineers in open Area 11. He then moves them all into closed office Area 8, and then moves the three new Japanese engineers back to open Area 11. The remaining engineer, who handles Quality Assessment (QA), returns to his original office in Area 7.

In keeping with public corporate ideology regarding 'localization' – and, after all, neither the Japanese nor the experiment with the American succeeded in 'turning the factory around' – the decision is taken to formally make a Frenchman plant manager. Otake-san, who takes dictatorial control over the organization of TP3 office space, puts him into a connected office (Area 9), next to his. Meeting tables remain in Otake-san's large office (Area 10) with his desk. This is the first chance in his career for Otake-san to have his own office, and he keeps it for himself.

With the arrival of a new Japanese team, Otake-san – frenetically – rearranges their desks over the course of four months. He is awkward cross-culturally, and apparently wants distance from the French and an all-Japanese space close by him: thus, the construction of a barrier between himself and the French by placing all four Japanese engineers in Area 11. Experimenting rashly, he moves them to Area 8 and then returns three of them – the newest members – back again to Area 11, while the Quality Assessment engineer vacates Area 8 for his original desk in Area 7.

Making Context

Redesigning the social organization of the fourteen areas of the TP3 office space was a continuously available, and powerful, rationalizing tool at YamaMax. Of course, it is the longitudinal data that makes this appear obvious, for during any one period the 'movement' has largely evaporated. Only when spread across longer periods of time, punctuated by several sets of observations, does the rapidity, indeed the intensity, of organizational, cum social, cum physical changes in the social occupation of office space become apparent, especially when compared with normal transitions in the use of office areas in most 'domestic' Japanese, French, American or British organizations. YamaMax is an especially 'nervous system' (Taussig 1992): hotly contested and politically fraught, loaded with the possibilities for cross-cultural misunderstanding. Indeed, these data and the narrative stories attached to them could be extended and deepened in order to generate full analyses of cross-cultural, as well as general organizational, dynamics, as I do elsewhere (Sedgwick 2000, 2001, 2007).

Here, however, let me focus on the processes and meanings attached to the creation of the 'data', and the making of office space. While we may be familiar with ideas that appreciate technology, machinery, data, time, and space as media, or extensions, between persons, as socially constituted, and/or as 'agents' (Law 1986: 16) animated by social relations, in their work engineers treat technology, machinery, data, time, and space 'naturally': that is, as common sense objective forms for achieving rational goals (Orlikowski 1992). Why, then, were the French engineers' goals of data collection regarding technologies of mass production turned towards explicating social relations?

As mentioned in the second section of this chapter, these French engineers were the specially selected and highly skilled team hired in 1990 to work intensively with the group of Japanese engineers who came to YamaMax solely for the installation and the start-up of a new set of machines at TP3. The Japanese TP3 'start-up' team was there for about a year and, their task complete, disbanded back to Japan or on to other start-ups in other countries – of which there were many in the late 1980s and early 1990s. With YamaMax's line expanded for complete start-to-finish production, an expanded version of mass production – and its attendant search for predictability, consistency of output, cost-cutting, automaticity, internal organizational stability, and normalization – resurfaced as its core focus. With the structures of manufacturing processes defined, and, thus, the parameters of product 'specs' accounted for, younger, less highly skilled and lower paid French staff from downstream segments of YamaMax's production line, as well as from other factories in France, came onto TP3's new and more technically demanding line. They quickly gained experience and were rapidly promoted. Meanwhile, the disbanded Japanese 'start-up' team, with whom my French engineers/informants claimed to share considerable mutual respect, was replaced many times over by a cycle of Japanese engineers circulating on three to five year assignments, as well as a steady stream of short-term Japanese 'advisors'. When they arrived, none of these Japanese engineers knew the French engineers, or about their earlier, important work with the Japanese 'start-up' team.

With the 'start-up' completed, among the new tasks of two of my French engineers/informants was the redesign and improvement of technical linkages between particular machines at TP3. They worked in close contact with two other members of their party who focused on maintenance. Another dedicated himself to parts procurement. Another – the former aeronautics engineer – worked side by side with a series of Japanese engineers on process engineering of the delicate and dangerous first stage of production: the chemical mixing of magnetic paste. This latter work, however, was so critical to the entire production chain that Japanese engineers effectively controlled it. Thus, while my French engineers/informants were formally labelled, and defined themselves, to themselves, in technical 'advisor' or 'consultant' roles – and to an extent this was accurate – they gradually became marginal players in TP3 activities: technically, socially and, so, organizationally. Over the years, their declining position with regard to top-priority, core mass production tasks was also demonstrated in their stagnant progress up the hierarchical ranks and, accordingly, the relatively slow pace of their salary rises. They were, it appears, growing obsolete.

In retrospect, for the French engineers this is apparently about balancing the rational and often harsh justifications of formal organization. That is, in a turn of psychological compensation the French engineers' early days of mutual respect with the high-powered Japanese 'start-up' team were glorified, made nostalgic. In time the French engineers came to exaggerate the distinction between their superior capacity to *create* the methods or machineries of production and the limited capacity of rising 'Fordist' 'staff' who could only *oversee* (or 'do') production in TP3 and many of whom, furthermore, came to TP3 from the less technically demanding downstream segments of the factory production line, e.g., TP2. Over the years, it appears that the French engineers/informants did not push themselves onto the line – into YamaMax's core rational space – and they did not make the move – admittedly counterintuitive – of understanding that, while mundane on the surface, the maintenance of consistency (as mass production's central requirement) is an extremely challenging and complicated process, subtle and analytically interesting.[3] Effectively having become outsiders, the French engineers were bitter about their declining authority at YamaMax.

Immersions in Research

The tradition of key informants as outsiders to their own society is a strong one in anthropology (Rabinow 1977), but that is the sort of thing ordinarily realized, and reflected upon (by anthropologists), in retrospect. (In any case, it is worth mentioning that, unlike the French engineers on whom I focus in this chapter, most of my informants at YamaMax were 'right in the middle' of things.) When I arrived at YamaMax, five years after the 'start-up' was complete, comparatively speaking the French engineers/informants had time on their hands, and they were prepared to talk about (their understanding of) YamaMax. As described in the introduction, as an ethnographer I 'naturally' began my discussions with the French engineers with an interrogation of the present in which I could at least literally see things, even if I had no idea 'what was going on'. Although my evolving observations of, and discussions with, other people – as well as coming to grips with organizational charts, job descriptions, machinery, and other

3. I, too, as a social analyst, and accustomed to focusing explicitly on the exigencies of 'change', have had to 'back my way' over some years into an appreciation of this point.

artefacts – brought on the confused information overload typical of the early stages of fieldwork, 'the present' gradually took its place for me at YamaMax. A better appreciation of the present's fullness suggested accounting for its past, a subject about which the French engineers were in principle, as we have seen, very accommodating, even insistent.

As I have suggested, the dissociation of formal organizational charts from actual patterns of communication and power among members of YamaMax quickly ruled them out as texts worthy of much attention. Rather, we organized our discussions around the movement of persons within the 'unchanging' walls of the office space. Practically speaking, I recognized that this literally contained, or 'canned', history would of necessity require thickening through a long series of discussions between us. While that would be interesting, frankly this work was not an obvious priority of my research: I was, rather, obsessed with the details of social relations lived day-to-day in the present. Thus, although from time to time we discussed the past, and I took notes, the information somehow did not organize itself: perhaps there was too much detail and density for me to understand how it might hang together. Furthermore, though we kept going with our history project, I was unsure what would emerge from it beyond overarching statements about a cross-cultural enterprise that would be, in any case, relatively thin compared to my participant-observations. In retrospect, however, this ambivalence is indicative of a transition in my understanding of YamaMax. The rational/technical framings of our discussions through the presence of the walls and desks – stable and obvious to the fresh observer – seemed 'canned', or 'tinny', because they were evaporated, or displaced, as my knowledge of 'the office space', over time, was reproduced as social space (Lefebvre 1991).

One Monday the former aeronautics engineer – my key informant among the French engineers – who was perhaps, also, frustrated by our research, showed up with the blueprint of the TP3 office with numbered office spaces, the time chart of the seven 'steps', and a set of handwritten comments on each step (apart from the seventh, when I was there): an entire time and motion tool box (Figure 9.1). He had apparently spent the weekend putting it together at home. While the blueprint was already present in our heads, as it was ever-present before our eyes, I was impressed with its work in combination with the time chart in bringing order to our discussions. Allow me to elaborate on this point.

In their day-to-day work, I had watched engineers producing and discussing data that reported on engineering processes – the temperature of polished rollers compressing plastic backing film and magnetic paste, the frequency of breakdowns on particular machines under particular conditions, etc. – which became records that assisted in organizing plans (Latour and Woolgar 1979; Latour 1986, 1987, 1988; Callon 1986). It was apparent that the engineers were keenly aware of the implications to analysis of the qualities and interactions making up data and calculations in the apparatus of material production. However, although I could read their data, and see its linkage to actions, I could not comprehend, and so fully appreciate, the organizing properties of their formulae: what was gained or lost in any particular, usually mathematical, form of data production. That is, until an operation of this kind was translated through the raw material of social relations, about which I had many other sources of knowledge with which to triangulate their forms. In their seven-stepped time chart the French engineers importantly called for each step to overlap at the margins – via the x's – as an expression of their sense of the analytical tension between providing chronological demarcations to 'fix' observations – the steps – and the 'continuousness' of movement in office, cum social, cum architectural, arrangements. This was an explicit, visible representation of the tension between social change and pressures towards continuity that are, of course, present throughout social relations, but fundamental to the rationalizations of social relations in modern organizations. Indeed, had I decided to divide the historical material by 'steps' over time, I probably would have strictly annualized them for 'clarity'. (I was implicitly – if meaninglessly – doing so by simply recording dates.) Their form for organizing the time and motion model of office space – softening the edges of those very demarcations in order to account for the rise and fall of tensions, adjustment and movement in social relations – was very satisfying, and accurate.

With these tools to hand, we shared a 'coeval' medium to speak through (Fabian 1983) and, so, quickly increased the quantity of detail while also enhancing the quality of our reflections. Based in what they recounted about the organizational episodes, the French engineers were interested in my views of how work at YamaMax, and living in France, may have been perceived among YamaMax's series of Japanese managers and engineers – as well as those back in Japan with whom the Japanese were in close and deliberate contact. In our research project, or dialogue and negotiation of technical and social languages, we continued to embellish the stories of office dynamics and, ever more interestingly, the tensions of overlaps – the overlapping x's – between each demarcated step.

In retrospect this seems a 'natural' process of research stimulated through the combination of observation and reflection. However, the low probability of having done this research may be best appreciated by way of contrast with other YamaMax engineers' accounts of the past. While in the field, and chock-full of an ethical stance vis-à-vis my host community, I of course never considered asking the opinion of the successful, rising French engineers, or indeed the Japanese, of my French engineers/informants' time and motion diagrams of TP3's office 'social space'. To do so would have risked sharply undermining mutual trust with my French engineers/informants. However, as I was learning a great deal about YamaMax's past, when I did press other engineers to reflect on it they would often mention transitions due to changes in top leadership at YamaMax and suggest that further detail could be acquired though a review of old organizational charts. That said, they had discarded their own old charts – as each was superseded by whatever rarely consulted organizational chart represented the present. They guessed, however, that old organizational charts were held on record somewhere at YamaMax. They were, in short, dismissive of such queries about the past. These other engineers also, eventually, became good informants, and I am confident of what they would have felt about their colleagues' time and motion diagrams. They would have been briefly amused, but seen the production of such diagrams as a waste of time, an analysis fully irrelevant to the present and future: YamaMax's rationally conceived, and continuously progressive steps towards increasing mass production.

Movements of Knowledge

Questions remain as to the quality of my French engineers/informants' anxiously acquired social knowledge articulated in their time and motion data. What are the implications of fact that it was produced because of their alienation from their authority over the types of rational knowledge that their organization explicitly rewarded? What was the use for them of transforming forms of engineering knowledge into explicit interest in and interpretation of other sorts of knowledge?

In coming to terms with these questions we might ask how it was made and used differently from knowledge generated for the academy. A key challenge to anthropologists lies in combining the positional realities of visitations for distinct periods of time in the field – sharing time and speech, as Fabian would have it – with professional obligations to stand apart from, but represent, the subjects they have studied with, when 'at home'. The French engineers/informants, however, unlike scholars, were unintentionally made into observers and analysts of that environment that so poignantly affected them – their own – while continuing formally in situ as organizational 'members'. Once made organizationally marginal they were good at explaining their organization to themselves. After all, they had exact 'native' knowledge of it. (Indeed, how could they not?) It is no wonder, then, that they were quite clear about the meaning of the Japanese term 'window promotion'. Perhaps not unlike ethnography, they knew that *observing* action – even if live and unpredictable – was like participating through glass: they could see it, but were not meant to touch it.

The French engineers/informants' process of making explicit new kinds of knowledge was possible, and necessary and – presumably aided by our joint research – was also increasingly poignant to the French engineers *because* their colleagues had gradually taken their social 'place' 'right in the middle' of YamaMax's core rational goal of mass production. This explanation is suggested by a key artefact of their time and motion chart. Apart from one move of the entire group between Areas 12 and 13 – which elicited no comment in our discussions – the French engineers/informants do not themselves appear as actors in any of their stories of the six steps in the office area of TP3: in their 'data' they represented themselves as non-artefacts. Even though, unlike the (visiting) anthropologist, they were continuously at work at YamaMax, they analysed themselves into the position of purely scientific, rational observers. It was as if they were invisible, having no effect on the subjects of their studies: their own colleagues at YamaMax. Unlike scholars, who strive for the success represented by grants and research time for going away and coming back and productively writing, the French engineers/informants were moved by the interactions within their own organization, which decontextualized them socially away from – and, effectively, freed them from – their organization's rationalized, and powerful, core formations. The organization delivered time to them for reflection and, so, the motivation for calibrating their distressed self-perceptions in altogether fresh ways. My temporary interventions, as an outsider, encouraged development of their time and motion chart – a temporary realignment of their professional (working engineers') forms of representation. And, of course, our sharing of time and speech unfortunately came to an end when I left the field. How the group communicated after my departure I do not know. I suspect that, as before my arrival, rather than making research explicit, they relied again upon speech with each other about their social situation.

I would have missed out on these recontextualizations of knowledge, however, if we had not been able to co-produce the convergences of so-called technological and social forms of knowledge (Grint and Woolgar 1997). On their time and motion chart the French engineers literally connected the dots – or, in this case, the x's – for me, and those x's overlap at the margins of chronological categories – or steps – thus accounting in a particularly evocative way for tensions in the movement of social relations at YamaMax. While, especially among relatively highly ranked persons in modern organizational settings, the collective situation of the French engineers was perhaps unorthodox, who would, after all, be expert (Bauman 1987, 1993; Beck 1992; Wynne 1996; Berglund 1998; Lee and Hassard 1999) – an anthropologist or the engineers – in progressing such forms of knowledge in a factory?

References

Bauman, Z. 1987. *Legislators and Interpreters: On Modernity, Postmodernity and Intellectuals.* Cambridge: Polity.

———. 1993. *Postmodern Ethics.* Oxford and Cambridge, MA: Blackwell.

Beck, U. 1992. *Risk Society: Towards a New Modernity.* London: Sage.

Berglund, E. 1998. *Knowing Nature, Knowing Science: An Ethnography of Environmental Activism*. Cambridge: White Horse Press.

Callon, M. 1986. 'Some Elements of a Sociology of Translation: Domestication of the Scallops and the Fishermen of St. Brieuc Bay', in J. Law (ed.), *Power, Action and Belief: A New Sociology of Knowledge?* Sociological Review Monograph 32. London, Boston, and Henley: Routledge and Kegan Paul.

Czarniawska, B. 1997. *Narrating the Organization: Dramas of Institutional Identity*. Chicago: University of Chicago Press.

Fabian, J. 1983. *Time and the Other: How Anthropology Makes Its Object*. New York: Columbia University Press.

Grint, K. and S. Woolgar. 1997. *The Machine at Work: Technology, Work and Organization*. Cambridge: Polity.

Latour, B. 1986. 'The Powers of Association', in J. Law (ed.), *Power, Action and Belief: A New Sociology of Knowledge?* Sociological Review Monograph 32. London, Boston, and Henley: Routledge and Kegan Paul.

———. 1987. *Science in Action*. Cambridge, MA: Harvard University Press.

———. 1988. *The Pasteurization of France*. Cambridge, MA: Harvard University Press.

———. 1999. 'On Recalling ANT', in J. Law and J. Hassard (eds), *Actor Network Theory: and After*. Oxford: Blackwell.

Latour, B. and S. Woolgar. 1979. *Laboratory Life: The Social Construction of Scientific Facts*. Beverly Hills and London: Sage.

Law, J. (ed.). 1986. *Power, Action and Belief: A New Sociology of Knowledge?* Sociological Review Monograph 32. London, Boston, and Henley: Routledge and Kegan Paul.

Lee, N. and J. Hassard. 1999. 'Organization Unbound: Actor-Network Theory, Research Strategy and Institutional Flexibility', *Organization* 6(3): 391–404.

Lefebvre, H. 1991 [1974]. *The Production of Space*. Oxford: Blackwell.

Orlikowski, W. J. 1992. 'The Duality of Technology: Rethinking the Concept of Technology in Organizations', *Organization Science* 3: 398–426.

Rabinow, P. 1977. *Reflections on Fieldwork in Morocco*. Berkeley: University of California Press.

Sedgwick, M. W. 2000. The Globalizations of Japanese Managers', in H. Befu, J. S. Eades, and T. Gill (eds), *Globalization and Social Change in Contemporary Japan*. Melbourne: Trans Pacific Press.

———. 2001. 'Positioning "Globalization" at Overseas Subsidiaries of Japanese Multinational Corporations', in H. Befu and S. Guichard-Anguis (eds), *Globalizing Japan: Ethnography of the Japanese Presence in Asia, Europe and America*. London: Routledge.

———. 2007. *Globalisation and Japanese Organisational Culture: An Ethnography of a Japanese Corporation in France*. London, New York: Routledge.

Sorokin, P. and R. Merton. 1937. 'Social-Time: A Methodological and Functional Analysis', *American Journal of Sociology* 42: 615–29.

Taussig, M. 1992. *The Nervous System*. New York: Routledge.

Watson, T. J. 2000. 'Ethnographic Fiction Science: Making Sense of Managerial Work and Organizational Research Processes with Caroline and Terry', *Organization* 7(3): 489–510.

Wynne, B. 1996. 'May the Sheep Safely Graze? A Reflexive View on the Expert/Lay Knowledge Divide', in S. Lash, B. Szerszynski, and B. Wynne (eds), *Risk, Environment and Modernity: Towards a New Ecology*. London: Sage.

Yeung, H. W. 1998. 'The Social-Spatial Constitution of Business Organizations: A Geographical Perspective', *Organization* 5(1): 101–28.

Chapter 10
Making Space in Finland's New Economy

Eeva Berglund

Co-ordinates

This chapter focuses on the Finnish province of Kainuu.[1] For me, Helsinki-born, Kainuu, with its expansive forests and almost empty roads, was long associated with remoteness and poverty. Numerous trips since 1996 have modified, if not completely overturned, these associations. My travel has transformed the vastness of its undifferentiated forested landscapes into landmarks like roads, fells, mires, lakes, and small towns that help me orient myself. I have invested them with significance and recognized that they are resources for managing life. In this process, the 'mediatized' imagery of Kainuu's burgeoning tourist industry, an international music festival, and other 'landscapes of publicity' (Paasi 2003) have become entwined in encounters with people and the environs, including visceral ones experienced in the freezing cold of midwinter and the continental heat of late summer. Besides forests and towns, my ethnography has taken me through airports and bus stations as well as into homes and government offices. The 'here and now' of the endeavour has been routed through a dense network of information and communications technologies – emails and websites – that seem to make distance unimportant. The result has been an experience of place as a multiple and sometimes clashing array of possible backgrounds to current activity, from deeply sensed places to what Marc Augé has termed 'non-place' (1995). The soundtracks of this travel have included a constant stream of political rhetoric according to which the world, Finland foremost perhaps, is on the move, hurtling towards a glorious future made up of cleaner and greener ways of life that enhance everyone's connectivity.

The dominant message is that inescapable technological innovation has relegated the fixities of modernity to history. Success in global competition

1. It is not, strictly speaking, a province. However, regional political boundaries are not comparable across countries and they also change as they did in Finland in the late 1990s. By using this term I hope to imply a certain peripherality yet internal and administrative unity.

through the capital-intensive and knowledge-powered industries promoted as part of Finland's National Innovation System (NIS) has put the country onto an accelerated path to global markets.[2] Flux, novelty, and speed are its virtues. They are also ends in themselves: in fact, they are becoming the co-ordinates for orienting and for conducting one's behaviour. In a country where the name Manuel Castells is known well beyond social science audiences,[3] the idea that society is a network or a space of flows has taken over from older sociological and policy co-ordinates like status hierarchies and bounded spaces, leaving the impression that modernity was about stasis, but that now we are on the move (Berglund 2007). In this new era of globalization, Finland is at the forefront, so the media reports. Since it emerged out of a huge recession in the early 1990s, massive intellectual energy and collective wealth has been invested in the business of innovation but also in monitoring the productivity of these investments and making the nation aware of home-grown successes. International indices of competitiveness, wealth, and well-being, where Finland features at, or near, the top, are published with ritual fervour. Finland might once, they seem to say, have been on the edge and far behind, but no longer.[4]

With the celebrated success of Finnish brands around the world and the ever more conspicuous circulation of knowledge workers into and out of Finland, the burden of distance appears to have been conquered.[5] Although the 'global' is talked about as emanating from elsewhere, Finland and Finns actively participate in it. 'Globe' and 'globalization' have taken on a massive symbolic weight, putting the ambiguities and complexities that such abstract concepts involve into service as co-ordinates for collective action here and now. If the global network presents few, if any, spatial limits, technology also allows society to sidestep questions of exhaustion, death, and decay (see also Pedersen, this volume).[6]

2. For an account that is both academic and policy-relevant see Schienstock and Kuusi (1999).
3. Castells co-authored a book with a Finn, Pekka Himanen (see References), and has often been referred to in management and public discourses on the social transformation Finland has experienced.
4. I have written in detail elsewhere of Finland's shift towards an information society (Berglund 2003, 2007). The key issue is that for any significant transformation we must look back to the period between the late 1980s and the mid-1990s. In the early 1980s the economy was still treated as a national project tied to the forest products industries. In the wake of 1989 there was a massive recession that fuelled fears of marginalization and economic decline. Instead, however, of being ignored or, worse still, being seen as backward (maybe even 'Eastern European'), Finland emerged out of the recession as a high technology exporter. High-tech exports jumped from 4 per cent in 1988 to 19 per cent in 1998 and have continued to grow. Oriented towards a volatile international market for forest products, the Finnish economy has long been dependent on events far away (Lehtinen 2002). Where the forest sector used to argue that it had no choice but to dance to a global tune, now the same justification is used for the constant upgrading of the knowledge-intensive industries.
5. As Massey (2005) points out, distance is not always a burden.
6. This is inspired by Teresa Brennan's original and insightful thoughts on modernity (e.g., 2000).

This chapter follows existing critiques of the common, but incoherent, ideology that treats globalization as 'a historical queue' (as Doreen Massey (2005) puts it). In this understanding globalization is a process that collapses the discrete spaces of a receding modernity into one space and one history, that of the 'advanced' countries (2005: 68). In this conceptualization there is only one history and one future. Those who are not recognized as being global moderns are assumed to be not elsewhere or even on their way somewhere else, but simply lagging behind. Indeed, some of the people I describe below are, or have been, seen by others as not only being of the backwoods but being backward. Following Eric Wolf's (1982) meditation on European conceits, they may not quite be people without history, just people with somewhat less of it. At best, they are minor players in somebody else's history.

'We haven't got all those country estates like you have', I was told. The reference was to southern Finland, historically wealthier than the country's northern parts. But it was the 'green gold' harnessed from all over the country that allowed the southern estates to flourish. As elsewhere, those at the front of the queue owe much of their well-being to others.

Whereas once it was a national imperative to help support the forest industries, now Finns do their civic duty by trying to out-compete each other in innovativeness and entrepreneurship. This makes the past look static and the future predetermined. It also gives rise to nostalgic remembrances of past social and spatial orders.

Looking back on it, Finland's forest-dependent economy appears as a combination of place-bound agrarian culture and the stifling social relations of industrial production. Looking forward, government discourse celebrates post-industrial success, where everything seems connected to everything else in fluid, horizontal, democratic and always positive sounding networks. Now culture and technology, meaning and technique, identity and citizenship blur into each other and replace bounded territories with spaces of flows (see, e.g., Castells and Himanen 2001). This optimistic view is further bolstered by a scholarly emphasis on transnational flows that create compressed and monolithic space-times (Kirby, Chapter One, this volume). By following movements whose context is both the hyper-mobility of this twenty-first-century social model and the embodied memory of proximate landscapes, I seek both a more realistic and less constraining account, one where space is relational and alive. At the same time, I can discern ways in which the rhetoric of flow and connectedness obscures a reality of control and constraint.

My tool is ethnography. It draws attention to the way interactions, movement, encounters, and forms of knowledge make places, and to how social relations are made together with spatial relations. It challenges the homogenizing geography of global-speak, and aims to present geography and history as multiplicity. This offers the possibility of a more open future (Massey 2005).

Massey is a geographer, but her principles fit with (and owe a lot to) what ethnographers do so well – tracing partial connections. Anthropologists, whose research tends to generate great detail, do this routinely and explicitly. From the creativity of everyday life they can then articulate a valuable corrective to the monolithic voices that proclaim either total gloom or naive optimism. In the humanities and social sciences, the impulse generally has been to argue for a future that is open and unlimited by narrow philosophies and that does not serve even narrower economic interests. Anthropological practice has already pursued this by moving from an ethnography of locations to one of circulations (Appadurai 2002: 23). This is not to deny the significance of non-place, in Augé's terms, but to reassess the continuing work that makes space and that takes place even in an age imagined as freed of spatial constraints.

I present four accounts of making space. They show that space is not only a daily preoccupation but one whose sustainability is constantly in question. The regionalist discourses and practices that I describe unfold in relation to significant geopolitical shifts. These enhance old forms of interconnectedness yet nurture mutual desires to exclude. Regionalist discourses, for example, often serve to obscure consequential rematerializations and remarkings of the environs. But I want to highlight possible ways that heightened awareness of one's surroundings also expresses and creates sustainable space (Berland 2005: 55). Put another way, if my informants tell me that they are concerned to protect their world by learning to manage what they consider their space, at some level I must take them at their word.

One reason why I decided to carry out fieldwork in Kainuu was that so many people I spoke to told me of the difficulties of living there under globalization while remaining committed to staying. I discerned a constant and noteworthy need to elaborate on spatial and temporal co-ordinates and people were, on the whole, keen to talk about their predicament. Their self-consciousness about their identity might be considered postmodern in its anxiousness yet rather non-modern in its disregard for external validation. It is perhaps unremarkable also in the sense that at the margins geography is harder to overlook than at the centre. I write this recalling the woman in the kiosk where I once bought a copy of Finland's only national newspaper, *Helsingin Sanomat* (Helsinki News). 'Ah', she said winking at another customer, 'so you're from there, that far-away town. From where we are, it's Helsinki that's the periphery'.

If space is something lived and felt, as it evidently was for her, it becomes easier to theorize about it without falling into the tunnel-view of globalization where only the one spatial order is possible. Ethnography and descriptive narrative may also help avoid discriminating against textual and other cultural practices associated with modernity (Harvey 1996: 181). After all, cultural theorizing notwithstanding, there remain risks for both author and reader of collapsing notions of authenticity and locality into each other and of seeking to either vindicate or demonize the self-exoticization that, as elsewhere, is ubiquitous in Kainuu. Undoubtedly my own affective relations to the material presented will be apparent. Hopefully they will assist rather than hinder the aim of making emerging spatial experiences discussable (cf. Hastrup 1989: 7), helping people, including social researchers, to 'find [their] feet in a strange new world' (Gupta and Ferguson 1997: 26).

I begin with an interview with a professional in a high-profile job in the regional Forestry Centre. When she was a child, her parents' work carried the family around the small towns of the region. Eventually, like many others, together with her sister, she went to live with a relative, her grandmother, in the one largish town where there was an upper school.

She used a common expression to refer to her experiences of natural environments: she said she 'moved in nature' (*kuljin luonnossa*), a phrase perhaps more idiomatically translated as 'spent time outdoors' but which in the Finnish renders alive the movement that is part of engaging with the environment.

> An ordinary family from Kainuu like us, we berry-picked and fished, and so I've really grown up on this natural bounty (*luonnon antimet*). We had lots of game and fish at meal times. My cousin, uncle and grandfather were hunters and I used to go with them. So my uncle ended up saying I should get a hunting permit too, after all, he said, I always had hares practically running at me. I wasn't that enthusiastic about it at first, but then at 16 I got my permit and I've had it ever since. As a young woman I was a keen hunter. It was fun. I went on my own to catch birds, and with the boys we chased hare. … Well, as I think of my childhood and a personal relationship to the forest. You know that Puolanka is by a lake with the forests right there, so we played a lot in the forest, climbed the trees. I remember for example the Saturdays (when my mother worked), the neighbours looking out for us, but I do remember that there were times when she [the neighbour] just didn't have the time and we'd climb into the trees. … We had lots of tree houses, and I remember what it's like to climb up an aspen and what it's like to climb a spruce and what it's like to climb a pine. In Germany today they have these 'forest kindergartens' but for us it was just natural growing up in Puolanka. And when we played, we usually created [a world] in the forest. Little towns or houses out of wood, sculpted stuff out of snow. We had living rooms … we made dolls for ourselves out of twigs and logs … or pets, and pine needles and sticks were for household things.

I have heard many such accounts in Kainuu. They belie a romanticism and nostalgia for a past not dissimilar to the wilderness ideals described by critical environmental historians, particularly of North America (Cronon 1995). However, local discourses in Kainuu present nature/wilderness and culture/people as one unity, neither conceptually nor geographically severed. To give an example, Kainuu's long dependency on forests means that nobody but an outsider could assume that they are untouched by humans. To learn about life and livelihood in places that are economically so dependent on natural resources means understanding forests and nature as thoroughly implicated in human affairs and vice versa.

Anthropologists know that for many the landscape is still experienced explicitly as part of social relations (Hirsch and O'Hanlon 1995; Kirsch 2001; Anderson and Berglund 2003). For instance, in his essay, 'Wisdom sits in places: notes on an Apache landscape', Keith Basso (1996: 54) notes the following:

> [N]ow and again, and sometimes without apparent cause, awareness is seized – arrested – and the place on which it settles becomes an object of spontaneous reflection and resonating sentiment. It is at times such as these, when individuals step back from the flow of everyday experience and attend self-consciously to places – when, we may say, they pause to actively sense them – that their relationships to geographical space are most richly lived and surely felt.

The Apache Basso describes appropriate features of the landscape – cottonwood trees, hills, and so on – in conversations about moral conduct. Basso gives the example of a young man whose behaviour elicits condemnation. Once the youth has acknowledged his transgressions, his friends have no wish to humiliate him further. Instead they make reference to a trail between two hills, a place where in the past a badly-behaved old man suffered for his transgressions. In the social interaction, it is the landscape that tells the important part of the story.

Basso's description emphasizes the interanimation of the physical and the imagined or symbolized. 'Locked within the mental horizons of those who give it life, sense of place issues in a stream of symbolically drawn particulars – the visible particulars of local topographies, the personal particulars of biographical associations, socially given systems of thought' (Basso 1996: 84). For him, sense of place is about connection to the past via the landscape, and therefore about selfhood, but it is also, as his title indicates, a resource, a form of wisdom, a form of thinking about thinking itself (1996: 86).

Basso draws on the kinds of insights that ethnographic research routinely generates: attention to practice in contingent yet culturally anchored co-ordinates, spatial and temporal. Ethnographic attention will inevitably emphasize the embodied experience of space, a stance that can be glossed as phenomenological. Yet what expresses itself as a visceral experience – the moving in the forest – is an ongoing social relationship that weaves together past people, future possibilities, and topography. As Kirby's introduction (Chapter One) to this volume argues, social theory is increasingly concerned to highlight that space is never uniform or universal. How it appears depends on how, when and by whom it is perceived, and on what hopes, dreams and powers of control inform this. I want to suggest that the physical and social are interanimated here too, just as Basso described. I suggest, further, that awareness is seized in other ways, using and creating other co-ordinates, from other spatial orders, including those that originated in the flattened-out spaces of government expertise. Even mapping, that quintessentially colonialist, modernist practice, can become resource for making space that is 'richly lived and surely felt' (Basso 1996: 54).

Mapping 1 – Land

At the level of regions and communities, spatial arrangements in Finland are largely the product of what, for convenience, I term the Forest State. Throughout most of the twentieth century, and particularly from independence (1917) onwards,[7] it seemed that Finland was, and always would be, a forest economy. Exceptionally among forest-exploiting economies, Finnish forests are, and have been, overwhelmingly in small-scale ownership, even though their management has been overseen by state experts. Despite ownership being fragmented, since the 1850s management has been standardized across the nation (Laitakari 1961; Lehtinen 1991).

Finland was constructed as a nation through weaving together nature, technology, and people. With the aid of modern, topographic maps, the co-ordinates of the Forest State became isomorphic with national boundaries, the borders of the Finnish state marking where Finnish forest management reigned sovereign (Michelsen 1995). A wonderful illustration of this is a sketch-map from an industry brochure of the mid-1990s, where a tree-covered Finland is suspended in limbo with no neighbouring countries or other geographical features marked at all. Like forest administrations elsewhere (Lowood 1990), the Finnish state institutionalized rationality and progress in the routine measurement of land and its produce.

The history of the Finnish Forest State can be read almost as a caricature of Foucauldian governmentality (Berglund 2000b), with maps and censuses in place in Finland since the sixteenth century, when it was part of the Swedish empire (Paasi 1996; Häkli 1998). Official maps served some interests better than others, but new divisions notwithstanding, modernity and modern spatial techniques became widely embraced as meaningful and technically indispensable. For the state, maps made control from a distance possible.

7. Until then Finland had been an autonomous Grand Duchy of the Russian Empire.

Modern mapping is considered above all a colonialist, modernist technology of control. Often stirred by Heidegger's critique of the concept of a 'worldview' (1977), scholars have shown how frameworks like the urban plan, the map, or the school curriculum, made the world into something to be managed through expertise (Mitchell 1988). In the colonizing schema everything must have its place or it poses a potentially terrible risk. This anxiety is still with us, perhaps even more than before. For whilst hyperglobalization is celebrated, refugees, infectious disease, toxic wastes, and other frightening pollutants proliferate. These 'problems' are above all problems because they are the wrong kind of overspill, the wrong kind of flow, seeping across national borders, making the maps useless, no longer corresponding to the reality they are supposed to represent. As these processes are debated by 'communities', politicians, and scholars, invocations of mapping, both literal and metaphorical, are ubiquitous.

Overturning once-unquestioned assumptions about the neutral relationship between the world and maps, mapping has been rightly identified as a deeply political act (Mitchell 1988; Winichakul 1994; Häkli 1998). Against the background of such a robust academic deconstruction, any defence of boundaries or marking territory based on maps is bound to at least raise suspicions of parochialism and xenophobia. The current politics of demarcation, whether as control of space or as mapping culture, cannot easily distance itself from a legacy of territorial relations that was achieved only with great violence. Even when they are not imposed as state technologies, boundaries can be violently ethnicized and anxiously policed (Sivaramakrishnan and Vaccaro 2006) and so it is understandable and important for scholarship to continue questioning the imputed 'naturalness' of any map.

Yet there is more to this story. As well as being tools of government and domination, maps and mapped knowledge can also be a form of resistance (e.g., Berglund 2000a; Appadurai 2002). In Finland they underpinned the prosperity of the twentieth century. Not to be forgotten, they also played a part in Finland's successful bid to break free of Russian domination (Paasi 1996; Häkli 1998). As key technical aids of forestry, maps symbolized and materialized national consensus on resource-use. To put it another way, they mediated the social contract in which the discipline required by the Forest State was traded for forest-based wealth, security and self-esteem among the population.[8] Finally, maps and the territory to which they refer have affective power, not least because they symbolized independence and freedom as precarious, but therefore all the more precious, achievements at national level.

8. Which is not to ignore the civil war or the painful internal divisions elaborated on by Paasi (1996).

The Finns became passionate about inventorying and mapping. In the late twentieth century, this passion spread to environmentalists, as most of those involved in forest conflicts now embrace mapping as the way to an accurate understanding of the true state of the country's forests. Although there is continuing disagreement on what the maps are saying (Berglund 2000a, 2000b) all parties remain committed to using them. Furthermore, everyone in Finland knows that maps are not the same thing as terrain. Finnish forests are generally unfenced and unmarked, and every person's rights to move and even pick berries and mushrooms, even in privately owned forest, remain cherished. What is interesting, however, is that since the late 1980s conflicts over land-use have been leading to pressure to parcel out Finland's forests into spatially segregated and ever more regulated areas, here for industrial use, there for strict conservation. There is some irony in the fact that the era of the Forest State secured relatively free movement through Finnish forests, whereas in the supposedly eco-friendly era of the network, the possibility of literal enclosure seems more real than before.

To return to the childhood recollections I quoted above, at the time my interviewee was working for the regional forest administration, where her job involved overseeing a constant process of map-making. Rather than assume her passion for moving in nature to be some kind of moral compensation for a life of map-making, I would argue that the two go together. Her own view is that working for the forest administration is seamlessly tied to her childhood experiences. I suggest that maps, even modern maps, can intertwine with meanders and generate new ways of making space and meaning.

Mapping 2 – Culture

Society has changed in many ways, but Augé suggests that what has really changed is the meaning of meaning. It is not that 'the world lacks meaning, or has little meaning, or less than it used to have; it is that we seem to feel an explicit and intense daily need to give it meaning' (1995: 29).

This resonates powerfully with my experience of travelling around Finland, encountering people and places, all eager to promote a particular image of themselves and their homes, and often keen to enter into dialogue with an anthropologist interested in the changing meanings of forest, resources, place, identity, nationhood, and technology.

The website of the small town where I did much of my fieldwork states the following:

> Prizes for being Finland's most creative municipality, for developing a successful image and for municipal development all testify to the open-minded, lively and bold activities of Sotkamo Municipality. The

> Vuokatti area ranks as one of the world's most versatile tourism centres offering activities all the year round while Sotkamo as a whole boasts high quality municipal and private services. Here you'll find an excellent environment both for living and for conducting business amidst beautiful unspoilt nature. The constant stream of events and happenings throughout the municipality add attractiveness and spice to life here in Sotkamo.

Sotkamo is situated, the reader is told, right in the middle of Kainuu, which is also energetically envisioning its future and representing itself. This is part of a frantic process going on across Kainuu, all of Finland, maybe even Europe, of making economic and political security as evident as possible. It is about planning for flux and constant innovation.

Rural and sparsely populated, Kainuu suffered from entry into the European Union (in 1995), with unemployment (over 20 per cent in 2000) continuing to be significantly higher than average. Until the 1960s, the majority of men in the region earned at least some income from seasonal forestry work but since 1963 the population has been declining. Since 1995, farm sizes were increased, further reducing the need for agricultural and forest-related labour. Kainuu's problems are not altogether new, nor are the tensions between stability and mobility novel. Proximity to the Russian border means that the Second World War is still actively remembered, particularly in the towns and villages that were destroyed or (temporarily) evacuated. After the war, the government relocated thousands of refugees from areas ceded to the Soviet Union in the Second World War, to establish farms in difficult conditions at the edge not only of Finland, but of the 'West'.

Joining the European Union was widely opposed and has meant severe readjustments. Life seems to be gravitating towards spatial clusters of innovation elsewhere. But regional policy and science and technology policy remain integrated and geared towards minimizing regional inequalities.[9] The aim is to improve the economic, social, and cultural competitiveness of the regions based on their own resources, characteristics, and needs.

Preoccupation with competitive advantage goes together with the increasing visibility of territorially specified identities. Simultaneously, contests over images of place are on the rise and cities, regions, and countries are giving themselves quasi-brands. Finnish publicity materials yield the following examples: Helsinki is the innovative city, Uusikaupunki the innovative engine of south-west Finland, and Kainuu promotes itself with the slogan 'Kainuu:

9. In Finland, regional policy and science and technology policy have always been closely intertwined. (See Pesonen and Riihinen 2002; Science And Technology Policy Council Of Finland 2003.)

renowned for its nature'. There is little, in fact, to distinguish these places, and the quotation above could be from almost anywhere. Interestingly, the first or nearly first 'attraction' to be mentioned is generally that municipality 'X' is located centrally/conveniently/close to somewhere else. So much for the reduced importance of place in the new economy!

These slogans and brands form what Anssi Paasi (2003) calls landscapes of publicity. From a critical social science perspective, such commodification might be expected to have an enfeebling, not enhancing, effect on sense of place. Particularly where identity politics and environmental politics come together – as they often do in Kainuu – media circuits exact their own price in decontextualized and always already self-conscious images that often play on the exoticism or naturalness of their object (Kirsch 2001; Nugent 2003). Religious and community observances also get caught up in the sign economy of consumer capitalism. It has fostered self-exoticization, made manifest in images that make a virtue of rurality, marginality, naturalness, and authenticity, and even quiet, remoteness, and slowness. Tourism, which primarily fuels this discourse, is, however, only one way in which Kainuu hopes to commercialize its natural resources. It is equally preoccupied with making visible the forest products industries and food processing, its other key economic assets. Natural capital then, and not intellectual capital, is poised to remain Kainuu's source of economic security.

Understood in context, such landscapes of publicity cannot be reduced to the 'inauthentic' half of a dichotomy between image projected outwards versus reality experienced on site (cf. Harvey 1996). Despite the intensifying interest in regional identities, ideas of landscape and identity – and therefore spatial imaginations – are very much open to challenge and reinterpretation (Paasi 2003) and to material reworking. That maps are made and remade as part of such a project is as unremarkable a fact of life now as is the fact that forests grow, are cut down, and grow back again.

Learning 1: Schools

Regional and local self-awareness have been enhanced by the province's Schools Forest Week for some years now. An annual event, it promotes forestry as a viable and important economic activity. In an already apparently forest-saturated region of an equally forest-obsessed country (at least until recently), this initially appears strange, but is but one response to the relative decline of the industry and to the need for some kind of consensus surrounding the question of conservation. Its originator, a historian and a regional public intellectual,[10] sees it as a way to introduce school-goers to the forest as a

10. Sakari Virtanen, who was my host and who opened many doors and suggested many roads. To him, my grateful thanks.

package of 'nature, economics, society and the human spirit' in Kainuu (personal communication). It is also a way to make explicit possible ways of connecting up to the network society. Since the late 1990s it has been run every year in a different municipality. Events have been aimed at all age groups, from pre-school day-care centres to old-people's homes, and all aspects of the school curriculum are covered. Mathematics teachers teach about methods of calculating increments of timber; history teachers about the various ways life has been embedded in forests; language teachers about the vocabulary of forests, and so on. Most classes are also taken on a field trip. The one I describe took place at the start of the 2001 school year.

The situation resembled modern tourism as a form of travelling elsewhere to experience the sublime (Cronon 1995). Over thirty 12-year-olds piled into a bus with representatives of the local forestry association, the Forestry Board, and the environment section of the Forest and Park Service. Besides myself, several other hangers on and a journalist were also present. By the time they spilled out into a forest plot on a local farm, the children had been introduced to the facts and figures of forestry in the area, from privately owned to state and corporate owned lands, and from intensively managed forest to conservation zones.

Visual contemplation (as of a view), the mode of relating to landscape said to be typical of modern nature lovers, is compromised in much of Finland by the closeness of the forest on either side of the road. Only at hilltops or lakesides can one usually enjoy a vista. The expanse of forest nevertheless has the capacity to impress the traveller. Such experiences are commonplace for locals, given that trips of 100 km or more to the theatre, parties or other social events are considered unremarkable, thus creating dense social networks that cover vast distances. The point is that on this trip as on others what might appear as monotonous landscape was narrated and, I can only infer, also apprehended as a social milieu laden with history and with plans for the future. This means that the social fabric these movements weave is quite different from that generated in city-dwellers' periodic efforts to 'get away from it all' in the wilderness (Cronon 1995: 85).

The speakers referred to maps where the municipality and the whole of Kainuu were shown divided into various shades of green to designate the different management categories. State-owned forests were presented as collective heritage, with emphasis laid on the responsibility that the younger generation now has for caring for it. However, rather than simply a process of imprinting upon impressionable minds the appropriate understandings of territory, proper management, and, of course, use or ownership rights, reading the maps also created an idiom for understanding belonging: we are part of this area; we are here.

A few children appeared to be indignant that they were being treated as if they did not know what it was like to work with forests, to live on a farm, to sell timber or to apply for EU (European Union) funds and so on. However, as the children were introduced to machinery, old and new, and to the techniques for measuring the age and size of trees, some of the older people present wondered in whispers to each other whether this generation, brought up on computer games, would ever be inclined to follow its forefathers. The secure past of the Forest State was receding into memory, and here its slipping into the past was practically being performed before their very eyes. Only recently useful chainsaws were displayed as if in a museum.

The event created a landscape of publicity, but for local attention. It was a response to a local need to safeguard important elements of sociability. It was a way of highlighting the need to create and recreate space sustainably within the co-ordinates set by national and international economic arrangements. So although such self-exoticization could be read as nostalgia or as a denial of local agency, even as something submitting to the desires of audiences and consumers elsewhere, from within Kainuu forestry is neither exotic nor historic. The large paper mill in Kajaani is expected to remain a going concern, despite the globalization of the forest sector too (see Lehtinen 2002). It may require less labour than before, but it still needs forests.

Moving in nature in this context wove together considerations for affect and economic survival. Such events make explicit differences between types of mobility, reminding participants of the spatial and temporal commitments of forestry, and also of the limits to the flux of the network. Furthermore, it recalls the continuing material needs of the network society, global paper consumption continuing to be on the rise. Thus the event expresses and affirms the sentiment that Kainuu, as it is, is neither backwoods nor backward. Its future, furthermore, lies right here.

As Basso describes sense of place, it is a form of wisdom, an understanding of life's spaces and times. What I have described is just this. Certainly it is informed by the landscapes of publicity that impinge on all of the projects underway as part of Kainuu's regeneration efforts. As well as meaning and new self-knowledge, however, events like the Schools' Forest Week are about acquiring the necessary skills for living, including those of nationally and internationally oriented schooling, as well as those that are regional and place-specific. Thus at issue is not just forest management but the reproduction of social relations.

This can also be seen in yet another form of contemporary self-knowledge, a 1997 survey on Kainuu's relationship to its natural resources. It provides ample evidence that for the vast majority of Kainuu's people, forests remain both meaningful and useful in commercial and non-commercial senses (Mäntymaa 1998). Undoubtedly there is politics, perhaps even exclusionary politics, involved in such research, but the point is that such mixes of pedagogy and affect open up and invite a range of possible futures that are not collapsible into the 'centre's' self-deluding narratives of homogenous globalization.

Learning 2: High-tech

In his influential work on perception and culture, Tim Ingold has abstracted out a distinction between a Cartesian ontology that separates subject and object, culture and nature, and an alternative ontology, the dwelling perspective, where natural and social history are seen as mutually constitutive, even continuous (Ingold 2000: Part II). This means that people and their surroundings exist in continuous intercourse and thus mutual dependency, acknowledged or not. However, those with spatially large-scale powers of control, colonizers particularly but moderns generally, imagine that their lives unfold according not to animal instinct or even tradition or convention, but to rational planning. Anthropologists have echoed this view, according to Ingold, whenever they have supposed that truly modern societies inhabit 'artificial' worlds whereas others, notably hunting and gathering societies inhabit 'natural' ones (2000: 181). The creation of imagery and landscapes of publicity subsumes the natural into the artificial, making it, in Marilyn Strathern's terms, 'after nature' (1992). And yet, as I hope my ethnography has indicated, this has not meant erasing landmarks, forgetting social histories or acquiescing to the network society's need for mobility. Like the woman I quoted at the beginning, many people are making a choice to 'move in nature' in Kainuu.

In Sotkamo there is a biotechnology laboratory. Since 2000 it has employed about sixteen people. It is the municipality's most obvious information-based economic unit, if not the most artificial. Sotkamo also boasts an indoor ski tunnel and an all-year tropical spa! The laboratory was founded in 1996 as part of efforts to reorient the regional economy away from primary production towards the knowledge society. Its remit was technology transfer, supporting the commercialization of local nature, notably berries and herbs, but initially also the dairy products that were processed in the dairy in whose buildings the laboratory was housed. It was not a completely new departure for the town, since the dairy had had research facilities there before. The rationale for high-tech here was inextricably tied to natural resources. As interviewees and the media put it, the challenge was a spatial one: how to transport Kainuu's riches elsewhere in exchange for money.

By the time I went there in 2000, a decision had already been taken to close not only the dairy's own research unit, but eventually the entire plant. By 2002 rumour had it that the former dairy was to be used as a call-centre. The closure would raise unemployment but some local farmers should benefit from the resulting economies of scale. The situation was often seen as a case of competition between industrial workers and agricultural workers which, this time, the latter won. That such dilemmas are a part of life was an oft-stated axiom. Indeed, one of the phrases I most came across in all my encounters was that, 'Well, we're living in a market economy now'. It reflected a sense that guarantees once provided by the forest-state and its agricultural supplements were being eroded.

The laboratory's task has been to find in the surroundings, with the help of modern techniques, raw materials with beneficial properties, e.g., berries, pine tar, that could then be systematically isolated and rendered into commercializable cosmetic and food products. Regional policy sees the laboratory as a node in the information network. Yet it is constituted as movement of information and matter, including people, that become resources for making sustainable space right here in Sotkamo and its surroundings.

Most of the workers were extremely pleased to have found jobs that fitted their training in such an unlikely place. Depending on their particular remit in the laboratory, some had more interaction with colleagues via the Internet or on trips to other research units than others. They claimed they had no problem negotiating the geographical location of the laboratory and its anchoring in local and regional natural products at the same time as playing a role in international networks of plant and food scientists. This mixture of places and networks is, after all, how science has always operated (Ingold 2000: 299). What did worry many was that the globalized, market-oriented universe of the laboratory that employed them was potentially precarious, whereas the socially embedded but economically depressed world within Kainuu was so solid. Optimism was nurtured by tourism and the continuing liveliness of Oulu University and Kajaani (the regional capital), the two largest nearby conurbations, and regular nodes in the weekly (or at least monthly), if not daily, routines of the workers.

Although the atmosphere at the laboratory always appeared optimistic, the spatial challenge has become worse, not better, as national and international food markets continue to move towards larger units at greater distances from each other. Because dairy production was once quite significant to the laboratory as well as to the region, its logics and logistics were a constant topic of conversation. As the director explained, raw materials for the dairy have come largely from Kainuu but are processed increasingly far away in Oulu and even further afield. 'Freight distances will therefore grow, and the situation is most miserable in Lapland. This year or next year they'll cease operations in Rovaniemi. All the way from the north then, milk will travel to Oulu [for processing] and be brought back as cartoned milk to the shops'. He went on to complain that the overall politics of centralization was itself misguided, implying that the somewhat foolhardy project of the laboratory itself was at least some kind of effort to halt or modify it. His ultimate vision was of a Finland with perhaps only one cheese-making plant in fifteen years – maybe not even that – when Finland as a 'market' will be treated as a 'far too small operating environment' and 'the whole of Scandinavia will have one plant, and then one day… They always find the justifications, don't they'. At the laboratory, the madness of global trade in food was a source of endless jokes: 'I wonder at which point the Finnish ferry-load of yoghurt passes the Swedish one [making the identical trip in the opposite direction]'.

The laboratory is also caught up in landscapes of publicity. As funding is increasingly organized around projects that compete for attention, even within the regional framework of science and technology policy, energies are required to publicize the potentials and results of the laboratory. The challenges they face are not so much scientific or technical, as to do with marketing. To put it in spatial terms, to make their lives and their space sustainable, they must travel elsewhere, virtually or in person, to find markets. Here is anxiety and a fear of losing control. Against such a background, the use of modern resources to plan the future, such as capital-intensive technology or marketing tools, becomes fused into the dwelling perspective. Whether moving in nature or moving around the Internet, the guiding principle of their activities is making space that is sustainable.

Moving Forward

Economic agendas are now routinely set in relation to the imagined placelessness, timelessness and, indeed, the unitary time of globalization. This encourages a nostalgia for the future that sets impossible goals. Nostalgia for the past meanwhile feeds selective amnesia. As rhetorics, both have the effect of occluding dependency on space and time and of fudging differences in entitlement to space and time. The practices they foster are intensifying contests over localized identities, so that people are compelled constantly to demonstrate that they exist and matter. They must represent themselves so that the fast-moving and perhaps distant audience stops to take note. Their choice is not whether or not to represent, but how. Everywhere one encounters a plethora of spatial representations that render questions about authenticity outdated.

Such attention-seeking seems necessary now to survival. It makes it almost impossible not to be preoccupied by space. Drawing on a society that is particularly vexed by spatial issues, I have sought to discuss space not as a context for action or as a static background, but as a set of practices, as movement. I have described everyday routes on which people employ the skills and wisdoms necessary for reproducing society. I have, furthermore, described how they also manipulate landscapes of publicity oriented towards those elsewhere. The future depends on their ability to keep doing this, consciously dependent on far-away decisions, but equally conscious of needing to work at making space.

Much has changed in the last two decades. The Cartesian co-ordinates of the Forest State definitely imposed order from above, but the fluidity and fragmentation of the network are just as problematic, perhaps even more so. If the Forest State imposed a rigid framework, survival in the network means acquiescing to the imperatives of globalization even whilst receiving little if any guarantee of reward. The high cost of reproducing society explicitly as everything from image to matter is particularly noteworthy. Yet, like the Apache described by Basso, I would argue that the people I have described live and feel their social as well as their spatial relationships richly and surely. Even an occasional visitor moving in Kainuu's nature learns to read this in the landscape. The irony is that the state-sanctioned, business-promoted discourse of global competition and context-free communication is in danger of displacing place-based learning and narrowing down options all over the world. Even those who consider themselves fortunate, like the people I have described, put huge energies into the one overriding spatial imperative of globalization: to find markets.

This is exhausting (cf. Brennan 2000) and somewhere there has to be a loss.

Acknowledgement

Besides all who have contributed to my ethnographic understanding, I wish to thank the Joint Committee of the Nordic Social Science Research Councils for funding through the network project 'Bodily Commodities: Ethical Concerns about Biotechnology and Market Exchange', and the Wenner-Gren Foundation for individual research grant 6936.

References

Anderson, D. G. and E. Berglund (eds). 2003. *Ethnographies of Conservation: Environmentalism and the Distribution of Privilege*. Oxford and New York: Berghahn Books.

Appadurai, A. 2002. 'Deep Democracy: Urban Governmentality and the Horizon of Politics', *Public Culture* 14(1): 21–47.

Augé, M. 1995. *Non-Places: Introduction to an Anthropology of Supermodernity*, trans. John Howe. London: Verso.

Basso, K. 1996. 'Wisdom Sits in Places: Notes on a Western Apache Landscape', in S. Feld and K. Basso (eds), *Senses of Place*. Santa Fe, NM: School of American Research Press.

Berglund, E. 2000a. 'Forestry Expertise and National Narratives: Some Consequences for Old-Growth Conflicts in Finland', *Worldviews* 4: 47–67.

———. 2000b. 'From Iron Curtain to Timber-Belt: Territory and Materiality at the Finnish-Russian Border', *Ethnologia Europea* 30(2): 23–34.

———. 2007. 'Information Society Finnish-Style', in J. Edwards, P. Harvey, and P. Wade (eds), *Anthropology and Science: Epistemologies in Practice*. ASA monographs 43. Oxford and New York: Berg.

Berland, J. 2005. 'After the Fact: Spatial Narratives in the Canadian Imaginary', *New Formations* 57: 39–55.

Brennan, T. 2000. *Exhausting Modernity: Grounds for a New Economy*. London and New York: Routledge.

Castells, M. and P. Himanen. 2001. *Suomen Yhteiskuntamalli*. (*The Finnish Model of the Information Society*. Simultaneously published in English.) Helsinki: WSOY and SITRA, Finnish National Fund for Research and Development.

Cronon, W. 1995. 'The Trouble with Wilderness; or, Getting back to the Wrong Nature', W. Cronon (ed.), *Uncommon Ground: Rethinking the Human Place in Nature*. New York and London: Norton.

Gupta, A. and J. Ferguson (eds). 1997. *Culture, Power, Place: Explorations in Critical Anthropology*. Durham and London: Duke University Press.

Häkli, J. 1998. 'Manufacturing Provinces: Theorizing the Encounters Between Governmental and Popular "Geographs" in Finland', in G. Ó Tuathail and S. Dalby (eds), *Rethinking Geopolitics*. New York and London: Routledge.

Hastrup, K. 1989. 'Nature as Historical Space', *Folk* 31: 5–20.

Harvey, P. 1996. *Hybrids of Modernity: Anthropology, the Nation State and the Universal Exhibition*. London and New York: Routledge.

Heidegger, M. 1977. *The Question Concerning Technology and Other Essays*, trans. W. Lovitt, New York: Harper Torch Books.

Hirsch, E. and M. O'Hanlon (eds). 1995. *The Anthropology of Landscape: Perspectives on Place and Space*. Oxford and New York: Oxford University Press.

Ingold, T. 2000. *The Perception of the Environment: Essays on Livelihood, Dwelling and Skill*. New York and London: Routledge.

Kirsch, S. 2001. 'Lost Worlds: Environmental Disaster, "Culture Loss" and the Law', *Current Anthropology* 42(2): 167–98.

Laitakari, E. 1961. 'A Century of Finnish State Forestry, 1859–1959', *Silva Fennica* 112.

Lehtinen, A. A. 1991. 'Northern Natures: A Study of the Forest Question Emerging Within the Timber-Line Conflict in Finland', *Fennia* 169(1): 57–169.

———. 2002. 'Globalisation and the Finnish Forest Sector: On the Internationalisation of the Forest-Industrial Operations', *Fennia* 180(1–2): 237–50.

Lowood, H. E. 1990. 'The Calculating Forester: Quantification, Cameral Science, and the Emergence of Scientific Forestry Management in Germany', T. Fränsmyir, J. L. Heilbron, and R. E. Reider (eds), *The Quantifying Spirit in the 18th Century*. Berkeley, Los Angeles, and London: University of California Press.

Mäntymaa, E. 1998. *Kainuulaisten metsäasenteet 1997* (*Attitudes of Kainuu People towards the Forest 1997*. Published in Finnish.) REDEC Kajaani Research Reports 5. Oulu: University of Oulu, REDEC Regional Development.

Massey, D. 2005. *For Space*. London, Thousand Oaks, and New Delhi: Sage.

Michelsen, K.-E. 1995. *History of Forest Research in Finland. Part 1: The Unknown Forest*. Helsinki: The Finnish Forest Research Institute.

Mitchell, T. 1988. *Colonising Egypt*. Cambridge: Cambridge University Press.

Nugent, S. 2003. 'Ecologism as an Idiom in Amazonian Anthropology', in D. Anderson and E. Berglund (eds), *Ethnographies of Conservation: Environmentalism and the Distribution of Privilege*. Oxford and New York: Berghahn.

Paasi, A. 1996. *Territories, Boundaries and Consciousness: The Changing Geographies of the Finnish-Russian Border*. Chichester and New York: John Wiley and Sons.

———. 2003. 'Finnish Landscape as Social Practice: Mapping, Identity and Scale', in M. Jones and K. Olwig (eds), *Nordscapes: Thinking Landscapes and Regional Identity on the Northern Edge of Europe*. Minneapolis, MN: University of Minnesota Press.

Pesonen, P. and O. Riihinen. 2002. *Dynamic Finland: The Political System and the Welfare State*. Helsinki: Finnish Literature Society/Suomen Kirjallisuuden Seura.

Schienstock, G. and O. Kuusi (eds). 1999. *Transformation towards a Learning Economy: The Challenge to the Finnish Innovation System*. Helsinki: SITRA/Finnish National Fund for Research and Development.

Science And Technology Policy Council Of Finland. 2003. *Knowledge, Innovation and Internationalisation.* Retrieved May 2007 from http://www.minedu.fi/OPM/Tiede/tiede-_ja_teknologianeuvosto/julkaisut/linjaus_2003.html?lang=en

Strathern, M. 1992. *After Nature: English Kinship in the Late Twentieth Century*. Cambridge: Cambridge University Press.

Winichakul, T. 1994. *Siam Mapped: A History of the Geo-Body of a Nation*. Honolulu: University of Hawai'i Press.

Wolf, E. 1982. *Europe and the People without History*. Berkeley: University of California Press.

Conclusion
Onward Bound: Ethnographic Perspectives on Space, Movement, and Context

Peter Wynn Kirby

Real life does not unfold in the hollow construct commonly called 'space', as these pages demonstrate. Neither does movement unfurl in a vacuum. Instead, the world we navigate in our daily experience is a concatenation of lived, interpenetrating social worlds as rich as they are diverse. Rather than objectifying, misconstruing, or otherwise distorting this difference, scholars' efforts would be better spent embracing and learning from such a multiplicity of perspective.

In this spirit, the preceding chapters present a broad range of ethnographic settings, meticulously studied, from which to draw some conclusions regarding the lived ontologies of varied social milieux and the topo-strategies of denizens there.

The most striking ethnographic contrast presented here is that of a hemmed-in Melanesian island sedentarism (Mondragón, Chapter Six) juxtaposed with a comparatively unfettered Mongolian nomadism (Pedersen, Chapter Seven). While land on the small island of Loh is subdivided into myriad zones (e.g., dwelling areas, ancestral grounds, cultivated gardens) for which access is customarily contingent upon kinship, remote areas of Mongolia can, by contrast, exhibit a disregard (and, reportedly, even ignorance) of boundaries that is striking. (This contrast is no doubt partly the result of the markedly different ecologies presented by each field-site, but only partly so. Denizens of equally vast and depopulated regions elsewhere are not necessarily so heedless of boundaries as the nomads that Pedersen describes. And spatial practice on small islands and other diminutive territories all over the world is often far less acutely confined [and confining] than the micro-archipelago that Mondragón analyses.) Yet while the organization of social space in the Torres Islands can be very restrictive – to the extent that islanders can feel loath ever to venture into numerous off-limits parts of their own small islet – Mondragón explains that other 'boundaries' non-islanders would see as self-evident are ignored: for example, neighbouring islands loom large in social life there and linguistic ties and relations of kinship, proximity, and exchange are such that in this 'local inter-island milieu … no single "island" is ever conceptualized as a self-contained entity'. Conversely, nestled along the Russian border, though utterly dismissive of the restrictions this might pose, Duxa nomads see their surroundings as 'ontologically neutral' and infinitely boundless yet interspersed with particular significant places – where, say, a mysterious death might have taken place, or an inauspicious supernatural sighting – that serve as crucial focal points. Rather than property or territory contained by boundaries of the sort more commonly found in sedentarist landscapes, life in a nomadic landscape revolves around places. As Pedersen explains, when on the move, these nomads feel compelled to pause temporarily at specific sites along the way, using ritual to 'bring about continuous re-evocation of the nomadic landscape'. These vital anchor points in a vast landscape structure Duxa movement, ironically, and appear to make nomadic infinitude tolerable.

As with other matters anthropological, context is everything. Just as 'space' is experienced very differently on a Melanesian island than in the Mongolian hinterland, movement and social action even in an established particular context remain sensitive to vicissitudes of relations and changes in surroundings. For example, in Kirby's Tokyo field-site, described in Chapter Eight, the miasma of toxic waste that enveloped a contemporary Japanese community swiftly undermined customary strategies of social distancing and lustral protocols and led to a subsequent remapping of the community, the effects of which were far-reaching. In response to this toxic blight, afflicted residents invented avoidance strategies (e.g., barricading themselves in their homes, or venturing out only when the wind was blowing from a 'safe' direction or when sequestered from the polluted air in sealed automobiles) and, in the face of ostracism by some, created novel political alliances that transformed relations in the community. Such contextual shifts, of course, certainly need not be the result of acute environmental changes or limited to the precincts of one community – a brief journey across a fraught boundary can be enough to impact comportment and movement dramatically. In Clarke's account, the difference between one side of the border or the other, between Israel and the Palestinian territories, was considerable, even during peacetime; the topo-mnemonic tourists he describes – retired Israeli soldiers – suddenly found themselves moving and responding differently to their surroundings on a highly visceral level due to the embodied legacy of rigorous military training and grim combat experience. These responses demonstrate the power of milieu and the eerily transporting ways in which bodies remember.

Boundaries and notions of sovereignty, particularly in colonial and/or military occupation of territory, are common triggers for tension, misunderstanding, brinksmanship, and conflict. Chapters Three, Four, and Five illustrate the frictions created by boundaries maintained between societies and the misapprehensions and hostility that can come from contact between divergent knowledge systems. The clear, if attenuated or vestigial, associations of ritual subjugation of lived territory enacted through contemporary, ostensibly peace-oriented, Tibetan-Buddhist rites, discussed by Mills, offer a glimpse of a system of belief and practices with notable differences vis-à-vis 'Western' conceptions of sovereignty over contiguous bounded space. Tibetan rulers, past and present, have – relatively speaking – tended to deemphasize territory circumscribed by fixed political boundaries in favour of extension and maintenance of vectors of power throughout a discontinuous realm. Such territorial ambiguity also surfaces, in turn, out of the divergent knowledge systems that collided before and during the Anglo–Gorkha War (1814–16), analysed by Michael. Discrete territories with fixed borders and unambiguous relations of fealty and tax were an English political import to the subcontinent that flowered with difficulty in the foreign soil there. Indigenous political mapping of unstable border regions fluctuated considerably with undulations of power and loyalty, and the imposition of Western European notions of rationalization and cartographic order became a literal war that would shape the subcontinent for decades to come. The contemporary battleground of the Palestinian territories, explored by Clarke, gives proof to the embodied toll of such divisions. Not just the occupied, but the occupiers as well, can find the imposition and maintenance of boundaries harrowing psychologically and physically. Clarke's Israeli soldiers lived with at least two very distinct regimes of movement, one enjoyed while in their relaxed 'home' sphere and one while on their guard penetrating enemy territory. But while this militarized Israeli case represents a perhaps unusually blunt contrast, most lives are, after all, a not dissimilar stitching together of numerous discontinuous modes.

Contemporary fascination with networks comes under repeated scrutiny and critique as it is contrasted, implicitly and explicitly, with movement and relation in several sites featured in the volume. Berglund finds her chosen field-site in rural Finland remotely, yet profitably, connected to the matrix of globalizing economies and deluged with rhetoric over globalization – the latter's promise of prosperity together with its cold, even threatening, market-driven processes. Finns have long felt stranded on the periphery, but their recent successes in high-tech, for example, have altered the co-ordinates by which they position themselves in the world. Ingold argues in these pages that, in the warped logic of 'space', movement resembles transport; residents of Kainuu, the affective heart of Finland's 'Forest State', balance nostalgia for the region's storied (but recently depressed) past – and the importance of 'moving in nature' there – with contemporary enthusiasm for global connectivity and its transport-like outcomes. Sedgwick's fieldwork in a France-based subsidiary of a Japanese multinational touches on similar questions. The performance and prospects of employees who jockeyed for position and promotion in the shifting political space of the factory's management ranks – metonymically represented by the France-based flexible office space that served both as organizational battleground and ethnographic stage – depended, in part, on how well the plant's production was comparing with other plants and integrating into transnational processes. In the age of cross-cultural networking, actors like Sedgwick's informants always seem to be balancing multiple frames of reference: their positioning in the organization, their ties of relation in larger networks, and their phenomenological iterations along the mundane plane of everyday movement through a culturally and politically contested zone, to name but a few. In all these accounts, we can discern the tension between the 'network', as commonly invoked in contemporary practice, and the 'meshwork', as Ingold puts it, of movement that more accurately characterizes human experience. While Pedersen's summoning of actor-network theory is understandable given the socio-animist contours of nomadic landscape ontology he finds in the field, Ingold's work reminds us that the routes we follow are not abstract ties in a network: 'They are the paths along which life is lived. And it is in the binding together of lines, not in the connecting of points, that the mesh is constituted'.

A lingering tension radiates from the two terms of the main title of this book, *Boundless Worlds*: indeed, why must they be boundless? To be sure, humans can never truly be free of the bonds of upbringing, social ties, and relational protocols; we live our lives, whether we like it or not, as products of embodied, socialized pasts. Moreover, as the contributions to this volume demonstrate, human interaction always takes place in particular social 'worlds' with their own histories, topographies, boundaries, and protocols. But if contemporary social developments – enhanced travel corridors, easy exchange of money and ideas, mobile communication networks, encyclopaedic knowledge at the touch of a finger or thumb – offer humankind anything, it is the increased potential to move between social frameworks and to experience the lively imbrication of social realms. Rather than be seduced by the apparent inevitability of heavily 'bound' regimes of territorial division chopped into small, restrictive zones under proprietary control (such as those Mondragón studied), restricting movement severely, or the heavily policed and socially quarantined Palestinian territories (explored by Clarke) in the age of counter-jihadist security, the volume gazes forward towards emergent social realms, with overlapping boundaries and expanding horizons, that are taking shape around us. Our future will doubtless have its security fences, its passport control, its clouds of surveillance, and (presumably) its Guantánamos. But fecund movement in between – including tourism, work, jet-setting, resettlement, intermarriage, pilgrimage, and vagabondage (but also smuggling, spying, trespass, human-trafficking, and asylum-seeking) – will continue on, reconstituting both sides of any line. While the world will always be to some extent bounded, those boundaries will continually be renegotiated and redefined.

For anthropology and other social science to add to this murk by leveraging restrictive, distorting systems of knowing – i.e., through overly zealous boundary maintenance between scholarly disciplines, or through imposing 'space' on field settings – is to move backwards. If there is just one anthropological approach to movement, it springs from anthropology's long-standing willingness – distinctive in the social sciences – to consider complex questions from indigenous perspectives. Yet anthropology seems always to eschew any monolithic structure or consensus views, preferring an acephalous, self-renewing process of interrogation and auto-critique that invigorates anthropology's theoretical and methodological practice and, in turn, bolsters anthropologists' ability to understand, through ethnography, ways of living, moving, and knowing. As the contributions to this volume demonstrate, an anthropological perspective on movement brings not only critique of 'space' but attention to difference.

In ethnography, then, anthropology possesses the methodological means to move forward, as the introduction to this volume avers. Of course, any attempt to 'freeze' a social milieu is doomed. In the living, shifting, messy state of becoming that is any ethnographic field-site, the responsibility and challenge is to move *with* the world we find.

Visual Appendix

Movement Studies

Christian Grou and Tapio Snellman

Images by
neutral

BRISTOL

A II

Notes on Contributors

Eeva Berglund trained as an anthropologist and taught for some years at Goldsmiths College, London. She also has a postgraduate urban planning degree. Most of her time goes into writing about society, space, and the environment, as well as into voluntary work. Her latest book, *Doing Things Differently: The Women's Design Service at 20*, came out in 2007.

Richard Clarke completed his Ph.D. in social anthropology at the University of Cambridge in 2001. His research focused on the relationship between place and knowledge in Israel/Palestine, particularly through the experience of Israeli peace and dialogue projects operating in the West Bank and Gaza in the late 1990s. He now works in the British Civil Service.

Tim Ingold is Professor of Social Anthropology at the University of Aberdeen. He has carried out ethnographic fieldwork among Saami and Finnish people in Lapland, and has written extensively on comparative questions of environment, technology and social organization in the circumpolar North, as well as on evolutionary theory in anthropology, biology and history, on the role of animals in human society, and on issues in human ecology. His recent research interests are in the anthropology of technology and in aspects of environmental perception. He is currently writing and teaching on the comparative anthropology of the line, and on issues on the interface between anthropology, archaeology, art and architecture. His latest book, *Lines: A Brief History*, was published by Routledge in 2007.

Christian Grou (born 1969 in Bucharest, Romania) and **Tapio Snellman** (born 1969 in Helsinki, Finland) have been working together as **neutral** since 1998. This London-based creative studio fuses film-making and architecture with art and design.

Peter Wynn Kirby is Lecturer in the Anthropology of Japan at Oxford Brookes University, Oxford, UK, and a research fellow at the Paris-based Ecole des Hautes Etudes en Sciences Sociales (EHESS). He has lectured at the University of Cambridge and he spent several years as a tenured assistant professor in Japan before returning to Europe. Drawn to the study of contemporary life and contemporary social problems in Japan and France, he conducts research on 'space' and 'environment' in their broad socio-historical contexts. He also scrutinizes the interplay between architecture, cities, discipline, movement, and resistance. He is author of the forthcoming book *Troubled Natures: The Politics of Waste in Japan*.

Bernardo A. Michael is Associate Professor of History at Messiah College and Director of the Center for Public Humanities. He is currently working on a book on state-making and space in colonial South Asia.

Martin Mills is Senior Lecturer in the Anthropology of Religion at the University of Aberdeen and co-director of the Scottish Centre for Himalayan Research. He received his doctorate in Social Anthropology from the University of Edinburgh. He is the author of *Identity, Ritual and State in Tibetan Buddhism: The Foundations of Authority in Gelukpa Monasticism* (London and New York: RoutledgeCurzon, 2003). His research interests include Tibetan monasticism and government; Buddhist ritual and geomancy; and anthropological theories of religion.

Carlos Mondragón is Associate Professor in Anthropology and History at the Centre for Asian and African Studies at El Colegio de México, in Mexico City. His principal research is based in Island Melanesia and focuses on human–environmental relations, social change and the early history of culture contact. He has also carried out fieldwork on the economy and ecology of pastoral populations in Tibet and is currently editor of the journal *Estudios de Asia y África*.

Morten Axel Pedersen is Associate Professor in the Department of Anthropology, University of Copenhagen. After several years of fieldwork among Darhad and Dukha nomads in Northern Mongolia, his articles on shamanism in post-socialist Mongolia have appeared in the *Journal of the Royal Anthropological Institute* (2001) and, more recently, in an edited volume entitled *Thinking Through Things* (Routledge 2007) and in a forthcoming special issue of the journal *Inner Asia* edited by Rebecca Empson, Caroline Humphrey, and himself. His monograph, *Not Quite Shamans*, is currently under review.

Mitchell W. Sedgwick is Senior Lecturer in the Department of Anthropology and Director of the Europe–Japan Research Centre at Oxford Brookes University. He was formerly Associate Director of the Program on US–Japan Relations, Harvard University. During the 1980s Dr Sedgwick was a consulting organizational anthropologist in South East Asia and West Africa for the World Bank, and later worked on Cambodia's first post-war election for the United Nations. He published his monograph entitled *Globalisation and Japanese Organisational Culture: An Ethnography of a Japanese Multinational Corporation in France* with Routledge in 2007.

Tapio Snellman (born 1969 in Helsinki, Finland) and **Christian Grou** (born 1969 in Bucharest, Romania) have been working together as **neutral** since 1998. This London-based creative studio fuses film-making and architecture with art and design.

Index